SUCCESSFUL TUTORING

SUCCESSFUL TUTORING

A Practical Guide to Adult Learning Processes

By

DAVID PRICE MOORE

Tutorial Coordinator
Academic Improvement Center
Metropolitan State College
Denver, Colorado

and

MARY A. POPPINO

Former Director
Academic Improvement Center
Metropolitan State College
Denver, Colorado

CHARLES C THOMAS • PUBLISHER
Springfield • Illinois • U.S.A.

Published and Distributed Throughout the World by

CHARLES C THOMAS • PUBLISHER
2600 South First Street
Springfield, Illinois, 62717, U.S.A.

© *1983 by* CHARLES C THOMAS • PUBLISHER

ISBN 0-398-04763-4

Library of Congress Catalog Card Number: 82-10800

Printed in the United States of America

I-R5-1

Library of Congress Cataloging in Publication Data

Moore, David Price.
    Successful tutoring.

    Includes bibliographies and index.
    1. Remedial teaching. 2. Tutors and tutoring.
I. Poppino, Mary A.   II. Title
LB1029.R4M66   1983   371.3'94   82-10800
ISBN 0-398-04763-4

To the hundreds of students who have tutored in the Academic Improvement Center at Metropolitan State College, Denver, Colorado (Formerly the Skills Reinforcement Center).

PREFACE

SUCCESSFUL TUTORING was written to increase the effectiveness of adult tutors. Most adults who wish to tutor have achieved a degree of expertise in their field of study or area of interest. Certainly, this is one prerequisite to tutoring. However, the authors have found through years of working with tutors that a working knowledge of the learning process is equally necessary for effective tutoring. *Successful Tutoring* is designed to develop this knowledge about learning for tutors in any subject area.

At present, many internally produced tutor training manuals exist unpublished in tutoring and learning centers throughout the country. The published materials available to educate potential tutors concentrate on adults tutoring children or children tutoring children. Those sources which are intended for adult tutors emphasize the helper/helpee skills such as good eye contact, positive body language and positive reinforcement. While these are important tutoring skills, the authors feel they only superficially address the complex situation called tutoring.

Successful Tutoring culminates the combined ten years experience of the authors in guiding hundreds of adults who have chosen to tutor. During these years, the authors have discovered that most tutors consider helping another learner one of the most satisfying experiences of their adult lives. Many of the experiences of these tutors have been incorporated into *Successful Tutoring,* and many of the chapters have been used and revised with tutor contributions. Thus, the text is primarily experience-based rather than theory-based.

The authors sincerely hope that the users of this text will

discover the satisfaction and rewards that accompany successful tutoring. The authors encourage correspondence from users of the book and look forward to corresponding with tutors who wish to make comments about tutoring issues.

David P. Moore   Mary A. Poppino
Tutorial Coordinator   Former Director

Academic Improvement Center
Metropolitan State College
1006 11th Street
Denver, Colorado 80204

ACKNOWLEDGMENTS

THE authors wish to thank the following reviewers whose comments and contributions improved the text through its several revisions:

Dr. Elaine Cohen, Santa Barbara City College; Dr. Susan Baile, Counselor, Special Services Program, Metropolitan State College; Dr. Elsie Haley, Director, Writing Center, Metropolitan State College; Dr. Susan Hofmann, Clinical Psychologist, Metropolitan State College; Kal Kallison, Tutorial Coordinator, University of Texas at Austin; Dr. David Marsh, Professor of Biology, Metropolitan State College; Kristy Anderson-Moore, former tutor, Metropolitan State College; Dr. Vincent Orlando, Associate Professor of Reading, Metropolitan State College; Ms. Avalon Williams, Assistant Professor of English, Metropolitan State College; and several tutors currently employed at the Academic Improvement Center, Metropolitan State College.

We also wish to thank the typists who worked patiently and diligently to produce the final manuscript: Ms. Harriet King, Ms. Cecilia Jones, and Ms. Lisa Gifford.

Other persons the authors wish to acknowledge are Ms. Yolanda Ortega, for her contributions to the tutoring manual from which this text has grown; and to Ms. Eva Dyer, Director of the Academic Improvement Center, Metropolitan State College and to Dr. Roberta Smilnak, Associate Vice-President for Student Affairs, Metropolitan State College for their continuing support and encouragement.

CONTENTS

Preface vii

Chapter

1. INTRODUCTION TO TUTORING. 3
   A Final Word 5
2. THE ROLE OF THE TUTOR 7
   Activity I. 7
      Tutoring Guidelines 7
      Tutoring Tips 8
   Activity II 10
      Ten Tutoring Situations 11
   Activity III. 15
      Suggested Answers to Ten Tutoring Situations 15
   Activity IV. 17
   Recommended Reading 17
3. LISTENING AND QUESTIONING. 18
   Open-ended Questions 18
   Feelings Versus Facts 21
   Reflection of Feeling 23
   Paraphrasing. 27
   Exercises on Listening and Questioning 29
   Recommended Reading 30
4. HOW ADULTS LEARN 32
   The Model 33
   Exercise One 33
   Exercise Two 34
      Enhancing Learning. 36

Exercise Three 38
Exercise Four 41
    Dialogue 41
Other Ways Adults Learn 41
    Applications to Tutoring. 44
Recommended Reading 45

5. LINGUISTIC, CULTURAL, SEXUAL AND AGE-ORIENTED
   ATTITUDES IN TUTORING 47
Linguistic Attitudes 47
    Inventory of Language Attitudes 48
Analysis A 49
Analysis B 49
Cultural, Sexual and Age-oriented Attitudes. 50
Recommended Reading 60

6. HELPING STUDENTS STUDY, READ AND WRITE
   EFFICIENTLY. 61
Twelve Case Studies of Tutoring (a) 61
Study Techniques (b) 68
    Textbook Reading. 71
    The SQ3R System 73
    Making Notes from the Text 78
    Taking Lecture Notes and Remembering Them 80
    Correlating Textbook Information and Lecture Notes 83
Recommended Reading 83
Recognizing and Strengthening Students' Weak Study Skills (c) . . 84
    Follow Your Intuition 85
    The Complete Study Picture 85
    Prompting for Information 85
    Five Troublesome Study Areas. 86
    Lecture Notetaking 88
    Preparing for Tests. 91
    Test Taking 92
    Time Scheduling 95
    Using Textbooks. 97
    Strengthening Weak Textbook Reading Skills 99

Tutoring Students with Serious Reading Problems (d) 104

    Helping Deficient Readers. 104

    Nonreaders. 108

    Guidelines for Tutors Majoring in Reading/Education. 109

Tutoring in Writing (e) 111

    Suggestions for the Writing Tutor 115

Recommended Reading 126

7. DEALING WITH PERSONAL PROBLEMS 127

Supportive Services 128

Identifying Personal Problems 129

Referring Students for Assistance 138

Steps in the Referral Process 139

Suggested Answers to the Six Situations 141

8. TUTORING APPLIED. 146

Respecting Fellow Learners. 146

Setting Goals for Tutoring Sessions. 147

Tutoring Techniques 148

    Question/Answer. 148

    Demonstration 149

    Illustration, Example and Analogy 149

    Induction and Deduction 149

Encouraging Thinking 150

Positive Reinforcement. 150

9. EVALUATING THE TUTORING PROCESS 152

Tutor Self-Evaluation 152

Evaluation by Tutor Supervisor 155

Evaluation by Students. 156

Index 163

SUCCESSFUL TUTORING

Chapter 1

INTRODUCTION TO TUTORING

SO you're thinking of tutoring? Probably, you've been drawn to tutoring for one or more of these reasons: academic credit, pay, to help another student or to review your own academic area. Many persons who have become tutors feel strongly that helping other students and having the opportunity to brush up on their own field far outweigh any considerations of credit or pay. In fact, many persons who have tutored remark that the personal fulfillment of helping another learner has been an important influence on them, sometimes affecting them so strongly that they have changed career plans because of their tutoring experiences. Other persons who have tutored consider tutoring the best possible method for reviewing their own academic knowledge.

What is tutoring? Many people think that tutoring is nothing more than one person's being courteous and positive toward another learner. Other people may think tutoring is identical to classroom teaching. Certainly maintaining a positive and encouraging attitude is an important trait for successful tutors, and like teaching, tutors are involved in the instructional process. But, there is more to tutoring than meets superficial examination. Successful tutoring incorporates positive and encouraging attitudes but is quite different from classroom teaching. *Successful Tutoring* explains those behaviors, attitudes and skills unique to tutoring.

The text considers tutoring to be an academically oriented, long-term effort undertaken by two adults,[*] one who wishes to

---

[*]Of course, these conditions can exist when one or both persons are children, but *Successful Tutoring* is intended for adults tutoring adults.

learn a new skill or body of knowledge and one who possesses that skill or who possesses some part of that body of knowledge. *Successful Tutoring* considers skilled tutoring to be a paraprofessional activity.* Because of this bias, *Successful Tutoring* is not one of many training manuals, most of which are designed to teach set behaviors for trainees to learn and to apply to every situation. Tutoring is too complex a relationship for "training," as we have defined it here. Rather, *Successful Tutoring* prepares you to respond appropriately to a variety of situations by using your educated judgment and to rely on professional staff persons when necessary.

Several other biases guide the text of *Successful Tutoring*. The text considers tutoring to be an effort by tutors to assist students to *learn to learn,* thus making them less, not more, dependent on tutors. For our purposes, tutoring also involves tutors' assisting students with their academic pursuits while also being acutely aware of the nonacademic aspects which affect most students: family and work obligations, personal goals, finances, and matters of health. This awareness allows tutors to make adjustments in the learning situation to accommodate the needs of students. Also guiding *Successful Tutoring* is the authors' belief that tutoring does *not* include the tasks of proofreading papers, grading exams, checking answers or proctoring exams. Tutoring is a much more substantive activity. Furthermore, since tutoring seeks to deal with the underlying learning problems which students may have, tutoring cannot be truly effective on a one-shot drop-in basis. Tutoring is a long-term substantive relationship between two people who are interested in learning.

Most of the chapters in *Successful Tutoring* are based on exercises which encourage you *to think* about the tutoring and learning process rather than having you memorize a body of facts or a series of set behaviors to use in every situation.† Tutoring also contains many exercises which ask you to think about what you

---

* Ursula Delworth and LuAnne Aulepp, *Training Manual for Paraprofessional and Allied Professional Programs*, Offset. Western Interstate Commission for Higher Education, Boulder, Colorado, 1976, pp. 1-5.

†Jerry Snow, *What Works and What Doesn't: In Community College Development Studies Programs,* Mimeographed. University of Texas at Austin, 1977, p. 6.

already know about a variety of behaviors and skills relevant to tutoring before the text presents any new information to you.

The chapters of *Successful Tutoring* are best used with a group of tutors in the order in which they are presented. This is not essential but is probably most productive. The first four chapters deal with the most fundamental and most quickly needed set of skills: knowing your role as a tutor, listening and questioning effectively, understanding how adults learn, and understanding your own linguistic and cultural biases. After Chapter 5, the text presents a five-part section on study skills, and how these skills may best be encouraged in students with whom you work. Not all students will need study skills help, but many will profit from it. An even smaller percentage of students with whom you work will need assistance with personal problems; for this reason Chapter 7 deals with personal problems and referral methods. Chapter 8 serves as a summary of the theories presented in the previous chapters and gives some quick practical applications of the ideas so that you will experience a boost in confidence near the end of the text. Finally, the text closes with a chapter on tutor evaluation.

A FINAL WORD

In *Successful Tutoring*, several terms appear which may not be in conventional usage. For our purposes, the term "content area tutoring" indicates tutoring within a subject area such as economics, chemistry, or management. "Basic skills tutoring" indicates tutoring in one of the basic skills areas: reading, studying, writing, or arithmetic.

For simplicity's sake, the authors have chosen to use the plural pronoun form as often as possible in order to avoid the gender-based pronouns "he" and "she." This may occasionally lead to less graceful prose.

Throughout, *Successful Tutoring* contains the personal pronoun form "you" in addressing tutors to establish a tone of familiarity and ease. This form appears in many of the sentences which introduce the chapters or which give directions (with the implied "you").

Most chapters contain a brief list of recommended reading at their conclusion for those of you who wish to read more about the subject of the chapter. These lists are not exclusive, and some supervisors will wish to supplement them.

For those who are using this text in an independent situation, a supervisor's guide is available from the publisher. This manual may provide added insights to those of you who are independent tutors and must guide yourselves.

Chapter 2

THE ROLE OF THE TUTOR

A S a beginning tutor, you will encounter situations that you have never faced before. Thinking about situations which are typical to tutoring will help you be more effective when you actually begin working with students. In this chapter, you will examine your role as a tutor. Exploring your role as the tutor beforehand can help you better focus your attention on the tutoring task itself.

ACTIVITY I

Read the Tutoring Guidelines that follow.

Tutoring Guidelines

The following informal guide has been assembled with the help of many persons who have served as tutors. Although tutoring relies on no hard and fast rules, the following guidelines represent the thoughts of many tutors from very different backgrounds and subject areas.

Most persons who have tutored agree that tutoring is primarily a close interpersonal relationship, the purpose of which is to help one or both of the participants succeed in a potentially difficult or challenging learning situation.

Although there may be useful "tips" which tutors can exchange with each other, the best way to succeed at tutoring is to *care* whether students learn. This is not exactly the same as caring about students themselves; it is more a conviction that learning is both possible and important for students and that it is worthwhile

7

to help them with that learning task. It is perfectly acceptable to care about students in a more personal way, of course, but caring about the students' *learning* seems to be the key. In an almost uncanny way, students seem to know if their tutor *cares* or not, so it is difficult to pretend a concern. If you care about learning, students may well care too. If you do not, students may learn anyway, or they may disappear after a few sessions.

Showing students that you are really concerned whether they learn can be done in many ways. Two of the indicators of caring which weigh heavily with most students are punctuality and reliability. If you make tutoring appointments, always keep them and be on time. Failure to keep appointments is not only rude, it also may permanently discourage students from seeking tutoring.

Tutoring Tips

1. As a tutor you have a dual role: to keep students up with the class and to help them with basic skills like reading, writing, and study skills for their subject area(s). (Chapter 6 deals in depth with tutoring in reading, writing, and study skills.)

2. Helping students feel confident about their ability to learn may be just as important as talking about the subject matter. Students who are made to *feel* stupid often act as if they were.

3. A pleasant, relaxed tutoring session often results in more learning than a grim-faced one. Relax and let yourself enjoy the session. Try to create a peer atmosphere, rather than an "I'm the teacher/you're merely the student" feeling. Sit next to students and on the same side of the table. Avoid facing them like a professor, standing above them, or turning your back while you write on the board.

4. In the first few sessions, use a little of the time to get to know students and to determine why they came for tutoring. It is always helpful to know how heavy students' time commitments are and to know generally how well they read, write, and organize studying. Students have a way of oversimplifying their study problems; they may say, "I just don't like this stuff," but you may see that they are weak readers with imposing textbooks facing them. It may be that students' "motivation" problems are

really reading problems or study problems. (Chapter 6 deals in depth with reading, study, and writing problems.)

5. Emotional problems may also be a part of the picture. Emotional blocks can prevent learning just as surely as poor reading or study skills. If you feel that students are caught in emotional blocks, seek the advice of your supervisor before prematurely suggesting a solution. (Chapter 7 discusses emotional problems at length.)

6. In general, try to help students *learn to learn*. Try to question, suggest, prod and guide rather than to tell, lecture and recite facts. (Chapter 3 provides suggestions on effective listening and questioning skills.) You are not the professor, so you don't have to have all the facts. Instead, you are in the unique position of helping students reach individual academic goals.

7. Don't blame yourself if students don't succeed. If you work hard at your tutoring job, students may work even harder. Occasionally, however, students have so many things on their minds that school is a low priority. You should examine your methods and efforts to see if they could be improved. If they reflect your best effort, do not waste time feeling guilty. If students do succeed, do not expect gratitude. Some students like to express thanks; others do not. (In Chapter 9, self-evaluation is discussed further.)

8. Many students are especially sensitive about their writing and therefore bruise easily. When tutoring writing, suggest changes instead of saying, "This sentence is completely wrong." On the other hand, do not give false praise. (Chapter 6 [Section e] addresses the special problems of tutoring writing.)

9. Respect students' regular language habits. Although those habits may not match yours, remember they will continue to be of prime importance to them in their neighborhood. Do not encourage students to forget their old language patterns, and learn the *right* way — standard English. Instead, encourage students to add standard English, which will be of use to them in academic situations, to their "regular" or everyday language, which will continue to be appropriate in other situations. Be careful not to embarrass students by correcting their oral speech patterns. (See Chapter 5 for a longer discussion of language attitudes.)

10. Be sure both you and students know what the assignments are and the purposes of the assignments before you tutor.

11. Visit students' teachers outside of class to see what they expect and to see the general layout and purpose of the course. However, do not mention students by name unless you have students' permission first. (Some students fear that the teacher will be prejudiced against them if they are being tutored).

12. Sometimes visiting students' classes will help you to see how the class operates and how the teacher presents material. Do not embarrass the student by disclosing to other students why you are there.

13. Work on one point at a time. For example, you might spend several weeks helping students learn capitalization rules. During that time, you may notice their spelling is also weak, but ignore that and concentrate on capitalization. Students cannot spread their attention over more than one or two items at once. You can work on spelling during subsequent sessions.

14. If students work very hard on academic tasks but seem to have a difficult time improving, you may be focusing on the wrong problem. Check with your supervisor to arrange for a new diagnosis. For example, you may be tutoring in spelling rules, when the students' real "spelling" problem is very poor hearing.

15. Become familiar with a few helpful resources in the tutoring center. Ask your supervisor for suggestions.

16. Be flexible in your use of resource materials. Some students prefer workbooks; others consider them a bore. Some students can learn from dictionaries and thesauri; others are merely confused by them. (Chapter 4 deals with the various ways in which adults learn.)

Hopefully, some of these guidelines will be useful; always remember that each situation is different, and each student you tutor is unique.

ACTIVITY II

Now that you have briefly considered some suggestions about tutoring, collated from the experiences of practicing tutors, you will be asked to examine tutoring situations which deal with some other aspects of tutoring. Examine each situation, considering how you would act or react in a similar situation. You may find it helpful to consult with another tutor who is working on the same chapter or has had some tutoring experience and discuss some of the options possible in each situation. As you consider your response to each situation, keep in mind any extenuating circumstances that will aid you as you make your decisions.

Ten Tutoring Situations

Situation 1

The tutor agrees to do one problem out of twenty homework problems for the student, just to get him started. (The homework will be graded by the instructor.)

Would you do the same? (Write your response here.)

Situation 2

The tutor meets with a student for the first time. As they talk, the student questions several facts that the tutor has stated about the subject matter. The tutor strives to impress upon the student that she is knowledgeable about the subject by using more technical vocabulary and mentioning facts that she feels the student could not possibly know.

What's your reaction to this?

Situation 3

The tutor asks a student to do one extra problem for practice. At the next session, the student says, "I forgot to do it!" The tutor lets the student know he is disappointed that she did not do the problem.

Would you let the student know how you feel?

Situation 4

The tutor, who feels he knows a student fairly well, is asked by the student, "I have a 'C' on the midterm and a 'D' on the practice quiz. I think I'll withdraw from the course instead of risking my grade point average on the final. What would you do if you were me?"

The tutor tells the student what he would do in that situation. Would you?

Situation 5

The tutor is working with a new student who lost the syllabus and style sheet for the research paper for his course. He wants the tutor to help him start the research paper. The tutor suggests he make a trip to the professor's office to pick up another style sheet. The student says, "I can't go; Dr. Brown will think I'm irresponsible!" The tutor agrees to go instead.

Would you?

Situation 6

Tutor A overhears tutor B praising her student for trying hard even though the student just failed a test. Tutor A resolves never to praise a student for failure.

How would you react?

Situation 7

The tutor, who is meeting a student for her second tutoring session, agrees to spend the hour telling the student all she remembers about Chapter Five because the student has a test coming up tomorrow and "didn't have time to read the chapter."

Would you?

Situation 8

The tutor has been working with a student whose time is limited but who has shown that he learns well by practicing and repeating. The tutor asks the student to do four extra practice problems (about 10 minutes apiece) and bring in the answers at the next session.

Is the tutor justified in asking for extra work?

Situation 9

The tutor is in a scheduled tutor meeting. Looking up, he sees one of his students beckoning to him through the glass door. The student doesn't have an appointment today. The tutor goes to talk with the student in the hall and learns she does have a crisis. "Word is out" that her instructor will give a "surprise quiz" in class the next hour. The tutor agrees to forgo the remainder of the meeting in order to help the student.

Would you?

Situation 10

A tutor has been working with twelve students regularly and so has a completely full schedule. Suddenly she realizes that four of the students are B+ or A students and have been so since she first met them. The tutor decides to tell the four brightest students she no longer has time for them so she can fill the four slots with lower achieving students who need more help.

Do you agree?

ACTIVITY III

After you have finished your responses, check your answers with the suggested answers below. As you compare your responses to the suggested answers, you may see that some of your answers closely resemble them; others may be quite different. The important thing to remember is that the suggested answers represent the collective experiences of many tutors who have dealt with similar situations.

Suggested Answers to Ten Tutoring Situations

Situation 1

Providing a model problem for a student to follow is a sound idea, because many students learn by imitation. Thinking through the problem entirely on one's own is ideal, but sometimes too frustrating. However, doing any part of *graded* work is inappropriate for the tutor. It is better to do a similar problem, not the homework problem, to get the student started.

Situation 2

It may be very ego-deflating to a tutor when a student questions everything the tutor says. On the other hand, tutors are not professors and should not expect to know everything. The question is: will impressing the student with big words and obscure facts erase the underlying cause of the doubts; many students feel that only the professor has the right answers. You may need to explain to the student that you are not the teacher and do not have all the answers; clarifying the role of the tutor may lessen the tension between the student and you.

Situation 3

Letting the student know you are genuinely concerned about her learning and doing well is usually helpful. However, letting negative feelings show will probably make the student feel either guilty or alienated. It might be profitable to find out why she "forgot."

Situation 4

It is best to encourage the student to explore all options and make up his own mind. In this way, the tutor avoids the student's returning and saying, "I took your advice and now I'm in a real mess. Thanks a lot for nothing!"

Situation 5

In order to get the term paper started, a tutor might elect to pick up the style sheet, although this is beyond the call of regular duty. The underlying problem, fear or anxiety, must also be dealt with. Tutors should consult their supervisors about referring the student for professional help with assertiveness skills.

Situation 6

In some situations, praising honest effort or partly correct answers may be appropriate.

Situation 7

Probably what this student needs in the long run is help in time-scheduling. The short-term problem, however, is the test. You might agree to help the student skim the chapter, but only after she agrees to work on her time scheduling with you after the test is over.

Situation 8

Reminding a student to repeat his new learning is usually a helpful procedure. Many students neglect this step and have to rememorize again and again. Some students are glad to do extra work, but some resent it. Also, be sure your student understands the psychological and physiological principles behind repetition, or he may think you're just asking for busywork. (Do you know those principles yourself? If not, you will find a discussion of study techniques in Chapter 6.)

Situation 9

Tutor meetings and preparation are vital to effective tutoring, so declining to help the student could be justified. Furthermore, most adults accept the responsibility to meet at appointed times.

Helping a student at such a time could encourage her to take further advantage of the tutor.

Situation 10

Is a tutor a person who helps low achievers only or who helps anyone who wants to learn? Do low achieving students take priority over high achievers? Short of turning away the high achievers entirely, the tutor might help them form a small group to tutor each other. Perhaps a tutor should consult the supervisor to see if the tutoring center has a policy which addresses this situation.

ACTIVITY IV

Now that you have compared your answers to the suggested answers, write your response to each of the ten suggested answers on a separate sheet of paper. Turn in your paper to your supervisor for evaluation.

Having explored your role should make you feel more comfortable as a new tutor. In the next chapter, "Listening and Questioning," you will explore some skills that will help you to feel even more at ease as you meet and talk with students.

RECOMMENDED READING

Danish, Steven J. and Allen L. Haver. *Helping Skills: A Basic Training Program.* New York: Behavioral Publications, Inc., 1976. Chapters one, two, three and six offer exercises which pairs of tutors may undertake, exploring such topics as motivations for tutoring, verbal and nonverbal behavior and helping relationships.

Chapter 3

LISTENING AND QUESTIONING

AS a tutor, listening will be one of your most used skills. Although listening to other speakers is something we all do everyday, the skill of being a good listener and questioner is especially important in the tutoring situation. When only two people are present, as in tutoring, conversational skills are much more important than in the lecture hall. Many beginning tutors foresee that their tutoring task will involve mostly talking, and they overlook the importance of listening. Students who come for tutoring may need to talk and be listened to in order to clarify their understanding of academic points or to ventilate their negative feelings about a school situation. Often, the best tutor is the best listener, not the best talker or lecturer.

Specifically, the objectives of this chapter are to help the tutor identify and use the questioning skill called "asking open-ended questions," and the listening skills of "reflecting the feeling" and "paraphrasing."*

OPEN-ENDED QUESTIONS

One of the ways to become a better listener is to become a better questioner, and one means to effective questions is the open-ended question. Consider the conversation below between a new tutor and a student.

---

*Allen Ivey and Jerry Authier, *Microcounseling: Innovations In Interviewing, Counseling, Psychotherapy, and Psychoeducation*, 2nd ed. (Springfield: Charles C Thomas, Publisher, 1978), pp. 64-85.

Tutor: Is biology the class you're having trouble with?

Student: Yes.

Tutor: Did you anticipate the class would be this hard?

Student: No.

Tutor: Had you already taken biology in your high school schedule?

Student: Yes, I did.

Tutor: Did you do well in the high school class?

Student: Yes, pretty well.

Tutor: Is this the book for the course?

Student: Yes, it is.

Tutor: Who's the teacher for your section?

Student: Dr. Hallett.

Tutor: Do you like her as a lecturer?

Student: I guess she's pretty nice.

Tutor: What sort of difficulties are you having with the course?

Student: I guess the worst part is figuring out the chemical equations. I do fine memorizing the phyla and doing the lab so long as it deals with the regular stuff, but when they start on the Krebs Cycle and the other chemical reactions, I get lost. I didn't take chemistry in high school, and I'm not particularly good at math either. I think I understand the "balancing" of the equations, and then I miss them all on the quizzes anyway.

This conversation is based mostly on one style of questioning. Needless to say, the conversation is mostly unproductive until the last interchange when some real information finally is extracted.

The following list of questions will give you the opportunity to probe deeper into the usefulness of various styles of questioning. Read through the list below and categorize the ten questions according to what type *response* they would call for. Be prepared to tell why you made the choices for each category; most people see two or three categories. (Hint: consider the *length* of the responses as a central factor when you develop your categories for the ten questions).

1. Are you having trouble with your biology class?
2. What type of difficulties are you having with the economics class?
3. Which term are you in at school?
4. How is your roommate interfering with your studying?
5. Did you do well on your last test?
6. Do you like your history teacher?
7. Why do you dislike your anthropology class?
8. Do you take notes in class?
9. What kinds of things do you do when you read your textbook assignments?
10. Is this the textbook for the economic class?

Group the questions in categories you develop and write the numbers of the questions below. (Hint: most people see two or three categories.)

One possible breakdown would be —

Category A: Question 1, 3, 5, 6, 8, and 10

Category B: Question 2, 4, 7, and 9

Or, another arrangement might be —

Category A: Question 1, 5, 6, and 10

Category B: Question 3

Category C: Question 2, 4, 7, and 9

The distinction behind the first set of categories is that questions 1, 3, 5, 6, 8, and 10 ask for a one - or two-word response, and questions 2, 4, 7, and 9 ask for a more substantial and therefore longer response.

The distinction among the second set of categories is the same as before, except that in the second set, category A and B make a finer distinction between types of short answer questions, i.e. between "yes" and "no" questions and those which provide a specific short answer such as "my first semester" for question 3.

The type of questions illustrated above have been called "open" and "closed." Questions 1, 3, 5, 6, 8, and 10 are examples of closed questions. Questions 2, 4, 7, and 9 are called open or open-ended questions.

Many counselors and psychologists recommend asking open-ended questions to start conversations and to gather facts from another person. In tutoring, it is usually up to the tutor to open the conversations and to gather from the students the facts about their study situations. Often, students are shy or simply do not know what sort of information to give the tutor.

As you meet with students, try to keep your questions open.

Ask: How are you doing in your economics course?
Not
Are you having trouble with the course?

Ask: How do you go about taking notes in the art history course?
Not
Do you take notes in the art history course?

Ask: What's your plan for getting ready for the mid-term?
Not
Are you getting ready for the mid-term?

Ask: Why do you think this part is the hardest for you?
Not
Is this the hardest part?

As you have probably already noted, open questions often start with a "how, what or why."

FEELINGS VERSUS FACTS

Just as asking open questions can make a tutor a more skilled questioner, being sensitive to messages of "feeling" and messages of "fact" can make the tutor a better listener.

Look at the list of statements below to distinguish those which communicate feelings:

1. I failed my biology test.
2. Boy, do I hate that course!
3. I finished reading my assignment for sociology.
4. Isn't this stuff boring!
5. Dr. Brown teaches our political science course.
6. What a chauvinist!

Most of you probably chose 1, 3, and 5 as those statements which communicate facts, while 2, 4, and 6 communicate feelings.

As a tutor, you will frequently encounter students who communicate to you both facts and feelings about their courses, instructors and experiences in learning situations. It is important to be sensitive to both types of messages. Before exploring further the reason for differentiating between fact and feeling messages, read this exchange between a tutor and a student.

Herb, an English tutor, has been meeting regularly with a student, Marilyn, who has been coming to the tutoring center for assistance in English composition. Today, however, Marilyn seems to Herb to be unusually upset. Her teacher, Dr. Allbright, has assigned ten practice sentences illustrating the difference between the similar use of the colon and the dash in sentences. As the session starts, Herb asks Marilyn how much of the lesson she thinks she understands so far. Marilyn does not reply immediately but looks disgusted and then exclaims, (1) "Who cares about this stupid stuff! (2) I did all right when we were working on paragraphs. (3) Now, we're supposed to figure out the difference between dashes and colons in sentences. (4) Who cares! (5) I never use either mark in my own writing anyway! (6) But this assignment's due tomorrow, so I have to do it this afternoon." Herb replies, "How do you think a dash should be used?" Marilyn frowns and then replies, (7) "Well, I think it always goes in the middle of a sentence, doesn't it?" In reply Herb says, "Yes, that's right, it can't start or end a sentence. But, can you just slap it in anywhere in the middle of a sentence?" Marilyn laughs, (8) "Of course not. (9) I've learned so far that it has to be close to a list of items." Herb says, "That's right; the list makes it necessary." With a slightly happier expression Marilyn says, (10) "Well I guess I can figure these out without too much trouble."

After reading the dialogue above once, return to the beginning of the conversation and record below the numbers of those sentences which express Marilyn's feelings.

You probably chose sentences 1, 4, and 10. Her other sentences are statements of fact. Notice that Herb replied deliberately to Marilyn's statements of fact only and not to her expression of feeling. In his way, Herb was able to keep the focus of the tutoring session on the task at hand and not on Marilyn's emotional reaction to the assignment. To be sure, she was a little annoyed, perhaps because she does not particularly like studying punctuation, but she was able to get on with the lesson after a little complaining about it. This is not very different from the way many of us act when we face an unpleasant task.

REFLECTION OF FEELING

Sometimes, however, students' emotional reactions are so strong that they must be dealt with before tutoring can continue. Suppose that the conversation between Herb and Marilyn had gone this way instead:

In response to Herb's question, "How do you think a dash should be used?" Marilyn reacts by wadding up her paper and stuffing it angrily in the wastebasket. She states adamantly, "I won't do this," and begins to look teary-eyed. Then she gets a tissue out of her purse and dabs her nose. Since it is clear to Herb that Marilyn intends to carry the conversation no further and that she is also unlikely to resume the work on the colons and dashes, he feels he must intervene in order to redirect the conversation toward punctuation. By responding to

Marilyn's strong *feelings*, Herb can get the conversation going again. To do this Herb might say, "The assignment's upsetting you, isn't it?" Or, he could say, "You look pretty upset. What's wrong?" Or, as a third alternative, he could remark, "You have some strong feelings about this, right?" These remarks "hold a mirror up" to help Marilyn become more aware of how much her emotions affect her studying. This is called "reflection of feeling."

In response to Herb's gentle, but frank reflection of Marilyn's feelings, she might reply, (1) "This is so frustrating because Dr. Allbright is making us *figure out* the difference between the dash and the colon instead of just telling us. Why doesn't he just *tell* us!" On the other hand, she might say, (2) "I broke up with my fiance last night, and I can't seem to stop crying. I'm awfully embarrassed to be crying at school like this." In either case, Herb's reflection of feeling to Marilyn has accomplished a resumption of the conversation, instead of Herb's sitting silently and feeling embarrassed while Marilyn sniffled. Further, the reflection has acknowledged that Marilyn is genuinely upset and, after her reply (whether number one or two), Herb will have a much clearer understanding about the source of her discomfort than if he had merely ignored the crying or said, "There, there," while patting her shoulder.

Either of Marilyn's responses suggests a course of action for Herb. If Marilyn had replied with sentence one, Herb could explain why some language teachers ask their students to *discover* language principles such as those behind the use of grammatical marks, as opposed to merely having students memorize a set of rules. If, on the other hand, Marilyn had replied with sentence two, Herb could suggest that they continue the session later that day when Marilyn was feeling more composed. Or, he could ask if she would like to discuss her feelings with someone else, perhaps someone from the counseling center.

Breaking an emotional "log jam" which has interrupted a tutoring session is one of the main purposes of reflecting someone's feelings. Many students have strong feelings about their school experiences, and these often erupt in tutoring sessions. Equally common is the sudden eruption of strong feelings from students' private lives. Reflecting the feeling often clears the way for resumption of tutoring. By acknowledging a student's strong feelings, a tutor can refocus the conversation on the facts of the lesson or postpone tutoring until a more propitious time.

Consider the following "mini-conversations" which illustrate reflecting feelings:

Student: I just hate this class. I failed the first test, and there's only one more, plus the book reviews for the grade. Dr. Green will probably hate my book reviews anyway, because they're all about women's lib books, and he hates all the women in the class; you can tell by the anti-feminist jokes he tells. You should hear him. I've got half a mind to go see the dean. Don't you think that's a good idea?

Tutor: Sounds like this course has been a bad experience for you.

Not

Tutor: I don't blame you for being furious. I'll bet the dean will hit the ceiling when he hears about it! (Remarks such as this will often be interpreted as advice. The students may genuinely feel that the tutor, whom they regard as an authority figure, is giving permission or even urging a visit to the dean's office. This can result in a tidal wave of reaction.)

Student: (Sniffling) I just can't seem to get anything right for this course. I gave my first speech on the Bill of Rights, and the teacher said, right in front of everybody, that I started too softly and nobody could hear me, and then when I got louder I was talking too fast. She used me as an example of what not to do. I just can't get up in front of everybody again. I don't see how all these other people can do it. Mrs. Banks criticizes everyone and they just laugh it off and act like they aren't embarrassed. (Blows her nose.) Maybe I'll drop the course. I just don't know what to do. (Cries afresh.)

Tutor: Having to give this speech is really making you feel miserable, isn't it?

Not

Tutor: Boy, you really must have messed it up the first time! (Levity is simply cruel at this juncture.)

And Not

Tutor: Let's get to work. Where's the outline for the new speech? (Ignoring the student's obvious and intrusive distress will not make it go away.)

Student: I guess I won't be seeing you for tutoring anymore. I've already looked in the catalogue to see how to drop all my courses. My health is so much worse now than it was at the start of the semester, and the doctor has upped the frequency of my medication. It's so strong that I'm afraid I'll get sick to my stomach and have to get out of class quick. That's not so easy in two of my classes because they're in that big lecture hall, and I sit in the middle. When everybody's seated, with their chair arms pulled up, it's harder to crawl out of there than it is to get out of a crowded theater. I don't know what to do except just chuck the whole semester.

Tutor: The problem seems pretty hopeless to you, doesn't it?

Not

Tutor: Come on now, it can't be that bad. Surely we can think of some other solution. (This remark denies the legitimacy of the student's very real feelings of desperation and implies that he or she is either faking or is a crybaby. The tutor should help him or her think up alternate solutions, but to do so before acknowledging the student's emotions is to put the cart before the horse.)

To summarize the section regarding reflection of feeling, it is enough to say that the primary aim of tutoring sessions is to focus on facts, not feelings. However, when students' feelings become an actual block to successful tutoring, they must be dealt with.

Reflecting the feeling is one way of dealing with intrusive negative feelings without committing the tutor to advice or a callous attitude. And, it sometimes clears the way for resumption of tutoring.

PARAPHRASING

Paraphrasing is another skill useful for tutors. It is closely related to reflecting the feeling. To illustrate, let us continue with the session between Herb and Marilyn. Suppose that Marilyn's real concern is that Dr. Allbright is making the students figure out the difference between the dash and the colon as used in the sentences above, and dealing with this ambiguity is very upsetting to Marilyn. She would rather be *told* the answer so she can simply memorize it.

As they continue their session, Marilyn says, "I see now, the dash is for a list, and the colon is for things in a series." Herb, realizing that Marilyn has not perceived the essential distinction between the two marks, replies, *"You mean that a list is different from a series of things . . . ?"* (Paraphrase 1) Marilyn says, "Well, I guess it really isn't, is it . . . ?" Herb continues, "So, that's not the big difference, right? Let me point out some examples. Take a look at numbers 3, 5, and 8 in the list, and then look at numbers 2 and 4. Can you see something similar in each bunch?"

No. 2 Philodendron, dracena, diffenbachia, and grape ivy — these are all plants which can tolerate low light.

No. 3 Tutors use these skills frequently: listening, clarifying, and encouraging.

No. 4 A human-like foot, thirty-two teeth, some capacity for language — these are the gorilla characteristics which make them akin to humans.

No. 5 Only the most skilled chefs can prepare these dishes: smoked shad-roe, pâté mousse, broiled filet of grouper oursinade, coquilles Saint-Jâcques, coquelet à la crème aux morilles, and mussels à la poulette.

No. 8 Many golfers have distinguished themselves during the last two decades: Miller Barber, Arnold Palmer, Jack Nicklaus, and Gary Player.

Marilyn examines the sentences, and ventures, "Well, I think that 3, 5, and 8 have a sentence and a list, but 2 and 4 are backwards." Herb responds, *"You mean that 2 and 4 are constructed in the opposite way from 3, 5, and 8?"* (Paraphrase 2) Marilyn continues, "Yeah, that's it! 3, 5, and 8 have a sentence with a list after it, and 2, and 4 have a list with a sentence after it. Now I see; the colon goes with 3, 5, and 8, and the dash with 2, and 4." Herb goes on, "I think you've got it. If Dr. Allbright asks you to tell how to use the marks, you'd say something like . . . ?" Marilyn picks up the cue, "I'd say *'When a list is preceded by a sentence, a colon is used before the list. But, if a sentence starts with a list, a dash comes before the sentence.'* " (Paraphrase 3)

As Herb and Marilyn have discussed dashes and colons, each one has been using paraphrases skillfully. The three paraphrases appear in italic print. Reexamine the sentences to see if you can determine the functions of the three paraphrases. Once you think you perceive their purpose(s), write an explanation of the use(s) of paraphrasing in the blank below:

You may have realized that the purpose of paraphrase 1 is for Herb to clarify Marilyn's thoughts by stating them in other words. When he does so, Marilyn realizes that her thoughts are not clear. This is one of the valuable uses of paraphrasing; i.e. to help students clarify their own understanding.

The purpose of paraphrase 2 is for Herb to clarify his own understanding of Marilyn's statement. This use of paraphrasing is equally helpful in that it clears up misunderstandings before they cause confusion in communication.

The purpose of paraphrase 3 is quite different from the uses illustrated in examples 1 and 2. Paraphrase 3 encourages students to think through and summarize the points of a tutoring session in their own words. This is one of the most decisive proofs of students' understanding. Skilled tutors often request paraphrases from students to check their comprehension.

Consider the following interchange between two tutors. One tutor is describing the type of professor she prefers:

Carol: I particularly enjoyed Dr. Howe's seminar. He's such a personal sort of teacher. You might enjoy his class too.

David: Well, maybe I will sign up spring semester! (During spring semester, Dave runs into Carol again and they discuss school matters).

Carol: I bet you really like Dr. Howe!

David: Well, he really knows his stuff, but he's not at all personal in my estimation. In fact, he seems downright unfriendly. I prefer teachers who take time to talk personally to students — you know — chat before class and such.

Carol: Oh! What I meant by personal is that Dr. Howe makes the class relevant to you personally. He gives lots of real life examples that you can apply to your personal life.

Dave could have saved himself a disappointing experience if he had paraphrased Carol's statements about Dr. Howe before taking action on her suggestion.

EXERCISES ON LISTENING AND QUESTIONING

Write the answers to Exercise A on a sheet of notebook paper and turn them in to your supervisor.

A. Change the following closed questions to open questions.

1. Do you underline in your textbook?
2. Have you written your outline?
3. Do you read your assignments before going to class?

Write a response that reflects the feeling(s) expressed in the following statements.

4. There's no way I'll pass this dumb test! I think I'll sneak in a crib sheet!

5. I'm never going back to the reserve desk in the library again, even if I do have to finish this term paper! Miss White implied that I tore a page out of *Chemical Abstracts*. What a nerve!

Write a short paraphrase of the following statements made by students.

(Refer to sample paraphrases 1 and 2 on pages 27 and 28 to guide you).

6. I think I'd like best a class where there's lots of freedom.

7. I'm really going to study for this test.

8. Dr. Agnew's a really tough teacher.

9. My sister's been helping me with my Spanish papers.

10. I'm doing really well in all my classes.

B. After you have completed Exercise A, find a tutor who has completed it also. Arrange to meet for a one-half hour conversation to discuss any topic with which you are both familiar. If possible, make arrangements to record your discussion.

During the discussion, concentrate on asking open questions, reflecting feelings, and paraphrasing.

After completing your discussion, listen to the tapes. Then write a short summary to be turned in to your supervisor. In the summary, assess your strengths in the three skills: asking open questions, reflecting feelings, and paraphrasing. Also, indicate the areas(s) where you feel you need more practice.

Now that you have developed better skills in communicating effectively with students, in Chapter 4, "How Adults Learn," you will gain insight into the various ways that people learn.

RECOMMENDED READING

Ivey, Allen E. and Jerry Authier. *Microcounseling: Innovations in Interviewing, Counseling, Psychotherapy, and Psychoedu-*

cation. Springfield: Charles C Thomas, Publisher, 1978. Although Ivey and Authier's book was originally intended for peer counselors, the important techniques for listening and questioning effectively are dealt with at considerable length.

Chapter 4

HOW ADULTS LEARN

MOST tutors feel comfortable about the extent of their knowledge in their major field due to the number of courses they have taken and the in-depth readings they have completed. But, is this enough to make a tutor effective? Does a person's knowing a great deal about a subject area necessarily mean that person is able to share knowledge with others?

We have all known the teacher or professor who was an indisputable expert in his or her field, but who could not effectively help students learn about the subject. Clearly, being an expert in a subject area does not always make a person good at facilitating learning for others. Facilitating learning is a skill in itself. Several factors affect this skill of teaching; understanding how adults learn is one of the most important factors involved.

No one knows precisely how all adults learn; however, many researchers have broached the question, and several models of learning have been developed. These models attempt to illustrate graphically how adults go about taking in and processing information. In this Chapter, you will examine in depth a basic model of information processing and briefly review several other models. Learning is a complex phenomenon; no one model of information processing is definitive, but exposure to several of the models will help you to visualize the variety of ways adults deal with information.

Specifically, the objectives of this Chapter are that you become familiar with several models of learning and learn how to apply them to improve your tutoring, whatever your subject area.

THE MODEL

The late Swiss educational psychologist and researcher Jean Piaget developed a model of learning based on stages;* Piaget believed that all learners progressed through a series of successive learning stages as they grew older, culminating finally in a stage characterized by mature thinking and creative problem-solving abilities. Other researchers have shown that many persons, even those enrolled in college or adult basic education courses, have not yet reached the final mature, problem-solving stage. Still other researchers working in educational psychology have recommended ways to apply Piaget's stage theory in practical learning situations in order to help learners become mature problem-solvers.†

Another important component of Piaget's model of learning deals with the importance of letting learners think material through, even though they may become frustrated as a result of the process. Because thinking things through is so vital to the learning process, it is important that tutors do not succumb to the temptation prematurely to provide answers for students who are struggling to learn.

EXERCISE ONE‡

To complete this exercise, first obtain from your supervisor a small mirror set aside for this exercise. You will also need a sheet of blank 8½ x 11 inch paper and a pen or pencil. Place the paper in front of you on the desk and place the mirror at the top of the sheet facing you so that the surface of the sheet shows in the mirror. Now, your task is to draw on the sheet the figures below, so that they appear *in the mirror* as they appear below. Try to watch the mirror only. Do not watch your hand. The figures must be right side up and have the same size and orientation of parts as do the figures below.

---

*Mary Ann Spencer Pulaski, *Understanding Piaget: An Introduction to Children's Cognitive Development*, (New York: Harper & Row, 1971), pp. 41-77.

†Robert Karplus. *A New Look at Elementary School Science*, (Chicago: Rand McNally & Co., 1969), pp. 81-97.

‡Mirror exercise adapted from learning cycles developed by the ADAPT Program, University of Nebraska, Lincoln.

Keep trying until you can reproduce all three figures tolerably well. As soon as you finish the drawings, stop briefly and consider what your feelings were while you were completing the figures. Below, note the continuum. Above the continuum appears a list of descriptive words representing emotions you might have been feeling. Think back over your feelings at the beginning, middle and end of the drawing exercise. From the list of words, choose only three to write on the continuum: one to represent your feelings as you started the task, one to represent your feelings as you worked on the task, and one to represent your feelings once you had successfully completed the drawings.

WORD LIST: challenged, expectant, angry, frustrated, annoyed, pleased, self-assured, discouraged, determined

as you started   *as you finished*
drawing   *drawing*

_____

_____

EXERCISE TWO

Your next task is to consider the three verbal puzzles which follow. For puzzle two, the answer is given in the footnote at the bottom of page 35. The answer for the other two puzzles you must provide yourself. Write all three answers in the blanks provided.

Puzzle One:

If in legal terms, there is the lessor and the lessee, then in tutoring there is the tutor and the_____

Puzzle Two: *

$$\frac{plant}{weed} = \frac{mushroom}{?}$$

Puzzle Three:

Question: When is a door not a door?

Answer: _____

The answer to Puzzle Three is available from your supervisor; however, try your best to deduce the answer before requesting it. Once you know the answer to all three puzzles, consider the following questions:

a. As you worked on each puzzle, what were your feelings?
b. Was there a difference in your feelings as you dealt with each puzzle?
c. As you dealt with the figure drawing, were your feelings more like your feelings as you worked on Puzzle One, Two, or Three?

Now that you have worked with several learning tasks of varying difficulty, stop to consider the range and movement of feelings which learners may experience. Consider how learners might feel in encountering (a) a *simple problem* which they *can solve* (Puzzle One); (b) a *problem* for which the *answer is immediately revealed* without the students' having to think it through (Puzzle Two) and (c) a *difficult problem which they solve only after much mental work* or not at all (Puzzle Three). As you consider these points, you may find it helpful to talk with another student who has completed the Chapter up to this point, or to talk with your supervisor.

Record here a short statement summarizing the range and movement of your feelings as you worked on the three puzzles:

_____

_____

_____

*The correct answer to this analogy is "toadstool." Try to think through the puzzle before looking at the explanation on the next page, at NB

Now that you have experienced anew the feelings of frustration which can accompany any person's efforts to learn a new task or to find a difficult answer, read below a discussion of how this frustration can enhance learning.

Enhancing Learning

In Piaget's model, the process of learning with the help of frustration is called *self-regulation* and includes three stages: *assimilation, disequilibration (frustration)* and *accommodation.*

As learners take in new information, they seek to fit it with their existing knowledge. If the new information or idea fits, learners can merely log it into their thought banks. This, Piaget called *assimilation.* However, if the new material does not fit, then learners are apt to experience a kind of mental frustration known as "disequilibration." This feeling is probably most akin to your feelings during the figure drawing or the solving of Puzzle Three. During these two activities, you likely experienced a sense of frustration caused by the lack of "fit" between your mental expectations and the new situation. In the figure drawing, your mental expectation was that left was left and right right. Using the mirror, however, made it necessary that left became right, and that down became up. As you solved the third puzzle (if you did) you had to deal with a contradiction about a word "door" with which you had been familiar for many years.

Feelings of disequilibration can impel learners to discover ways to make new information fit into their mental expectations. However, this can only be accomplished if the learners are willing to make changes in their mental expectations. Making such changes is called *accommodation.*

NB: In reference to the analogy, the term *plant* relates to the term *weed* in the same way that the term *mushroom* relates to the term *toadstool.* *Weed* and *toadstool* are commonly used to indicate nondesirable plants. Additionally, botanists ignore both terms because they have no scientific definition. Both *plant* and *mushroom*, however, are scientifically accepted terms.

*As you read, be sure you understand the terms *assimilation, accommodation*, and *equilibration* and how they relate to each other.

For example, students who attempted the figure drawing task must have felt a great deal of disequilibration when they discovered that the normal signals of "left," and "right," "up" and "down" which they gave to their drawing hand would not produce the desired results. Most students continue to struggle with the task, in spite of their frustration, until they have succeeded by discovering that left has become right, and up down. Students who make these mental adjustments have successfully accommodated; they have altered their existing mental structures or expectations to allow new information to "fit in."

By the same token, those tutors who pondered the riddle of the door which is not a door must have felt disequilibration also. How could a door not be a door? In English, this is an impossibility. Only altering of expectations will allow a person to solve the puzzle, thus accommodating the new concept that the door can indeed not be a door, if it is ajar (a jar).

When the accommodation is successful in the eyes of the learners, then equilibrium or mental balance is reached, and they feel success instead of frustration. If successful accommodation is not reached, then learners either continue with the process until accommodation is reached, or give up seeking the answer. For these learners, the frustration has become too great. As a result, they choose other means to reach accommodation. At best, they seek tutoring or conferences with their instructor.

In the best of all possible worlds, learners could simply assimilate all new knowledge, but this is not always the case. No matter how intelligent we may be, all of us occasionally encounter new information which seems to contradict some preexisting thoughts in our minds. When this occurs, we feel disequilibrated. This disequilibration is the catalyst that changes us from lackadaisical thinkers into those who are working hard to find a way to accommodate the new information with the thoughts we previously had. Thus, a certain amount of disequilibration is desirable, as it is one of the forces which moves learners through the learning process; without this tension, learning of difficult material may fail to occur.

EXERCISE THREE

How can you apply your new knowledge about assimilation, disequilibration and accommodation to the tutoring situation? The following exercise will illustrate how a tutor, Ernest, uses his knowledge of Piagetian learning theory to assist a student.

The student, Pamela, has been working regularly throughout the semester with Ernest, a third year math major. Pamela rushes in one day to her tutoring session visibly upset. She has just come from her math class and explains to Ernest that her teacher has introduced to the class the terms "mean, mode and median." Although Dr. Robbins spent 20 minutes explaining the three terms, Pamela discovered that as soon as she left class she did not understand the terms clearly. She also began to doubt her understanding of the process of averaging numbers, which she previously thought she understood. Pamela requests that Ernest explain the four terms for her "in real simple words," so that she may write the definitions down in her notebook.

In this situation, it is obvious that she was already in a state of disequilibration when she entered the tutoring center. She had evidently heard new information during her lecture class and, to her dismay, found it did not fit with her previous math knowledge. Thus, she could not assimilate it and in frustration sought help from her tutor.

She thought that she remembered what an "average" was from her days in grade school. Suddenly, she was presented with three new math terms, one of which she did not realize was the same as "average." Thus, she thought that her conception of "average" was wrong all along. How could two terms mean the same thing?

Being an experienced tutor, Ernest would not attempt immediately to *tell* Pamela the correct definitions nor to redefine averaging for her. Instead, he would seek to discover what mental operations Pamela has employed so far in her effort to understand. Consequently, Ernest would start the session by *asking Pamela to tell him what she understands so far about each term*, one by one, beginning with the points about which she is surest. In this way, he can ascertain what she heard and what attempt she has made so far to accommodate the new terms (how was she going about making the information consistent with her previous knowledge?). The next part of the conversation might be as follows:

Ernest says, "What part is confusing you the most?" Pamela replies, "I always thought that an average was adding together a bunch of numbers and dividing by the number of numbers. But now (looking at her notes) Dr. Robbins says that the mean is found by adding numbers and dividing by the number of items added, thus trying to find the midground. But he also said the median is the mid-point. So if that's true, then what's the average?" Ernest says he can explain this best by an example. He then writes a series of ten numbers quickly and asks Pamela to find the average of the list. This she does correctly, and Ernest tells her that she is correct. Then Ernest asks her to apply Dr. Robbins' directions for finding the mean to the list. With a small frown, Pamela adds the numbers and divides the total by the number of items she added (10). The results are, of course, the same as she found for the average. Ernest queries, "Is that the same process?" Pamela replies that it is, and Ernest confirms to her that the mean is just another term for an average. Thus, Ernest has allowed Pamela to think through her confusion without barraging her with definitions to memorize. He is also sure that Pamela can find the mean of a series of numbers, because she can perform the operation on paper without error. Before they go on, Ernest may ask Pamela to explain what usefulness she thinks a mean may have in her class, so that she has a reason for remembering the term.

Once Pamela has demonstrated that she understands average and mean and can actually do the arithmetic to find the mean, Ernest can continue his questioning to help Pamela verbalize the difference between the informal term used by Dr. Robbins (midground) and the more formal math term (mid-point), so that Pamela can differentiate mean and median.

Notice that Ernest has employed his understanding of Piagetian learning theory by questioning Pamela about her grasp of new information. As the session proceeds, Ernest thereby helps Pamela to regain equilibration so that she feels confident about math terms.

It is important to note that Pamela understood much more than she thought she did, and Ernest's primary function was to show her that this was so, not to simply copy Dr. Robbins' behavior and *tell* her the four definitions over and over. It is a common occurrence in tutoring situations for a new tutor to *tell* a student the "right answer" before checking what the student already understands. Often students exclaim, "I don't understand any of this!" when, in reality, they understand at least part of the material; your questioning will bring out the student's understanding.

The example below presents another instance of a student's feeling disequilibration because of encountering new ideas which do not fit with previous knowledge.

Charles, a student who is taking beginning accounting, is struggling to understand the basic terms "debit and credit." Charles' general understanding is that credit works for a person and debit works against a person. However, when Charles' instructor announces that increases in assets and expense accounts are debits, while increases in liability and revenue accounts are credits, he is dismayed. He wonders how can an increase in assets be a debit? And how can an increase in liability be a credit? These ideas contradict his general understanding.

Charles seeks tutorial help. He meets with the accounting tutor, Myra. In this session, Charles immediately brings up his confusion over the terms "debit" and "credit." Instead of explaining the terms to Charles right away, Myra proceeds to question Charles to ascertain his understanding of the two terms. As a result of her questioning, Myra is able to discern the cause of Charles' confusion and to clear up the confusion by showing Charles the new meaning of the two terms by use of examples. As soon as Charles realizes that in accounting these two terms have a special meaning, his disequilibration should begin to fade and accommodation begin.

These two examples illustrate the importance of understanding Piagetian principles for effective tutoring. Tutors who wish to be more effective *question* their students about the source of their confusion *before* they begin tutoring on the subject at hand. Because students may already be disequilibrated, nothing is more disheartening to them than to have a tutor launch into repetitions of what the professor has already said or overwhelm them with additional information.

EXERCISE FOUR

Your final task in this part of the Chapter is to develop a tutoring situation along the lines of the tutoring sessions illustrated above. Below, fill in the blanks as indicated and compose the first few sentences of the conversation between the student and the tutor.

Dialogue

_____: "Hi: Here I am again. I've

any student's name

just come from a heavy lecture in_____.

your subject area

Am I ever confused about_____

two or more vocabulary terms

_____!
I sure hope you can help me. Just tell me the answers and then
I'll go catch my bus."_____

your name

replies: "_____

_____

_____

_____

_____."

When you have completed the dialogue, turn it in to your supervisor.

OTHER WAYS ADULTS LEARN

Many factors exist which affect the ways in which people learn. We have already considered the model of Jean Piaget. Below, we will consider five other factors that bear on learning: (1) auditory learning, (2) visual learning, (3) kinesthetic learning, (4) inductive learning and (5) deductive learning.

All five of these factors are likely to affect each learner to some degree or the other; they do not contradict the model of Piaget, but rather complement his theory. Furthermore, none of the five factors contradict one another; all learners are affected to some degree by all five factors.

AUDITORY LEARNING. Are you skilled in auditory learning, i.e. learning by listening? For example, do you take lecture notes with ease? Do you remember things you have been told? Do you like to study by discussing ideas with others? Do you remember the words to songs you've heard? Can you remember spoken telephone numbers without writing them down? If you answered "yes" to most of these questions, you probably have strengths in auditory learning.

VISUAL LEARNING. Even though you may have strengths in auditory learning, you may also have strengths as a visual learner. For example, do you learn more from reading textbooks than from listening to lectures? Do you prefer to read written directions as opposed to having someone tell you how to proceed? Do you know how words look when they're spelled right? Can you visualize maps and charts after you have looked away from them? Can you recall telephone numbers you only saw once? If you answered "yes" to most of these questions, you may have a good visual learning aptitude.

KINESTHETIC LEARNING. Some people have strengths both auditorily and visually, but, there is a third avenue for learning. This avenue is called "kinesthetic." Kinesthetic learners learn from tactile stimulation, i.e. from touching or using their muscles. To determine whether you are strong in this area, ask yourself these questions. Do you doodle a lot? Did you learn your spelling words in grade school by writing them over and over? Do you enjoy handling the equipment and materials in classes such as chemistry and biology? Do you prefer to take your lecture notes home and type them out? (These situations offer stimulation to the muscles of the writing hand and arm). If you answered "yes" to most of the questions above, you may be skilled in kinesthetic learning. However, it is unlikely that students who have reached adult learning tasks would be exclusively kinesthetic. Most students possess strengths in auditory and/or visual areas, with some smaller degree of strength kinesthetically.

In addition to the three areas considered above are the areas of inductive and deductive learning.

INDUCTIVE LEARNING. Inductive learners enjoy being given academic problems *to solve*, whether in math or humanities classes. To determine your strength in this area, ask yourself the following questions. Do you like to gather small bits of information and build them into a bigger comprehensive idea? Do you enjoy the challenge of a crossword puzzle and prefer to struggle with an entry instead of looking at the answer puzzle? Do you prefer to learn the rules of a new game by watching and then just plunging in? Do you have little trouble following lecturers who give all the details before talking about the main point?

DEDUCTIVE LEARNING. Some persons are strong deductive learners; they prefer to have the whole picture, not just the details, as they are learning. Do you sneak a peek at the answer puzzle when you are working on a crossword puzzle or look at the answers at the end of the book when working math problems? Ask yourself the following: Would you rather have a comprehensive idea in mind before gathering details to explain or support the larger idea? Do you prefer to learn new card games by being told, "The object of the game is . . ." before you hear the details about bidding and play?

Even though some of the questions about the five factors above seem to indicate opposite or even contradictory skills, some persons can truthfully answer "yes" to almost all of them. These persons have strengths in all five areas and are able to capitalize on their strengths to meet the demands of the situation. Others answer "yes" to only some of the questions. These persons may have limited skills in some of the five areas mentioned and therefore be less able to learn efficiently. As a result, they may not perform as well in certain classes or at certain academic tasks. It is likely that students who request tutoring could evidence weakness in one or more of the five areas; it is important, therefore, that you be attentive to which areas represent strengths and weaknesses for students with whom you work.

Applications to Tutoring

An effective way to discover which modes of learning students favor is to ask questions much like the examples above. Another way to supplement your perceptions about your students' learning modes is to observe the things they do as students. Do they have many pages of notes in their lecture notebooks? Do they allow you to finish your explanations to them before attempting to take down every word in their notebooks? Can they reiterate the contents of a lecture they have just heard without looking at notes? If so, these students have auditory strengths.

This strength would suggest that in your tutoring you should promote as much discussion of ideas as possible. Instead of asking these students to do extra reading on the subject, question them orally about the material they have already read. Get a discussion going. If a student is somewhat shy, consider pairing one student with another from the same course to make a small discussion group. Ask the students frequently to reiterate or paraphrase what they have heard in lecture or lab in order to take advantage of their auditory strength. (Use your skills in paraphrasing to check the students' comprehension of material.)

On the other hand, do you find students hurriedly writing things down while you are in mid-explanation as if they fear they will not remember what you said for more than a few seconds? Do they sometimes say, "That word doesn't look like it's spelled right." Are they often unable to repeat the contents of a lecture but are skilled at telling you what they read in their text? If so, these students have visual strengths.

Visual strengths suggest that you focus your tutoring on writing, whether on the board or on paper so that students have ample opportunity to see what the written information looks like. This is crucial to visually oriented students. They could also be encouraged to use flashcards and other visual representations of information.

As a third possibility, your students may have strongly kinesthetic skills. If this is so, encourage students to write problems, notes, spelling words, and definitions repetitively on the chalkboard or in their notebooks.

It is relatively easy to assess students' auditory, visual and kinesthetic strengths, but the inductive or deductive strength of learners is more difficult to observe. Often, you will work with students whose learning strength in this regard is not clear to you. It is important, even so, that you be aware of the way in which you go about presenting material.

Are you already in the habit of making mostly inductive presentations, i.e. helping students think through details to reach a main point? Or, do you usually proceed deductively, i.e. telling main points first?

As you learned from the first part of the Chapter, presenting material inductively is usually best, because it allows students to think through the material. However, in some cases this may not be effective. Some students will be unable to tell the tutor what part of the lesson they do understand and which part is still confusing. They may simply say hopelessly "I don't know" to any question the tutor puts to them. If students are so confused or panicked that they cannot even frame a reply, then proceeding deductively may be necessary.

In the case of Pamela and Ernest, for example, suppose that Pamela had been so disequilibrated and distraught that she was only able to exclaim, "I'm so confused" and show Ernest her notebook in despair. If his questioning of Pamela produced no results, Ernest might have to proceed deductively in order to lessen Pamela's anxiety. In this case, he could simply tell Pamela the definitions of the terms, *average*, *mean*, *median*, and *mode* and then work some examples with her to illustrate the concepts, returning to a more inductive approach in later sessions.

Just as your understanding of the ways adults learn will affect your tutoring, your feelings about linguistically or culturally different persons may affect the way you behave in the tutoring situation. The next Chapter deals with this aspect of tutoring.

RECOMMENDED READING

John Dewey on Education: Selected Writings. ed. Reginald D. Archambault. New York: Random House, Inc., 1964, Archambault's introduction and Dewey's essays, "Progressive Education and the Science of Education," "School Conditions and the Training of Thought," "The Child and the Curriculum," and "The Process and Product of Reflective Thinking" will be of most interest. Although Dewey speaks mostly of children, his ideas have been found to apply equally well to learners of any age. Although Dewey is usually classed as a philosopher and Piaget a researcher, their ideas on learning are similar.

Messick, Samuel, and associates. *Individuality in Learning.* San Francisco: Jossey-Bass Publishers, 1976. Although it is advanced reading, Messick's book, especially Chapter Three, is valuable for readers who wish to learn more about learning styles.

Piaget, Jean. *To Understand Is to Invent: The Future of Education.* New York: Penguin Books, 1977. The first essay in this volume, "Où va l'éducation?" or "a Structural Foundation for Tommorow's Education," centers around Piaget's belief that thinking through academic questions is more valuable than memorizing facts.

Pulaski, Mary Ann Spencer. *Understanding Piaget: An Introduction to Children's Cognitive Development.* New York: Harper & Row, Publishers, 1971. Piaget's stage theory and its implications for teaching are clearly elucidated.

Chapter 5

LINGUISTIC, CULTURAL, SEXUAL
AND AGE-ORIENTED ATTITUDES
IN TUTORING

INEVITABLY, adults in most formal educational settings come into contact with other adults who differ from them in many ways. Indeed, this "confrontation" is one of the most stimulating side effects of being on a college campus or in an adult education center where a number of adult students are gathered. With equal inevitability, differences will emerge, notably in language and cultural habits, and in attitudes toward sex and aging. Although these issues are outside the realm of education in the formal sense, they often have an impact on the tutoring situation.

Most people expect some differences to emerge when they meet persons from another country, but it is as often true that persons from ostensibly the same culture will manifest many differences in their attitudes toward a multitude of subjects. Indeed, some social scientists are fond of saying that the differences among members of different cultures or different countries are no larger than the differences among members of the same culture.

LINGUISTIC ATTITUDES

By adulthood, most persons have developed deeply embedded attitudes about language and language habits. Some of these attitudes are nearly unconscious, while others are closer to the surface and easier for a person to articulate. The objective of the following language inventory is to help you bring to a conscious level some of your attitudes about language. The inventory consists of a number of statements. Read each one and consider how much or little you agree with it. Circle the phrase most closely matching your reaction to the statement.

Inventory of Language Attitudes

1. Persons who have British accents often sound very intelligent and well-informed.

   definitely   somewhat   agree   somewhat   definitely
      agree   agree   disagree   disagree

2. All adult students should be able to sound out and pronounce new words from their courses, even difficult vocabulary.

   definitely   somewhat   agree   somewhat   definitely
      agree   agree   disagree   disagree

3. Southern drawls and dialects always sound slovenly or sluggish to me.

   definitely   somewhat   agree   somewhat   definitely
      agree   agree   disagree   disagree

4. I grow impatient (inwardly) with people who talk very slowly and stop to think a lot after they begin talking.

   definitely   somewhat   agree   somewhat   definitely
      agree   agree   disagree   disagree

5. Dialect jokes may be unkind, but they're often very funny.

   definitely   somewhat   agree   somewhat   definitely
      agree   agree   disagree   disagree

6. I'm secretly annoyed when people mispronounce words, especially when I know they've heard them said correctly.

   definitely   somewhat   agree   somewhat   definitely
      agree   agree   disagree   disagree

7. Nonstandard dialect phrases like "I be studying," "don't have none," and "youse" (for you plural) make persons who use them sound like they're not intelligent (even though they may be quite intelligent).

definitely agree	somewhat agree	agree	somewhat disagree	definitely disagree

8. All adult students should be able to spell with accuracy or at least to use a dictionary well enough to correct their own misspellings.

definitely agree	somewhat agree	agree	somewhat disagree	definitely disagree

Now that you have completed the inventory, read the following analysis.

ANALYSIS A (Items 1, 3, 5, and 7)

Persons who agree with these items are acutely aware of accents and dialects and seldom fail to notice them. Whatever their outward reaction, their inner reaction to persons with accents and nonstandard dialect patterns is one which has been formed by what they imagine the dialect or accent to represent, for instance, the British accent representing intelligence. Even though the persons who agree with the statements may not actually be prejudiced, they have done some pre-judging. This capacity to prejudge could make them act prejudicially, although this is not inevitable.

Consider how much you concur or differ in opinion from the above analysis and circle the appropriate response. If you answer "disagree mostly" or "disagree thoroughly," write out your basis for disagreement on a piece of notebook paper.

Agree Thoroughly	Agree Mostly	Agree	Disagree Mostly	Disagree Thoroughly

ANALYSIS B (Items 2, 4, 6, and 8)

Persons who agree with these items could be described as having high language standards for themselves and equally high expectations for other persons. They believe that adults should be able to function skillfully with language tasks and that persons who cannot may have lower intelligence or perhaps just do not belong in a college or adult education center. However, persons who agree with these items may be quite discreet and no one knows they have these opinions.

Consider how much you concur or differ in opinion from the above analysis, and circle the appropriate response. If you answer "disagree mostly" or "disagree thoroughly," write out your basis for disagreement on a piece of notebook paper.

Agree Thoroughly	Agree Mostly	Agree	Disagree Mostly	Disagree Thoroughly

When you have completed the Chapter to this point, find another tutor in your center or program who is ready to discuss the inventory and the analyses. Meet with your partner and compare your responses. Remember that there are no right or wrong answers or attitudes about language. There are merely many possible attitudes and some of them are more helpful to tutors than others. You are the best judge of this. Also keep in mind that the analyses were written rather emphatically and one-sidedly in order to evoke a strong and honest response. Some tutors are annoyed that the inventory is too short and encourages a superficial response. Even if you are somewhat annoyed with the analyses, please recall that the point of reading them is to give tutors the opportunity to make a thoughtful self-analysis about their language attitudes.

If you are like most people, somewhat less than perfect, you may have discovered in yourself some attitudes that you would describe as less than ideal. If you did find evidence of prejudice in yourself, however, you are not alone. Most adults, and therefore most tutors, are like you. The important thing is not to let the students with whom you are working be aware of your feelings if they are negative. Regardless of your hidden feelings, you can project a positive and supportive linguistic attitude toward students if you respect students' regular language habits. If they are preparing a formal English paper or a speech, it is appropriate for you to correct their language. Otherwise, it is best not to comment on another person's oral language, particularly in the presence of other people.

CULTURAL, SEXUAL AND AGE-ORIENTED ATTITUDES

Just as most people have deeply embedded attitudes about language, they have also developed rather fixed attitudes about cultural, sexual and age differences. Although we try to avoid prejudging other persons, most of us have some stereotypes in our minds about the opposite sex, older or younger people, or persons from cultures different from our own. These deeply embedded attitudes may have an impact on tutoring situations if we allow them to color our actions, speech or decisions about matters related to tutoring. Because of this possibility, it is imperative that tutors examine their thoughts on these topics.

The situations below represent the meeting of persons from differing cultural backgrounds, age-groups, or sexual orientations. They have been taken from actual tutoring records. Read each situation with two concerns in mind:

1. What beliefs about behavior, aging or sex are illustrated by each situation? (In each case there will be at least two beliefs: one for the tutor and one for the student.)

2. Should the tutor attempt to do anything to alter the belief or attitude or, in other words, to change the situation? If yes, what?

Write your answers on a separate sheet. The first one has been done for you by a former tutor.

Example One

An older woman visited the tutoring center for academic assistance. She was paired with a younger woman who tutored in the subject area. Although the older woman was talkative and pleasant when she registered for tutoring, her tutor noticed she was withdrawn and silent during their first session. The next day, the older woman came into the center and asked to be assigned a different tutor, in her words, "an older person who knows more about the subject."

1. What beliefs about behavior, aging or sex are illustrated by each situation? (In each case there will be at least two beliefs: one for the tutor and one for the student.)

This situation centers around attitudes toward aging. The older woman obviously thinks that someone nearer her own age would know more (not an uncommon attitude in many cultures and in the United States). Probably the tutor knows as much as necessary or she would not have been accepted to work as a tutor.

2. Should the tutor attempt to do anything to alter the belief or attitude or, in other words, to change the situation? If yes, what?

Probably, the tutor should step aside and let another tutor take over the assignment, so she actually doesn't have to do anything. She may feel somewhat frustrated or perhaps insulted. I myself would feel more insulted, but I would try to keep saying to myself that the "rejection" had nothing to do with me personally and that the lady probably wouldn't have liked anyone under her own age.

Example Two

A female tutor nicknamed "Mickey" accepted an assignment pairing her with a student, Bob, for assistance in Speech 101. During their first session Mickey helped Bob revise his speech outline which had come back from the instructor with directions to revise. Bob was cooperative, but Mickey was a little uncomfortable because the subject of the speech was "the natural inferiority of women." During the session, when Mickey asked Bob if he meant his delivery to be ironic, he said of course not, that he truly believed the ideas and wanted to sound sincere. He also said that he thought Mickey was very helpful even though he had been unpleasantly surprised to find that someone named Mickey was not male.

1. What beliefs about behavior, aging or sex are illustrated by each situation?
2. Should the tutor attempt to do anything to alter the belief or attitude or, in other words, to change the situation? If yes, what?

Example Three

A tutor had been working with two students (in separate sessions) who were friends. Both usually had appointments with the tutor on the same day at adjacent hours. On one day, without explanation, both students were absent. The next week, both were present at their expected hours. When the tutor asked what had been amiss the week previous, both students said, "Didn't my friend tell you? We were at my third cousin's daughter's christening in a neighboring state. I'm sure I told you about it a long time ago, and it was last week. I hope you didn't wait around for us." Then the tutor faintly did remember a mention of a christening, but he hadn't imagined that anyone would give up classes in order to attend such a function.

1. What beliefs about behavior, aging or sex are illustrated by each situation?
2. Should the tutor attempt to do anything to alter the belief or attitude or, in other words, to change the situation? If yes, what?

Example Four

David, a biology tutor, was assigned to assist a female student, Penny. After several weeks, David found that Penny was making up excuses to stay late after tutoring sessions and sometimes patted him on the hand or shoulder when it did not seem necessary. One day in the lunch room Penny found David at a corner table and invited herself to sit down. She asked David to go to dinner with her. When he declined with a polite excuse, to David's horror Penny began to pout and then to sniffle and use a tissue. Although she took no for an answer that day, she continued in subsequent weeks to repeat her request, often with tears.

1. What beliefs about behavior, aging or sex are illustrated by each situation?
2. Should the tutor attempt to do anything to alter the belief or attitude or, in other words, to change the situation? If yes, what?

Example Five

A tutor at the tutoring center took on an assignment to assist another student who was on a temporary student visa to study in the United States. When she met the student, she liked her immediately except for one thing. Whenever Farana met with her tutor it seemed Farana's voice volume rose with her level of excitement and interest until she was virtually shouting, or so it seemed to her tutor. Her voice could be heard all over the tutoring center and into the hall. Sometimes other students looked up from their books as if they were annoyed by the noise. Otherwise, she was a very intelligent and cooperative student and was always on time for her appointments with her homework done. Her tutor was uncertain about whether to broach the subject with Farana when one day she observed Farana talking with some other exchange students in the hallway. At once, the tutor realized that Farana was talking at the same volume as the other foreign students in the group.

1. What beliefs about behavior, aging or sex are illustrated by each situation?
2. Should the tutor attempt to do anything to alter the belief or attitude or, in other words, to change the situation? If yes, what?

Example Six

A young married woman came into the tutoring center for her first session with her accounting tutor. The student brought her husband with her. As soon as the tutor, Dennis, and the student, Marliss, were seated, Marliss' husband, Lonnie, began to say, "The problem with Marliss is that she went through high school in a very small town and they didn't expect very much from their graduates. Marliss is very smart, you understand, but she has lots of trouble with math. Actually, I think she isn't even very sure of her times tables, isn't that right, honey?" Dennis turned to Marliss to see what she would have to say, but she had nothing to add. Then Lonnie took up the conversation again, and monopolized most of the hour with a recitation of Marliss' academic faults. Finally Dennis could stand it no longer and turned dramatically to Marliss, asking, "What do you think about all this, Marliss?" Marliss answered precisely, glancing toward her husband, "I think what he says." Dennis was so surprised that he had no reply, but he had plenty of time to think after the couple left the center.

1. What beliefs about behavior, aging or sex are illustrated by each situation?
2. Should the tutor attempt to do anything to alter the belief or attitude or, in other words, to change the situation? If yes, what?

Example Seven

Jana had been working as an undergraduate teaching assistant in one of the computer programming courses at her institution, and the students in the class had been instructed to seek her help when they had difficulty with their programs. Jana enjoyed her work very much until she encountered Robert, a student from the class. Robert was very polite during the first session; however, once he learned that Jana was a single woman, his behavior changed radically. He developed a habit of patting Jana on her knees and of edging closer toward her whenever they were in the study lounge. When Jana ignored his overtures, Robert resorted to telling suggestive jokes, offering sexual compliments about Jana's body, and commenting loudly about the charms of other young women who passed by their study table. Jana was accustomed to this type of behavior in bars and cocktail lounges (she had been a cocktail waitress during the summer to pay her tuition), but she had never had to deal with it in an academic situation.

1. What beliefs about behavior, aging or sex are illustrated by each situation?
2. Should the tutor attempt to do anything to alter the belief or attitude or, in other words, to change the situation? If yes, what?

Example Eight

Henry, an aviation tutor, was given the opportunity to work with a student, Daniel, who was new to the United States. During the first two sessions, they got along very well and enjoyed discussing aviation as well as the native costume and jewelry that Daniel wore. At the third session, however, Daniel was twenty minutes late. When he arrived he did not apologize, so Henry ignored the lateness, and the session went very well (although Henry was forced to be late for his next class). At the next session, Daniel was nearly thirty minutes late, and Henry knew that they did not have very much time to work because his own class was now only twenty minutes away. He was about to explain to Daniel that his lateness created a problem, when suddenly Daniel produced a little box, which was a present for Henry — an ivory hand-made ornament from Daniel's homeland. Then, Henry did not know what to do.

1. What beliefs about behavior, aging or sex are illustrated by each situation?

2. Should the tutor attempt to do anything to alter the belief or attitude or, in other words, to change the situation? If yes, what?

After you have completed your responses to each of the eight examples, find another tutor who has completed the assignment to this point. Exchange your answers so that you can each read and discuss the other's responses to the eight situations. Remember, there are no right answers. Probably you will agree on some points and not on others. When you are finished with your discussion, consult the Sample Answers that follow to see what other tutors answered. Of course, these are not right answers either; they are composites of several tutors' responses.

Example Two

1. What beliefs about behavior, aging or sex are illustrated by each situation?

   This situation concerns Bob's beliefs about the natural inferiority of women.

2. Should the tutor attempt to do anything to alter the belief or attitude or, in other words, to change the situation?

   In this case, Mickey should probably let well enough alone. Although she may not like Bob's attitudes about women, it is not appropriate for a tutor to challenge students' private beliefs if they do not jeopardize their performance in class.

Example Three

1. What beliefs about behavior, aging or sex are illustrated by each situation?

   In this situation, it seems that the students' attitude about their obligation to attend a family gathering was different from the tutor's. Because of this, the tutor had not paid attention to the mention of the christening and expected the students to appear at the usual time.

2. Should the tutor attempt to do anything to alter the belief or attitude, or, in other words, to change the situation?

   Since the incident has already occurred, there is not much the tutor can do except remember that not all persons see non-school obligations in the same light. The whole situation might have been avoided if the tutor had clarified, maybe by paraphrasing, what the students meant by mentioning the christening in the first place.

Example Four

1. What beliefs about behavior, aging or sex are illustrated by each situation?

   In the situation between David and Penny, she evidently thinks that it is appropriate for a student to go out with the tutor with whom she is currently studying. For some reason, David is reluctant to accept the invitation. Maybe he thinks it is inappropriate for a tutor to date a student he works with, or maybe he is married or involved in another relationship.

2. Should the tutor attempt to do anything to alter the belief or attitude or, in other words, to change the situation?

   David probably should explain his reasons to Penny for declining the date. Maybe once she understands why he won't go out with her, she will stop asking. Possibly David could use some of his skills at reflecting feelings in order to deal with the issue of her crying occasionally in tutoring sessions.

   If Penny continues to ask David out, and David feels that she can no longer benefit from his tutoring, he could ask Penny to meet with another tutor.

   Although David has declined to date Penny, it is not unknown for teachers and students and for tutors and students to date each other. For some people this may be all right. However, dating persons with whom you are working in a tutoring relationship can cause the roles to be confused.

Suppose you date a student and then have a lovers' quarrel? How would you feel the next day when it came time for your tutoring session?

Example Five

1. What beliefs about behavior, aging or sex are illustrated by each situation?

   It seems that the appropriate voice level in Farana's culture and in the tutor's culture are different.

2. Should the tutor attempt to do anything to alter the belief or attitude or, in other words, to change the situation?

   Probably, the tutor should ignore the issue, unless other people studying nearby are disturbed. In that case, maybe she could say something like, "I think we're talking too loudly. I see other people looking at us." Or, if the tutor is not personally disturbed by the loud volume, she could simply make plans to tutor in a non-study area where loud voices are not an issue.

Example Six

1. What beliefs about behavior, aging or sex are illustrated by each situation?

   In this situation, Lonnie and Marliss must think it is appropriate for a husband to speak for his wife. Dennis, on the other hand, is surprised by this behavior; probably he thinks most people should talk for themselves.

2. Should the tutor attempt to do anything to alter the belief or attitude or, in other words, to change the situation?

   He will not need to do anything unless Lonnie shows up at every session and continues his present behavior. If Lonnie shows up and talks for his wife all the time, Dennis will have to confront the situation. He could explain that it is imperative that all tutors talk directly to students with whom they work so that the tutor can hear how the student paraphrases the points of the lesson. Since this discussion between Dennis and Marliss might not be very interesting to Lonnie, he could suggest that Lonnie listen in, or wait in the lounge.

If husband Lonnie still refuses to let Dennis talk directly to his wife, he will just have to make the best of it. Perhaps he could give lots of written homework or problems to work on while Marliss is present, so that he could check her understanding in that way.

Example Seven

1. What beliefs about behavior, aging or sex are illustrated by each situation?

   Obviously, Robert thinks that making sexual innuendos is appropriate in the tutoring situation. Jana apparently thinks it is inappropriate, if not insulting.

2. Should the tutor attempt to do anything to alter the belief or attitude or, in other words, to change the situation?

   In order to stop Robert's advances, Jana could explain to him that she thinks sexual talk is not appropriate for a tutoring situation where the focus is supposed to be on academic matters. If Robert persists even after this talk, Jana may request that Robert meet with another tutor, preferably a male.

Example Eight

1. What beliefs about behavior, aging or sex are illustrated by each situation?

   In this example Henry and Daniel must have different expectations about the importance of being on time, or maybe they just do not define "on time" in the same way.

2. Should the tutor attempt to do anything to alter the belief or attitude or, in other words, to change the situation?

   Henry needs to bring up the topic of being on time for appointments. He could explain that the tutoring center is run on the expectation that students and tutors are meeting at the appointed times. At some centers, it is probably the policy that students who are chronically late or absent for appointments have their appointment times given to other students who request tutoring. Whatever the policy is, Henry should explain it. However, if Henry is tutoring

Daniel independently and is paid directly by Daniel, then it is up to Daniel to take advantage of the time he has paid for. But, even under these circumstances, it is still not Henry's obligation to be available for tutoring except at the appointed times.

At best, analyzing the situations above has increased your awareness of the possible impact that linguistic, cultural, sexual and age-oriented attitudes can have on tutoring effectiveness. Perhaps it has also given you some idea of what to expect when you become a tutor. Having thought through these situations will, hopefully, help you deal competently with similar situations in the future.

Up to this point in the text, you have been considering the essential skills of tutoring. Now, we will turn our attention to the ways in which tutors can help students study, read and write with greater skill.

RECOMMENDED READING

Allport, Gordon W. *The Nature of Prejudice*. Massachusetts: Addison-Wesley Publishing Company, 1954. Although dated, this work surveys prejudicial thinking; Part Three may be most useful to you as a tutor.

Chapter 6

HELPING STUDENTS STUDY, READ
AND WRITE EFFICIENTLY

TWELVE CASE STUDIES OF TUTORING (a)

ONE of the distinct pleasures of the tutoring situation is getting acquainted with a variety of other learners in a close friendly relationship. Unfortunately, this is one of the aspects of education that teachers with classes ranging from twenty-five to 300 persons usually miss. Because of the one-to-one relationship allowed by the tutoring situation, you as the tutor can bring to other students perhaps their only opportunity for individually assisted learning. For some students who are experiencing academic troubles, this can make all the difference.

Students who wish to work with a tutor come (or sometimes are assigned by a faculty member) to the tutoring center for a variety of reasons. It would seem that the only logical reason for seeking tutoring would be for assistance with an academic subject. However, many students experience academic difficulties because of their weak study skills. No matter how bright students may be, weak study skills will hamper their ability to perform well in demanding college classes. As a tutor with a particular academic specialty(ies), you may feel that study skills are unrelated to achievement in a subject area. Nothing could be further from the truth. Tutors should not consider their subject area as their only area of responsibility. All tutors should consider themselves responsible for helping with study, reading and writing strategies as they apply to the content areas.

As successful students, you have undoubtedly employed many of these study strategies yourselves and therefore are aware of their value in academic success. Chapter 6 will help you to develop tutoring skills in studying, reading and writing to accompany your subject area expertise.

The objective of this first section of Chapter 6 is to introduce three areas of study-related problems: concept problems*, study skill problems and reading-writing problems. The following sections of Chapter 6 deal with ways to adjust your tutoring to take these areas into account.

These study-related areas will be illustrated by twelve case studies summarized below from tutoring records. In each case, the student has come to the tutoring center for a specific reason. Be cautioned that the reason the student describes may not always be the whole story. This is not to say that students consciously deceive tutors, but rather that students may not be fully aware of all the forces that are at work in creating their study problems. The problem which students state to be the reason for seeking tutoring is usually called the "problem of presentation." But behind the problem of presentation there may be more information of which the tutor would like to be aware.

This is not to say that the tutor is expected to "play the shrink" or to attempt to get at "deep, dark secrets." Deep probing into anyone's personal life is as much out of place in the tutoring situation as it would be at a dinner party. At the same time, it is less helpful for the tutor to work on one problem when the real trouble is something quite different.

After you have read all twelve cases closely, try to group them into similar types of cases, according to four categories: concept, study skills, reading/writing or personal problems.† When you have made the grouping, record the students' names in the spaces provided on page 66.

Case 1

Debbie comes to the tutoring center to see her education tutor, with whom she has been working for a month. As they

---

*I.e. problems caused by failing to understand important academic ideas.
†Personal problems will be dealt with in Chapter 7.

start the session, Debbie says, "I think I understood most of this new stuff, but I'm still not sure what the difference is between 'field dependence' and 'field independence.' "

Case 2

Vince has been visiting the tutoring center for almost the whole semester and usually seems interested and alert. One afternoon, however, he seems preoccupied as he works on chemistry equations with his tutor. When the tutor queries why he seems so "far away," he replies that his child was hospitalized early that morning to undergo an emergency appendectomy.

Case 3

Juan is relatively new to tutoring and is meeting his anthropology tutor for the second time. As they start the session, Juan refers to his text to find the vocabulary word he has intended to bring up to his tutor for clarification. The tutor notices that nearly every line in the book has been marked with yellow highlighter.

Case 4

Ruth has been visiting the tutoring center for assistance in sociology. She tells her tutor that this is the second time she has enrolled in the course, and she is determined to do well this time. However, whenever they start to talk about the important concepts from the chapters, Ruth sheepishly says that she has not "really tried" to do the assigned reading.

Case 5

Letti is studying literature, which she always remarks she enjoys very much, although the reading assignments are "awfully long." On one particular day she asks her tutor, "Can a 'simile' be a comparison and a figure of speech at the same time?"

Case 6

Sam has been a regular student at the tutoring center for several semesters. This term he is seeking help in Algebra 1. Although he seems to be highly motivated, his average on his daily algebra quizzes is below 50 percent. On this particular day, he is working very hard, as usual. During the session, he remarks earnestly, "I'm seeing you and the English tutor and the lady at the counseling center. With all that help, I suppose I'll get mostly A's this term."

Case 7

Mary has been coming regularly to the tutoring center to meet with a sociology tutor. Mary complains, "I studied so long for my essay test and look what I got on this part. See . . . I only got 10 points on this 25 point essay, and I knew the answer!" The tutor looked carefully at the teacher's comments; they said "What does this mean?" and "Not clear."

Case 8

Near the end of the term, Elaine is still working with her tutor in math in order to improve her average on the daily math quizzes. She has dark circles under her eyes and says in a very tired voice that she has not started the problems for the week because she had to move over the weekend. She continues, "This is the third time I've moved this year. What a drag!"

Case 9

Laura, with her tutor in biology, is working on distinguishing and remembering all the one-celled plants and animals she has been assigned for the mid-term. As they are discussing "euglena," Laura turns to consult her lecture notebook. As she opens it and turns the pages, she notes in an undertone, "Let's see . . . sociology . . . ah, here it is . . . no that's not it . . . oh darn, I can't find my biology notes. I don't remember just what day we did that part, or I bet I could find it."

Case 10

Christie, who has come to the tutoring center for assistance in economics, is working with her tutor Jeff. As they both look at a page in her text to see what the author has to say about the "cobweb effect" (which the professor mentioned several times), Jeff scans until he sees the term in boldface and then starts to read to himself. He glances up when he is through with the passage and can tell by the direction of Christie's gaze that she is reading from the column on the left side of the left page. (The cobweb effect does not appear until the right-hand column of the right-hand page.)

Case 11

Bill has been reviewing concepts in psychology with his tutor. On one day, he asks his tutor, "How can they apply all these labels? I don't see how you can tell where 'neurosis' leaves off and 'psychosis' begins."

Case 12

Kathy comes to the tutoring center very depressed. It is just after mid-terms, and she has received a "D" on her objective test for marketing. She complains to her tutor, "I can't imagine why I only got a D. I studied nearly three hours!"

Group _____A_____ _____Concept Problems_____

Students' Names:

Group _____B_____ _____Study Skills Problems_____

Students' Names:

Group _____C_____ _____Reading/Writing Problems_____

Students' Names:

Group _____D_____ _____Personal Problems_____

Students' Names:

One possible grouping of the twelve students is given below:

Group one: Concept problems
                  Debbie, Letti, Bill

Group two: Study skill problems
                  Juan, Laura, Kathy

Group three: Reading/Writing problems
                  Ruth, Mary, Christie

Group four: Personal problems
                  Vince, Sam, Elaine

Do not be concerned if your analysis is not identical to the listing above*. For example, some persons list Vince in a separate group called family problems, Ruth is sometimes listed with the study skill group, or Sam is sometimes separated out in a category called "unrealistic expectations," and so forth. The important thing is to become sensitive to the clues that students give so that you can assist them appropriately. And, you need not be a professional psychologist to perceive some of these clues. Most tutors learn to perceive them with great skill as well as to adjust their tutoring accordingly.

For the purposes of discussion, let us assume that the group listing above is approximately accurate. From this analysis, it is clear that the tutoring situation is multifaceted. A student may seek assistance ostensibly in "sociology," when the root of the problem is actually *reading* this particular sociology text, not any deep-seated confusion about sociological terms. Or, it might be that a student seeks assistance in "biology," when learning to

---

*In this analysis, Debbie, Letti and Bill are grouped because all are concerned about fine distinctions between concepts they have already read about or heard mentioned in connection with their courses. In the study skill group, Juan cannot decide what is important in his anthropology text, so he underlines everything; Laura is a disorganized note-taker; and Kathy has vastly underestimated the time necessary for preparing for a mid-term. In the reading group, Ruth may be avoiding her reading because it is so frustrating for her; Mary composes essay answers unclearly and Christie probably does not yet know how to scan, or if she does, fails to see that scanning is a skill she could use at the moment. In the "personal" group, Vince, who has a child in the hospital, and Elaine, who has just moved *again*, are obviously and maybe justifiably preoccupied with nonstudy concerns. Sam, for some reason, is relying too much on others or spending too much time as a "helpee," leaving him little time for study.

take notes efficiently would clear up the "biology" problem, at least to some extent. And finally, students who seek help in particular subjects may need only and precisely that – help in the subject. This can be seen in the cases of Debbie, Letti, and Bill, who are concerned about the clarification of key terms new to them. As far as can be assumed from the capsule information given, none of these three suffers from reading or study inefficiency or from overbearing personal problems.

Perhaps you as a sociology or biology tutor are thinking, "I'm not a study expert; why can't I just give my student a study skills manual? *My* interest is in my subject." The answer to the question is this: students learn study skills only superficially when they study "studying" in a vacuum. Only study methods in a subject area make sense. It is much better to tutor "notetaking in biology" than notetaking alone. Tutors are in the unique position to do this.

In the next sections of this Chapter, we will turn our attention to two of the three important tutoring areas suggested by the previous exercise: study skills problems and reading/writing problems. (By using your skills in paraphrasing well, you can assist students to clarify concept-related problems. To review paraphrasing, see Chapter 3.)

STUDY TECHNIQUES (b)

As a tutor, you have probably been a successful student in at least your major subject area or area of interest for many years. You may be quite successful in your minor areas of study or interest as well. In fact, you may be one of those people who is virtually an expert in the techniques of study generally and would therefore perform rather well in the study of almost any academic area. This "study sense" probably came from years of usually successful trial and error as you sought the most efficient way to learn academic material. Unfortunately, this very "study sense" may be the vital ingredient that keeps many students from achieving well in academic areas. Granted, talents vary from person to person and subject area to subject area for a single person, but having "study sense" can make the mastering of all subjects less painful and more efficient.

The objective of this section is to help you clarify and verbalize those successful techniques that you have always used to make your own study time more profitable. This section will also present some study techniques that tutors and learning experts have found to be useful. Of course, no technique can be guaranteed to work for everyone, but having exposure to several techniques to choose from has to be a tutoring plus. Since all content area tutors will want to help their students with study and reading skills within the subject area, knowledge of study skills strategies is vital to all tutors.

One of the most efficient ways for you to become more conscious of study techniques you have used successfully is to articulate and describe them. The following activities are designed to help you develop your personal profile as a successful student.

To complete the following activity, choose two of your current subjects as "test cases." If you are currently studying no subjects, consider instead any two academic subjects that you have studied successfully in the recent past. The activity will be more meaningful if you choose two subjects that you believe require very different study approaches, for example, literature versus biology, economics versus art history, or physics versus the history of computers.

The spaces below have been provided for you to record your approach to each subject. In these spaces, write the steps you follow in studying both subjects. Notice that there are spaces to enter not only activities you pursue during the actual study time, but also those activities that you carry out both before and after the study time *per se*. It is very important not to fool yourself during this activity. *Do not* record any behaviors you have not spontaneously used, merely because they represent the way study books you may have seen insist is the right way. As a successful student, the "right way" is most likely the procedure you have actually been following, regardless of its orthodoxy. After you have completed studying one of your "test" subjects, use the space labeled Subject A below to record *what you actually did*. Proceed to the second "test" subject and then fill in the second space provided (B).

Subject A

   Prestudy Activities

   Study Activities

   Poststudy Activities

Subject B

   Prestudy Activities

   Study Activities

   Poststudy Activities

Keep your responses for future reference as you continue on with this chapter.

The remainder of this chapter will concern three basic study areas: (1) textbook reading and noting in the text; (2) remembering and reviewing materials read; and (3) lecture notetaking. It is likely that you both read materials and made efforts to embed them in your memory as you carried out the two exercises above. You may not have included any thinking about the process of lecture notetaking in your two exercises, but lecture notetaking is such an integral part of the study process that this chapter will deal with this topic as one of the "three basics."

Textbook Reading

As a successful student, your techniques in getting the maximum from each textbook are probably highly developed. Next to attending lectures, reading texts may well represent the major investment of your studying time. In the space below, record what you consider to be the three most important steps in using textbooks. Again, these steps should represent your own priorities regarding this topic, rather than a study "authority's" priorities. You may wish to consult your answers to Exercise A or B to refresh your memory on your personal textbook approach. For example, you might list steps such as: (1) answer the questions at the end of each chapter or (2) underline important ideas with a translucent marker, etc.

Three steps for using textbooks:

a.

b.

c.

Your task now is to choose one of your own textbooks as a "test case." Ideally, you should try to work with a typical text, that is, one divided into chapters, with chapter headings and sub-headings, introductory and concluding paragraphs and with study questions at the conclusion of the chapter. If your text is not "typical," try to find one that approximates that familiar format. Choose a chapter that you have not read. Observe the chapter closely and completely, with an eye to using it to the best advantage; however, do not at this point take time actually to read the chapter.

Now, try to devise a system of at least five steps to be used by you or any typical student in reading the chapter in the most efficient possible way. Use all of the text aids provided with the chapter, e.g. vocabulary lists, study questions, illustrations, etc. Write out all your steps in the space below.

Steps for Reading

Textbook

Now that you have devised your own set of steps, you may wish to consider the merits of several other approaches to using textbooks. Numerous study experts and many students also have invented text strategies which others have thought helpful. Keep in mind as you review the following techniques that no one of them is perfect or relevant to all possible texts or all possible study styles or preferences. Also important to keep in mind is the general principle that *any* system is probably better than a random approach, regardless of the steps used in the system. Finally, the best judge of each study system is the individual user of that system. Some techniques work for some students but not for others; study systems originated by students may well be as useful as systems originated by experts. But, the experts have devised some effective study approaches too.

The SQ3R System

The SQ3R textbook reading system was first made famous by its designer, Francis Robinson, in 1941 and has remained one of the most popular systems ever since.* Many students find it useful. Others have considerable trouble with the Q step (question step). As mentioned before, it all depends on the student, the subject and the text.

The letters SQ3R stand for survey, question, read, recite and review. In general, this system asks the student to approach the text *actively* before actually reading much of anything. In order to "survey" an assignment, students should look through the chapter in order to identify its salient ideas. They should read only the chapter title and any other sub-titles, italicized terms, boldface type, and introductory or summary sections. From this activity, readers can be aware of the two to six main ideas presented by the chapter and can make mental predictions about what the titles and subtitles imply the chapter will discuss. Even though a reader's predictions turn out to be inaccurate, the process of predicting sharpens comprehension.†

---

*Francis P. Robinson, *Effective Study*, (New York: Harper & Row, Publishers, 1970), pp. 32-35.

†Yetta M. Goodman, and Carolyn Burke, *Reading Strategies: Focus on Comprehension* (New York: Holt, Rinehart & Winston, 1980), pp. 3-13.

Following this step, students should create for themselves a purpose for reading by making up questions (step 2) from chapter headings or subheadings. For example, one chapter heading of a history text might be "The Louisiana Purchase." From this sub-title, students should think up a question, for example, "Why is the Louisiana Purchase so named as opposed to Michigan Purchase or other name?" When students actually read the section entitled "The Louisiana Purchase," they should actively search for the answer to their question. There is no doubt that this activity, for those students who *can* frame profitable and relevant questions, is one that engages them actively in the reading process. Hence, they avoid the common pitfall of listlessly moving their eyes over and over the printed lines without actually engaging their brains at all.

Step three, "read," represents the familiar activity of reading the chapter section by section, for the purpose of answering the questions the students have formulated. (Answers may be written or oral, depending on the student). Combined within this activity is the next step, "recite." This step requires students to stop periodically during reading (say at the close of every paragraph for very difficult material and at the close of every section for simpler material) in order mentally to review, in the reader's own words, what the message of the printed lines has been and to ensure that they can answer the question they formulated for that section. This step again requires readers to be active and to have their brains "in gear." For this reason, the recite step is one of the most valuable, for it engages those readers who have been reading with the clutch depressed.

During the recite step, readers should write down very short (1 to 4 words) cue phrases on a notesheet to use in reviewing. An important point to remember is that students should never copy directly from the book. Instead, they should (1) read; (2) think about the meaning; (3) decide if it's noteworthy; (4) if it is, write the cue phrases in their own words — without looking at the text.

Students should repeat SQ3R steps 3 and 4 until they have completed the reading assignment.

In the fifth step, "review," students should spend five minutes immediately after reading the entire assignment to recall the main points (probably two to six) without peeking at the book or notes.

Additionally, students should try to state orally the relationship among the main points. Finally, they should try to state the sub-points for each main point, referring to text or notes only to check their accuracy. This process eliminates the time-consuming process of rereading or "looking over" the material endlessly without ever really testing the memory.

Several other versions of Robinson's original system have been introduced through the years. You may see some of them in various study books under the names of PQ4R, OARWET, and others.* All these systems emphasize the Robinson concept of *active* reading by questioning, thinking, evaluating, or relating ideas before, during and after reading. They also stress the importance of reviewing by testing one's memory rather than by reading over and over in the vain hope that the memory will be tested by reading.

As you read about the SQ3R system, you may have remarked to yourself that your own system closely resembles it. Or, it may be that your system is quite different. It is important to keep in mind that no two students or texts are quite alike, so no system is likely to be a perfect fit for every text or reading ability. There are difficulties in all the systems discussed above, and there may be drawbacks in your own system as well. Knowing about the possible difficulties in your own system and other systems can be

---

*PQ4R is a technique designed specifically for textbook reading. Using it will improve your concentration, reading speed and memory of that you have read. PQ4R stands for Preview, Question, Read, Write, Recall *and* Review. The first three steps are much like those of the SQ3R system. The "Write" step involves underlining and/or marginal noting and/or making of flashcards after reading and reflecting on the material. "Recall" is much like the recite step of SQ3R. "Review" stands for recalling all of a reading selection in a kind of summation exercise, plus periodic reviews up until test time. Minnette Lenier and Janet Maker, *Keys to College Success: Reading and Study Improvement*, (New Jersey: Prentice Hall, Inc., 1980), p. 83.

The six letters of OARWET form an *acronym*, which is a word made up of the first letters of the six steps involved. "O" stands for the "Overview," a process which gives you an overall picture of the entire chapter. "A" stands for "Ask," a step in which — before you read — you examine the questions usually found in the book. "R," the first letter of "Read," stands for reading in the regular sense. "W," for "Write," deals with the note-taking step. "E" is for "Evaluate," a most critical step in understanding (and remembering) what you read. And finally, you check yourself with "T," the first letter of the word "Test." Maxwell Norman and Enid S. Kass Norman, *How to Read and Study for Success in College* (New York: Holt, Rinehart, Winston, 1976), p. 50.

very helpful to tutors. For example, some students have trouble in formulating profitable questions in the Q step of the SQ3R procedure. They may make up questions, but perhaps not very helpful ones. To illustrate, a student surveying a history text might come upon the section with the boldface heading, "The Louisiana Purchase." From this heading, the student might ask the question, "What is the Louisiana Purchase?" If students read to find the answer, it is " . . . the vast territory (885,000 square miles) purchased in 1803 (April 30) for $15,000,000 by the United States from France. It extended from the Mississippi to the Rocky Mountains and from the Gulf of Mexico to British America;"* they have the bare bones of the situation at least but might not be able to answer an essay question, such as, "What have been the far-reaching effects of the Louisiana Purchase?" In other words, the SQ3R system can lead some students to overemphasize purely factual knowledge, perhaps at the expense of conceptual knowledge.

The next time you read an assignment, return to your own system of text reading, and proceed through the reading assignment as you normally would. When you have finished, evaluate your own system as objectively as you can and record your evaluation below.

My Own System:

Webster's New International Dictionary, 2nd ed., (Springfield, Massachusetts: G. E. Merriam Company, Publishers, 1958), p. 1461.

The next time you read a new chapter in one of your texts, apply the SQ3R system. After you have given it a fair try with one chapter at least, write a brief evaluation of its strengths and weaknesses relative to that text. Space is provided below for the evaluation.

SQ3R:

Finally, compare the two systems. Probably, they both have strong and weak points. Write your comparison below, noting the important advantages and disadvantages of both. For example, Robinson's system might be ideal for "typical" texts but be less useful for reading literature or math or physics texts.

Comparison:

Keep your notes relative to each system so that you can assist other students with textbook reading. Your supervisor will probably arrange a tutor meeting to discuss textbook strategies.

Now that you have started your student profile by examining your approaches to textbook reading, the next activity in this section will help you to extend the profile to include your perceptions about your system of making notes from textbooks.

Making Notes from the Text

Textbook reading systems can upgrade study efficiency greatly, but they are only part of the study picture. Making notes in (or about) the text and/or underlining in the text are also necessary steps for most students — only those with photographic memories escape them. As an introduction to this section of the chapter, return, if you will, to the section headed "the SQ3R system" on page 73 and proceed through it as if you were reading it in preparation for an upcoming exam that will test your factual recall of study-reading systems. Use your normal method, whether it be underlining, marginal noting, outlining, or other. Do this now.

Now that you have "made notes" on the chapter, consider what techniques you have used, and why you have done so. In other words, analyze the rationale underlying your "notetaking" system. Ask yourself questions such as, "Why did I underline this section as opposed to another?; why did I write this fact, date or figure in the margin?; why did I choose to outline as opposed to underline or make marginal notes?; why did I circle, star, box or otherwise differentiate one or another section or term?; what plans did I have for using my underlining, outlining or notes, etc., as reviewing tools?; will the system I used to mark the text prove to me that I can independently recall the factual portions of the test or only that I can recognize the facts when I see them again?"

After you have considered your own style of making notes, you may be interested in what a number of learning specialists agree are some of the most important facts about noting in (or about) texts.

First, most experts and most teachers agree that *active* readers learn and retain more. So, any activity which requires the reader to *do* something is probably better than the "do nothing but read" system. However, most students underline too much too soon and overburden themselves with trivia. Most study authorities recommend that underlining be done only after a whole page or section has been read and reflected upon a moment. Then, the reader can judiciously choose just *a few* words or phrases per paragraph to underscore or highlight with a translucent marker. Of course, careful underliners choose only those key ideas or words which represent the "gist" of the matter and not great gobs of words. After all, underlining everything means you have, in effect, underlined nothing. If it's all important, you're right back at the starting gate. Consider the next three paragraphs. Read them and underline the important information as you would in any text.

(1) Finally, an important distinction should be made between the mental processes of recognition and recall. Many students fail to make this distinction and study very hard, only to find that they can't quite remember the information they need at test time, although they are sure they did go over it several times. Students who suffer from this complaint have failed to provide opportunities to self-test. The principle of the self-test is the cornerstone of a study system called the Cornell System.* Although the Cornell system is actually designed for lecture note-taking, the procedure fits equally well to notes taken from texts.

(2) To use this principle, students should underline from each section of text several key words or phrases, then summarize the concepts represented by the key words and list them in the book margins or at the bottoms of pages. (If students are using borrowed or library books, then the key words must be written on notecards keyed to the appropriate page numbers.) The trick of using this system is to list very little and to avoid listing anything that might be an *answer* to a question.

(3) As an illustration, suppose a student is reading a textbook on psychology in which he finds a section on the famous psychologist Erik Erikson.† Erikson is remembered in his field for his

---

*Walter Pauk, *How To Study in College*, 2nd ed., (Boston: Houghton-Mifflin, Co., 1974), pp. 125-139.

†E.H. Erikson, *Child and Society*, 2nd ed., (New York: W.W. Norton and Company, Inc., 1963), p. 93.

theoretical model of the eight stages of psychosocial development, which most persons pass through as they move from infancy to late adulthood. Erikson represents each stage by two conflicting terms such as in stage one, "Basic Trust vs. Mistrust," or in stage eight, "Integrity vs. Despair." Students reading this portion of the text may choose to underline the names and characteristics of each of the eight stages. This is perfectly consistent with the principle of the Cornell system so long as the student also lists in the margin (or bottom of page or notecard) the words "Erikson's 8 stages?" During later review, students should not simply reread the passage to see if they recognize the stages upon reading about them again. This is mere recognition. Students need to know if they can independently recall the names of the eight stages along with their important characteristics and age ranges. Upon reviewing, students should cover the printed text, leaving the margin notes visible. As they come upon the phrase, "Erikson's eight stages," they can attempt to recite all they recall about the stages. If they can recall only five of the eight stages, they know exactly which ones they need to review and also which ones they need not waste the time to go over again. If the students had only underlined or written the names of the eight stages in the margin, they would have no opportunity to self-test, because they could not avoid seeing the answers written out for them as they reviewed the text pages.

Now that you have read and underlined the three paragraphs, what would you write in the book margin to jog the information out of your memory for a test a month away?*

Taking Lecture Notes and Remembering Them

Another big part of the study picture is the taking of notes during lectures and using those notes to prepare for tests. As a successful student, you probably have worked out a highly personalized system which you use most of the time in lecture situations. Notetaking systems seem to vary greatly, and many different systems work fairly well for their users. Assuming that you have at least one (probably three to five for full-time students) lecture

---

*Marginal notes for these three paragraphs need only say "Cornell System and how it works."

style class this term, your notetaking and note-using techniques may be easier for you to verbalize than some of your other study skills. (If you are taking no other courses, or have no lecture style classes this term, try to find an old notebook that you have used in the past for a lecture class.)

Glance through at least one of your notebooks as a first step to this section of the chapter. You may wish to proceed very quickly at this stage, leafing through to get a general impression, rather than actually reading any of the notes at this point. You may even wish to hold the notebook open at arm's length (too far away to read the handwriting) to see the configuration of the notes and the white space you left as you originally took the notes.

After this step, actually read through several typical-looking pages of notes to get an idea of the techniques you used on these pages to record what the lecturer was saying, demonstrating or writing on the chalkboard. Now, jot down on a sheet of paper a quick description of your technique. You might consider the following points as you write the description: Are you an outliner? If not, how have you differentiated the main from the subordinate points? How have you indicated relationships between the various ideas — by connecting balloons, boxes, hierarchies with sub-points beneath main points? How have you usually left white space? Are your pages loose and airy or filled with writing? How have you indicated especially important points — with stars, margin bars, exclamation points? These are not all the considerations, of course, but they may start your thinking.

After you have written this short description, think a moment about any pre-lecture behaviors you usually perform. Do you "go in cold," or do you prepare in any way for the lecture? Now, what about post-lecture behaviors? Do you typically follow any kind of procedure after lectures are over? Add these items to the description of your notetaking style.

Finally, consider your note-using behaviors. How do you usually use your notes during review time? Do your notes show any physical evidence of this? Are there highlighted portions, dog-eared pages, personal comments written in the margins? Even if your notes don't reveal their use, how have you used them? Have you typically differentiated the recall versus recognition function of notes? Have you reviewed in long periods of four to six hours or shorter periods of one-half to two hours? What memory tricks have been useful for you? Do you prefer silent reviewing or do you find group review or "stereo-assisted" review helpful?

From your description of your notetaking and note-using habits, extract those points that you think would be most helpful to another student. All of the points may seem to you to be self-evident and perhaps too obvious or simple to extract, but many students are relatively weak in their notetaking (and especially their note-using) skills when new to college. Techniques which you have found valuable may never have occurred to them.

Use the space below to record the points you want to be sure to mention to students whom you are assisting with notetaking. Some tutors prefer to record these points as do's and don'ts; others prefer only do's, to accentuate positive approaches.

Notetaking Tips:

Your supervisor will probably arrange soon for a tutor meeting so that all tutors can pool their ideas on notetaking techniques and textbook underlining and marginal noting.

Correlating Textbook Information and Lecture Notes

To continue your student profile, ask yourself how you have correlated the information from lecture classes and the textbooks accompanying them. For example, have you found that in some classes the lecture notes are simply a repetition of the textbook, while in others the lecture is an orderly amplification of points presented in the textbook? Still another style of lecture, and perhaps the most common one, is that which provides a whole new body of information pertinent to the topic of the course but not explicitly related to the textbook. In the latter case, the bodies of information must be brought together by the student who is to be a successful test-taker, for the professor may ask questions from both sources and may also ask questions which specifically require that students correlate the two areas of information. These are important considerations that many students never think of.

In this section of the chapter, you have been working on your own student profile. As you did so, you brought to mind a number of the study methods you have found successful in the past and have also read about some other suggestions for study success. With these ideas fresh in your mind, the next section will help you determine students' study strengths and weaknesses and help you develop strategies to strengthen their weak study skills. You have already considered textbook reading and lecture notetaking skills in detail. The next section will say more about the *application* of these skills to tutoring and will introduce the additional study skills of time scheduling and test-taking.

RECOMMENDED READING

Buzan, Tony. *Use Both Sides of Your Brain.* New York: E. P. Dutton and Co., Inc., 1976.
This simply written book approaches study skills by explaining physiological processes.

Lindgren, Henry Clay. *The Psychology of College Success: A Dynamic Approach.* New York: John Wiley & Sons, Inc., 1969.
Lindgren's book emphasizes positive attitudes.

Pauk, Walter. *How To Study In College.* 2nd ed. Boston: Houghton-Mifflin, Co., 1974.

This is one of the best books available on study skills.

RECOGNIZING AND STRENGTHENING STUDENTS' WEAK STUDY SKILLS (c)

This part of Chapter 6 concentrates on the application of those study skills and reading skills that you explored in the previous section, viz., textbook reading and noting, remembering and reviewing materials and lecture notetaking, plus two others, time scheduling and test taking. Before you as a tutor choose to concentrate on improving students' study and reading skills in the subject, you must have some information which indicates that students are suffering with weak skills in these areas. To gain this information, you can conduct an informal diagnosis. Therefore, the specific objectives of this section of Chapter 6 are that you will learn to conduct the informal diagnosis and then to apply to tutoring your knowledge of study and reading skills.

As a tutor, many times you will encounter students who seem to "have it all together." These students appear enthusiastic and motivated to do well in their academic careers; they seem to be emotionally stable, and their lives seem to be well-organized, with school concerns as a priority. In spite of this potentially excellent study picture, these students may not be performing as well as either they or you would expect, given the superficial circumstances. In cases such as these, development of study skills may not be sufficient for the rigors of a full schedule of studying, or even for a part-time study schedule combined with the duties of part-time employment, full-time spouse, parent or other role. Many of those students who are older than twenty-five performed well in their high-school classes but have been away from the study arena for so long that they no longer recall the study techniques that helped them in the past. Or, they may have been graduated from a small high school or one which put very finite demands on them, so the study skills they used at one time may no longer be sufficiently streamlined for the demands of college work.

Follow Your Intuition

Use your best commonsense judgment when deciding if weak study skills are significant contributing factors in students' study problems. It is not necessary to administer a full battery of formal tests in order to determine the study strengths and weaknesses of a fellow student. After all, you have been a successful student for a good while and can train yourself to recognize efficient and inefficient techniques for study.

The Complete Study Picture

If you infer from the students' overall behavior, or from specific statements, that study skills may be at the root of the problem, use some of your tutoring time together to get a complete study picture of the student. This process is sometimes referred to by the rather imposing name of "informal diagnosis," but it is nothing more than gathering information about the study process students follow and judging whether some other study techniques could be introduced to make the process more efficient.

The best way to develop a complete study picture is to question students to find out how they study and to examine the "artifacts" of the study procedure, such as notebooks, textbooks and notecards. Most students, approached in a frank, nonjudgmental way, are very happy to tell you to the best of their ability just what they do as they study. Some students are rather brief in their description, either because they are not conscious of their study habits or because they actually do approach their study time in a rather haphazard fashion. This very brevity in description can be a telling factor.

Prompting for Information

If students seem willing to give you information about their studying but are rather general or rather terse, you may have to do a little prompting. Request students to tell you what they do as they study, in increasingly small spheres of concern. For example, in response to your request to tell you about notetaking techniques, a student may promptly reply, "Well, I just try to keep up with the lecturer as best I can." Since this is generally true for all notetakers, more information will help make the picture clearer. You might then narrow down the area of query by paraphrasing, "I see, so you try to record Dr. McPherson's lecture word for word . . . ?" The student can then clarify by replying, "Yes, I try to get it all down verbatim, so I can think about it later," or he or she may surprise you and answer, "Oh, of course I don't try to take everything down — that's impossible — but I do try to anticipate Dr. McPherson's next topic." From these two responses to the paraphrase you made, there emerge two very different notetakers, one very literal and the other very sophisticated.

In another example, you might be examining the techniques students use when reviewing from the text. You might lead the conversation by asking, "How do you usually make use of the text when you're reviewing the assigned reading?" The student may reply, "I just look it over and over again until I know it." You may need to paraphrase by asking, "I see . . . you review the parts you've underlined with yellow highlighter?" in order to get at the more specific text-using skills involved. Or you could also narrow the topic by asking, "How do you use the questions at the end of the chapter for review?" If students say "What questions?" you have a valuable piece of information about their knowledge of the study aids present in the text. If they say, "Yes, I always use them," you can continue to narrow down by asking what particular use they make of them in reviewing. Thus, you can build up very small pieces of information which will eventually reveal the specific study steps students follow.

Five Troublesome Study Areas

Tutors and teachers have noted over the years that many students have weak study skills in one or more of the five following areas: (1) lecture notetaking, (2) textbook reading, (3) reviewing for tests (all of which were introduced in the preceding section of this chapter) and (4) test-taking and (5) time scheduling, two topics which will be introduced in this section. Before coming to the tutoring center, students may have already diagnosed the situation correctly and mention to you that test-taking, for example, is their weak area. Or, students may come to the tutoring center and only say something general, such as "I'm having trouble studying." In another case, they may say something more colorful such as, "Dr. Edgewater lectures so fast that everybody goes crazy during lecture periods." In another case, they may say, "Sociology has so many big words, I think if you would help me with my spelling, I could do better." All of these are common situations when students who have weak study or reading skills seek tutoring.

To determine how efficient the student is in study or reading skills, it is wise to check all five of the skill areas mentioned above. You may prefer to chat with the student about these skill areas in the order mentioned above, or you may work out your own personal order, whichever feels more comfortable. Naturally, if the student mentions a particular study or reading skill area, it is usually better to start by talking about that area first.

In general, these three guidelines will help you obtain useful information: (1) Attempt to get the whole study picture. Investigate the five areas mentioned in this chapter and any others which come up as you and the student talk. Many tutoring centers require that students fill out an information sheet when they come to the center.* This sheet often contains valuable pieces of information about students' schedules and extra-study obligations. If your center (or tutoring situation) does not provide you with a registration sheet, ask students if they will write out a schedule for you, so that you can see what other study obligations they have and what nonstudy obligations may intervene to take up time and energy. Most students do not object at all to recording their class schedule, their work hours, plus their outstanding home obligations. Of course, make it clear that you are not asking idly, but sincerely wish to see the whole study picture. (2) As you look over the students' schedules, ask about the study strategies they use. Ask open questions, listen closely and ask frequently for clarification or paraphrase the students' remarks, so that you are sure you know *exactly* what they mean. Also, be sure to give some reinforcement for study techniques which you recognize to be efficient. Compliment students for effective techniques and encourage

---

*See sample information sheet, page 103.

their continued use of the technique. At this point, some tutors prefer to say, "I like (or use) that technique myself," as a kind of reinforcement. (3) As you talk with students, ask if you might look at their study aids, e.g. lecture notes, notecards, textbook, etc. From these "artifacts" of student work, you can sometimes *see* factors which students did not mention. For example, you may work with students using notecards to learn biology vocabulary. However, when you look at the cards, you may see they have used them merely as substitutes for regular note-pages by writing a dozen vocabulary words on each, with the definition on the same side of the card, thus destroying their utility. (Needless to say, the usual format for notecards is one new word per card, with the definition on the back, to allow for self-testing.)

Lecture Notetaking

As you talk with students about their habits as notetakers, keep the following topics in mind to help you get the whole picture.

(Pre-lecture)

Do they:

- make friends with at least one other student in order to have a "buddy" to consult in case of illness?
- read the accompanying text assignment before class? If students find it impossible to complete the reading before the lecture, do they at least apply the survey step from the SQ3R system to the assignment?
- note the lecture title (from the syllabus) before class and make up at least one substantive question to guide their listening?
- try to recall everything they know about the lecture topic, or if nothing, try to predict what the lecture probably will contain?
- look over the previous day's lecture notes?
- have a notebook for this subject only, or at least a multi-section notebook?

- consider the purpose of the lecture, i.e. to reiterate the text? . . . to supplement the text? . . . or to present a whole separate body of information?
- consider the professor's lecture style, i.e. inductive, deductive, discursive, etc.?

(During lecture)

- write the date on the first page of notes?
- stick to a notetaking system?
- leave blanks for anything missed?
- ask the lecturer for clarification of any unclear points on the supposition that, if one student missed it, so did many other people?
- use a system of abbreviations?
- *above all, think before writing to judge the value of the information?*

(Post lecture)

Did they:

- reread the notes for legibility and completeness?
- see the "buddy" if the notes are incomplete or incoherent?
- *most important, as soon as the lecture is over, summarize mentally the main points of the lecture without peeking at their notes?**
- plan several study periods spaced at regular intervals prior to the test?
- plan to study by self-testing rather than looking over the notes again and again?

As you look at the student's notebook, consider the following characteristics:

- As you hold the notebook at arm's length, how do the notes look?

---

*Hermann Ebbinghaus, *Memory: A Contribution To Experimental Psychology* (New York: Dover Publications, 1964), p. 76.
Ebbinghaus' research (and that of other researchers in the field) confirmed that memory loss is greatest immediately after the initial learning and tapers off gradually thereafter unless review intervenes.

- Are they very dense and undifferentiated or random looking?
- Does the writing look arranged, patterned or systematized in some way, with a reasonable amount of white space showing?

Poor notetaking often shows even if the words are not immediately visible. It is often characterized by dense writing with very little white space left or by chaotic-looking writing. Good note-taking looks systematic and leaves room for interpolations and additional marginal comments; it is also best done on only one side of each sheet.

- As you read the notes, do you see that the skeletons of sentences imply meaning, or are the notes a mixture of short chaotic phrases alternating with partially completed verbatim sentences which end with a frustrated squiggle?
- Have students employed some method to indicate the less from the more important points? Some students use formal outlining, some an indenting system, some use signals such as stars or bars next to the main points, or other systems.
- Has the student employed some method to indicate the relationships between points . . . balloons . . . indenting . . . arrow, or others?

As you talked with students and looked at their notebooks, you probably noted some strengths and some weaknesses. With students make up a short list of strengths (so they have something positive from which to start) and a short list that you and they agree are the skills that most need to be strengthened. Do not try to strengthen six or eight notetaking skills at once. Concentrate on two or three. For example, the list you develop together may look like the following:

Strengths	*Things to Work On*
Has a system of abbreviations	Needs to think about the subject to warm up before lecture
Reads before lectures	
Has one notebook per subject	Needs mentally to summarize the ideas after lecture
Indents details and puts main points at margin	

This diagnosis should suggest some strategies for improving the weak areas. But, before you give students advice on how to strengthen the skills you have agreed to work on, encourage them to think independently of ways to improve. Many students *know* what they are supposed to do but do not really believe the approved techniques will help them or think that they are more trouble than they're worth. As an example, the student may suggest writing a summary paragraph of the lecture in the lecture notebook or writing two or three questions to be answered during the review for the mid-term. Write down these suggestions and keep them for future progress checks.

Notice that the process through which you have been guiding students encourages them to explore their own study profile and to be actively involved in thinking up solutions to their study problems. This is much like the process you completed in the last section of this chapter.

If the student needs more new ideas on how to improve, you should demonstrate and explain some techniques that you know to be effective. Two very different but effective notetaking systems are shown on pages 101 and 102. If the student seems to have a lot of enthusiasm, you may recommend a study skills book which you know to be helpful and, of course, which deals with the relevant points. (See Recommended Reading, pages 83-84 for suggestions.)

Set reachable time limits for the one, two or three areas the student should concentrate on improving. Do not expect too much too soon. As the weeks go by, check progress on the goal areas and praise any improvement you see. If there is none, continue to encourage until you see some.

Preparing for Tests

Preparing for objective and/or essay tests is another of the study skills that is frequently underdeveloped. Most students know they are expected to study hard before test time, but their conception of "studying hard" is highly variable. For some students, studying hard means looking through the book while watching television for two or three hours. Other students study hard by reading and rereading the same textbook passages from three to six times, even if they still fail to understand them fully. Still other students work hard by thoroughly memorizing their lecture notes, while ignoring the textbook, hoping that the professor will not test about anything not mentioned in the lectures.

If students mention to you that test preparation is a worry to them, or if you merely suspect that studying for tests is a weak skill, talk with them about study approaches for tests. As you investigate the situation, consider the following points:

Do they:

- complete the readings and get all the lecture notes?
- study in spaced periods such as two hours a night for several weeks as opposed to massed periods such as ten full hours just before the test?
- cram according to some system instead of randomly, if cramming were made necessary by illness or other unavoidable event?
- provide opportunities for self-testing, such as flashcards, using marginal key words in the textbook or the Cornell noting system in their notebooks to see if they can recite the relevant facts *before* peeking at the textbook or notebook?
- waste time trying to memorize something they did not hear clearly during the lecture?
- set realistic goals about the time needed to prepare for the test? (Many students underestimate from 10 to 50 percent the study time required.)

Test Taking

It may be that the students feel confident about their test preparation skills, but you discover later that they perform very poorly on tests for which you knew they were prepared, because you had studied and reviewed the material together. In this case, it may be that students are efficient studiers but poor test takers. Students with this fatal weakness say things like, "I knew it all pretty well, but when I looked at the testpaper, I just about passed out. I couldn't remember anything until after it was all over." Or, they may remark, "I really studied hard (and you concur), but the professor didn't ask the right things. When I studied, I skipped over the part that he asked the fifty-point essay on." These students are manifesting two of the most common ills for weak test takers: (1) tensing up and (2) studying the wrong things.

In the case of students who tense up, referral to someone in the counseling center is sometimes necessary. If the student almost always "blanks out" on tests in most subjects, the problem may be too chronic or serious for you to handle. In this case, consult with your supervisor about the procedures for referring a student for professional help. (Or see Chapter 7 of the text for more on referrals.)

If, on the other hand, students only occasionally have tension-promoted blank-outs or have them only in one particular area that they consider "my worst subject," then some words of advice from you may be appropriate. As you talk with students, keep these points in mind as indicators of those students who tense up and, as a result, forget material they knew perfectly well an hour before the test.

Do they do the following:

• go to the testing room early and begin to panic upon hearing the other students quizzing each other on esoteric points or upon seeing someone else's stack of 500 notecards? (Advise these students to avoid any situation which seems to increase their anxiety. If hearing other students before class shouting questions and answers across the room unnerves them, then they should avoid the testing room until the last minute. They should stay in the hall and walk into the room just behind the professor.)

• start at number one and proceed slavishly through to the last test item? (Advise these students to read the whole test before answering anything. This procedure is a confidence-builder; as the test-taker sees more and more familiar items, tension dissipates. This procedure also allows students to write down in the margin or on a note sheet anything they see they will be called upon to answer but are afraid they will forget before they get to the item.)

• get stuck on a two-point item and waste twenty minutes on puzzling over it? (Advise these students to calculate a minute per item figure for objective tests. As the test starts, they should look at the clock, note the number of test items and calculate how many seconds or minutes the test-maker intended test-takers should spend on each. They should try to keep pace. If they do not finish, they will surely lose points on those unanswered questions unless there is a specific statement that those items will not count against the test taker. On essay tests, students should be acutely aware of the point value of each essay question. In this case, they should use the point values to calculate the percentage of importance each question has been accorded and grant each the same percentage of time out of the whole test period.)

In working with students on test-taking, it is sometimes possible to glean information from an old test on which students reported that they were prepared but still did not do very well. Ask them if you might look at the test in order to gain more information. If they agree, you may be able to discover something that will be helpful. On objective test items that have been answered incorrectly and for which the right answer has been marked by the professor, or for which you yourself know the correct answer, ask the students to think aloud their reasoning as they made the original choice of answers. From this discussion, you may be able to see a pattern of which students were unaware. For example, they may say more than once, "I thought this was wrong, so I changed it, but I guess I shouldn't have." The converse of this statement is only slightly less common. You may perceive that a particular student makes best guesses on the first try, while another student may make best guesses on items where he or she changes an original choice. These individual traits will make a difference on students' test scores. In another case, students may say something like, "I thought this was right, but it seemed too simple, so I picked the other one." This is especially frequent on true-false tests. Students such as these are outsmarting themselves by assuming that the test-maker is trying to trick them.

Although these are by no means the only examples, when students become aware of these types of personal habits, they can become more successful test takers.

The best way to check for progress in test taking skills is to wait for the next test which students must take. Ask them to evaluate their behavior immediately after the test and then wait to see the grade. If it is higher than the last test, congratulations are in order. If it is not, try to help students analyze their behavior to find the problem. Perhaps they still need more practice, or some other skill not yet discussed may be causing the low grades.

Time Scheduling

Many students who seek tutoring complain that there is never enough time for them to complete all their tasks, to attend classes and to do homework. You will soon discover that some of these students are weak in background skills, so they move very slowly through their school tasks, thus giving them and you the impression that they are over-loaded with work. If they were more efficient in study skills or had better subject-area background, their tasks would not be so onerous. Occasionally, however, you will encounter students who are motivated, have good skills as note-takers and text readers, who still wish that there were twenty-eight hours in each day. Often these students seem harried and worn-out and nearly fall asleep during tutoring sessions. These students may be dissipated because they are spending time in frivolity and party-going. More commonly, over-worked students are employed at a full-time job, attend school and have a young family demanding their attention — all at the same time. Having responsibilities in all these spheres simultaneously would wear anyone out.

As you work with students, you may see that this is the case. But, it will be difficult for them to jettison any one of the roles they have taken on. Obviously, no students who have paid tuition for the term are anxious to drop courses they have already started, nor is there any acceptable way for them suddenly to stop being a parent, employee or spouse without contradicting society's rules.

In cases such as these, it is virtually impossible to find a full solution to the dilemma. Still, there are several tips that students might take into account. For one, they could use public transportation rather than drive to classes, if this is possible. Although this may take longer than driving, it allows uninterrupted time to read or review. Driving requires too much concentration to allow much thinking. Also, they could use the library or secluded corners of the student lounges as much as possible instead of waiting to study at home if home responsibilities make it nearly impossible to study there. They should try to keep up with the reading and with reviewing class notes, even if it must be done incompletely or hurriedly. Doing so takes advantage of the principle that several spaced periods of study are more efficient than waiting to cram all night just before the test. Even though all study experts advise reading materials before the lecture period, this is sometimes impossible for the parent/worker/student. When it is, it is still more efficient to preview reading materials (see Chapter 6 on the previewing step of the SQ3R system) rather than to go into the lecture cold. Finally, students should examine their schedules to find tasks which can be eliminated or delegated to someone else. During the years students are pursuing an academic program, children and spouse may have to take on more daily tasks to relieve the student. Or, tasks can simply be left undone. Needless to say, housework and yardwork have to be done *sometime*, but for the duration, bed linens can be changed less often, meals can be simplified and the lawn can be mowed less frequently.

Clearly, all these are only stop-gap measures. The only real solution is for students to plan fewer responsibilities for themselves. This usually cannot be done until the next term at the soonest. If the students with whom you are working seem amenable to modifying their school schedule for the next term, you can assist them by having them fill out a time schedule. Find a daily planner sheet or use a blank calendar or daily appointment book. On the sheet, they should first list all those items they cannot dispense with, such as job hours or daily duties such as picking up the children from the baby-sitter. Next, they should mark in times for meals and for sleep. Then, they should log in one hour per day of personal time — such as for talking with their spouse, relaxing, napping, taking a walk, etc. (Most students object vigorously to this, on the premise that they deserve no time for such extravagant self-indulgence. Request that they do so anyway.) When students complete this part of the task, request them to write in their class hours. Already, the typical over-worked students have filled in all the boxes available on the sheet and have to overlap tasks. Finally, ask them to multiply their academic hours by two, thus telling how many hours they should be spending in homework each week. (For example, students taking ten credit hours per term should be spending twenty hours per week study-ing outside of class). By this time, the page (probably all but obscured by the numerous tasks inscribed) will be ample evidence, without your having to say a word, that students have been too ambitious in planning tasks for themselves. Because of your help, perhaps the next semester will be more realistic!

Using Textbooks

Surprisingly, even many moderately skilled students are weak in textbook using skills. For some reason, *most* students who have not taken reading efficiency courses as adults approach textbook reading in an ineffectual manner, possibly because they have read so many textbooks through the years that have bored them thor-oughly. Consequently, they expect textbook reading to be a chore and never suspect there are ways to make it less so.

You may be working with students who are weak in text reading skills if they are typically behind in reading assignments, if they habitually complain about the book's being too hard or report that they read assignments over and over. Or, you may note that they seem generally unfamiliar with the component parts of the typical text. They may refer to the table of contents as "that list at the front that tells the chapters" or look at you in puzzle-ment when you mention the glossary or the index.

If this is the case, investigate further. Ask students to tell you what they do in reading a typical assignment. As they talk, you may have to probe to keep the conversation going because they may answer, "Well, I just start at the first page and read until I'm done." Needless to say, this is not enough for you to go on. If their answers are terse, ask how they use the specific parts of the book, such as the glossary, the index, the questions at the end of the chapter, the summary sections, etc. Of course, you must be familiar with the text or have it close at hand so you can ask appropriate questions.

As you and students talk, keep the following points in mind. Do they:

- do the assigned readings before they will be dealt with in lectures?
- read in a study atmosphere or in a sleep atmosphere such as on top of the bed or on the couch?
- read with a purpose in mind, such as "getting the general points plus the details," or "reviewing for an essay test," or "reviewing for an objective test," etc.?
- use *any* reading system other than starting at the beginning and going on until the end of the assignment or until sleep intervenes, whichever comes first?
- make some use of the questions at the end of the chapter or study guides at the beginning?
- make any use of titles, sub-titles, picture captions or other helps provided?
- make use of any vocabulary helps?
- review mentally every page to be sure to get the gist of the information?
- review mentally after the whole assignment to be sure to recall the main points?

During the conversation, look at the book with which the student is having trouble. As you glance through it, note the following points:

Do they:

- underline nearly everything on some pages?
- make no marginal notes?
- leave the book looking clean and practically unused?

After investigating these points, you will probably have found some students who are inefficient readers. If you do, you will naturally want to help them to become more efficient. Many students are especially sensitive about their reading skills, so it may be wise to avoid saying that they are "poor readers." It is more politic to speak of "reading efficiency" and to make clear you know that they are adequate readers, but the demands of college require special reading/study skills which few general readers possess. Also, it is helpful to mention to students that studies have shown some college freshmen have difficulty with their textbooks because the books are sometimes written with a vocabulary level appropriate for master's degree students.

Strengthening Weak Textbook Reading Skills

As you did in the note-taking diagnosis, you may want to ask students at this point if they can think of any techniques which might be of some help. However, in this sphere, students seem less able to think of methods that might be of help. They tend to suggest such things as "reading it over more times" or "reading more slowly." Since neither of these is an efficiency technique, you may have to offer more assistance in this case than in the case of note-taking (which is generally easier to improve).

Any of the following suggestions may be appropriate for students. Demonstrate a study/reading system to them. SQ3R, PQ4R, OARWET or another technique is probably better than their present approaches. Practice a technique with them step by step until they can go through it themselves. Request them to use the technique on their next reading assignment and to inform you how they like the results. It is often necessary to assure students that the technique seems time-consuming at first, but they will get better at it and eventually save considerable time. If the students seem enthusiastic about the technique, show them a study skill book detailing the study method you discussed. (See suggestions in the Recommended Reading, pages 83-84.)

While a study/reading method may take a while to master, the following tips in this paragraph can be used immediately by most students. Advise them to read in the same place all the time, whether it be their room, the library, or other place. The important thing is to get into an habitual pattern and stick to it. If the pattern is to study in bed, and this has not proved successful, a new habit will be more profitable. If, on the other hand, the students have successfully studied in bed for years, there is no dogmatic reason they should change just for the sake of form. Another bit of advice is to keep up with the reading, if at all possible, and to take advantage of the principle that short, spaced periods of study are more efficient than one or two long periods. During long periods of studying, fatigue is also such a strong negative factor that it causes reading efficiency to drop sharply. Finally, doing something reading-related while reading is a help to concentration and retention; advise students to underline (but only a few words per paragraph and only after thinking about the whole section they just read), take marginal notes or take notes on a notesheet to keep themselves involved. It is quite normal to "blank out" on material which is rather dry (as many textbooks admittedly are) and let the eyes move over the printed lines without the mind's absorbing anything unless some concentration tricks are used. Even the best and most intelligent readers agree this is so.

As in notetaking, list students' strengths and weaknesses in textbook reading. With them, choose one through three skill areas within the sphere of textbook reading as those to concentrate on improving. Ask them to suggest any ways they can think of to enhance the improvement program. Write the suggestions down. If they have trouble making suggestions, make some yourself. Set some time lines and check for improvement at future points. If progress is visible, congratulations! If not, keep encouraging until things improve.

Lecture Notes   May 1st "

Topic — <u>Cell Structure</u>

Cell Parts
   Membrane (80-100 Å thick)
   Cytoplasm (mostly H_2O)
     • Nucleus (primary organelles of cyt&8.)
       controls cytoplasm
       has nucleoplasms
         proteins
         nucleic acids
           like DNA, RNA
         chromatins
         nucleolis (1 or more)
     • Lysosomes
       have enzymes to break
       down cell parts or dead cells
       spherical
       single membrane
     • Chloroplasts (plants only)

Recall Column

tell 2
main cell
parts
_____
_____

second part
contains
3 things:
_____
_____
_____
↓
tell names,
components
& purpose

what's in
nucleoplasms
(4 things)
_____
_____
_____

This notetaker has used an airy, informal outline and indented from the left margin to show the relationship of cell parts of occasionally used arrows to clarify the outline. Notice the Cornell column the notetaker has made on the right hand side of the page. This notetaker leaves blanks for him/herself in the column to fill in as a self-test device. The column, as you will note, contains only blanks to be filled in mentally as reviewing is done for tests.

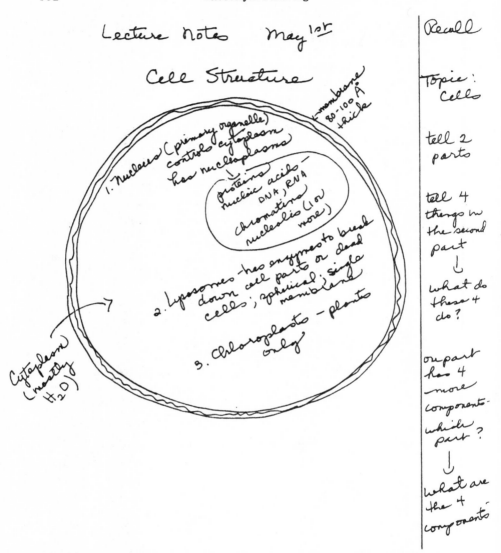

Lecture Notes   May 1st

Cell Structure

Recall

Topic: Cells

tell 2 parts

tell 4 things in the second part ↓ what do these 4 do?

one part has 4 more components which part? ↓ what are the 4 components

membrane 80-100 Å thick

1. Nucleus (primary organelle) controls cytoplasm has nucleoplasm ↓ proteins nucleic acids - DNA, RNA chromatins (1 or more) nucleolis

2. Lysosomes - has enzymes to break down cell parts or dead cells; spherical; single membrane

3. Chloroplasts - plants only

Cytoplasm (mostly H₂O)

This notetaker represents the cell more artistically, as it might really appear. Notice that he/she also uses the Cornell style recall column on the right by listing questions for him/herself to answer during later reviews.

Information Sheet

Today's Date:_____ Who Referred You To Us?_____
Self Referral?_____

NAME:_____ Social Security/
Student Number:_____

ADDRESS:_____
  (Street)   (City)   (State)   (Zip)

HOME PHONE:_____ WORK PHONE:_____

ETHNIC BACKGROUND: ___ Black   ___ American Indian
                   ___ Hispano/Chicano ___ Asian American
                   ___ Anglo   ___ Other

MAJOR:_____ Number of Credit Hours You Are
                               Taking:_____

                               Number of Hours Completed:_____

REQUESTING SERVICES FOR TUTOR:

  Course/Instructor: _____
  Available Days/Times: _____

CONTINUE BELOW IF YOU REQUIRE ADDITIONAL ASSISTANCE OR IN-
FORMATION

IN WHICH OF THE FOLLOWING AREAS DO YOU FEEL YOU NEED ADDI-
TIONAL HELP?

_____ Written communication   _____ Following directions
_____ Notetaking   _____ Understanding what has
_____ Pronouncing words when reading   been said
_____ Vocabulary   _____ Joining in class discussions
_____ Memory   _____ Attending Classes
_____ Spelling   _____ Work schedule conflicts
_____ Understanding what I read   _____ Understanding course con-
_____ Remembering what I read   tent

I WOULD BE INTERESTED IN LEARNING MORE ABOUT:

_____ Personal counseling   _____ Choosing a major/minor
_____ Class scheduling/registration _____ Handicapped Services
_____ Financial Aid assistance   _____ Locating a job
_____ Help with admissions forms   _____ Veteran's Assistance
_____ Finding out about community _____ Women's Center
         resources such as:
                    ___ Medical Services   ___ Day Care
                    ___ Housing   ___ Other:

WHAT DO YOU FEEL ARE THE REASONS FOR YOUR ACADEMIC DIFFI-
CULTIES?_____

HAVE YOU USED OUR SERVICES BEFORE?_____

TUTORING STUDENTS WITH SERIOUS READING PROBLEMS (d)

If you have been tutoring very long, you have probably encountered a small percentage of students who have excessive difficulty reading and understanding their textbook(s). You may have attempted to assist these students with their textbook reading by introducing the SQ3R or other textbook reading system and found the student unable to handle the system. Unlike those students who were discussed in Section 6b, these students have such weak reading skills that they are unable to make use of a reading efficiency technique such as SQ3R, which requires independent reading skills on the part of the student. Essentially, students with severe reading problems cannot read their text without individual guidance. Students such as these may have been passed through the high school system regardless of their reading problems and arrive at the doors of colleges and adult basic education programs with reading skills far below the requisite level. Therefore, the objective of this section of Chapter 6 is to illustrate techniques that any tutor may use to assist students who are virtually unable to read their assigned textbooks independently.

Helping Deficient Readers

Many adult students who are having serious trouble reading one or more of their textbooks can learn a simple three-step method which will improve their reading. In order to use this method, students must bring one of their textbooks to your tutoring sessions. At the session, ask students to open the textbook to the current reading assignment. You should first preview the chapter yourself as in the survey step of SQ3R (Section b of Chapter 6); then, ask the student to read silently the titles and subtitles of the first two or three pages. Give them as much time as they need. Now, you are ready for Step One.

Step One: Warming Up

Ask students to stop and think what they already know about the topic or the assignment. This may seem like a simplistic approach, but much modern research is indicating that "priming" the mind is an important first step to reading comprehension. At first, students may say, "But I don't know anything about stocks and bonds, (for instance); I haven't read the chapter yet." At this point you can help them "warm up" by probing a little. Ask students some leading questions, such as "Have you ever bought any stocks yourself?" If they answer "No," ask why. Many students will say, "Because it's too risky!" At this point, you can remind them that they do know something about stocks after all — that they involve risk of capital in order to make a financial gain. This is probably the most basic and valuable piece of information about stocks. Students may not have all the details, but they know the important general concept.

Once you have increased students' confidence a little, keep probing with questions until they have stated everything they can think of (no matter how simple) relating to the topic of the reading assignment. Some reading experts call this process "pre-thinking." * Do not jump in with information which you know is pertinent to the topic. The purpose of pre-thinking is not for students to learn new information from you; it is to make their minds active and to pre-dispose them to take in new information when the reading process does start.†

It is also profitable to encourage students to make predictions about what the chapter probably contains. Again, students may express reluctance to do so or profess ignorance, because they have not read the chapter already. But, many students find they can predict what kind(s) of information a chapter will contain merely from reading the title and the sub-titles on the first several pages with you. If they are reluctant to make predictions, hazard aloud a few guesses yourself.

After students have warmed up by pre-thinking and making predictions, (or hearing your predictions) you are ready for Step Two.

Step Two: Reading

This step will seem very familiar. All you and students have to do to accomplish this step is to read the chapter silently together.

---

*Goodman.

†P. David Pearson, Jane Hansen and Christine Gorden, "The Effect of Background Knowledge on Young Children's Comprehension of Explicit and Implicit Information," *Journal of Reading Behavior*, XI, 3 (1979), pp. 201-9.

Start reading the chapter simultaneously, not rushing, and with the intention of stopping every little while to discuss the ideas found in the text. If reading from the same book makes you or students nervous, find a second copy of the book or photocopy the first few pages of the chapter. Then, each of you will have a personal copy of the text. *It is important that you read material silently at the same time.* The reason for the simultaneity will become clear with Step Three.

The only caution to keep in mind with Step Two is not to read too much before stopping to discuss the ideas. At first, it may be enough to read just one paragraph at a time. (Do not stop at less than a paragraph; most authors cannot develop an idea in less than a paragraph, and it's counterproductive to stop reading in mid-idea). Later on, when the process seems natural and smooth to you and to students, you can try reading two or three paragraphs at a time, or even a whole sub-section between boldface headings. Agree with them on a prearranged stopping place before you start reading. If you finish the section or paragraph before students do, do not make it obvious that you have done so. If you gaze about the room, drum your fingers or sigh with impatience, students may feel so pressured that they will be unable to comprehend at all. Deficient readers may read very slowly and perhaps move their lips or slide their fingertips across the page as they read. Do not comment on their reading habits. Use the extra time to get ready for Step Three.

Step Three: Re-telling

In this step, ask students to tell you everything they remember from the paragraph they just read. This is a test of comprehension, not a test of memory, so it is all right for students to look back at the book occasionally as they retell what they read. But, it is important that students are actually telling about the information in the book *in their own words*. If they can do so, then you have the surest sign possible that they read and understood the material. If students are reluctant or unsure about what "retelling" requires, you might re-tell the first one or two paragraphs as an example.

To reiterate, retelling is restating in one's own words the ideas and details presented in a reading passage. It differs from summary in that it is a point-by-point restatement, not a condensation. It is not, however, necessary that the re-stater present the ideas in the same order as in the original.

As an example, consider the following oral restatement of paragraphs 2 and 3 from "Enhancing Learning" on page 36 of the text.

Restatement:

When learners understand what they hear or read, it is called "assimilation." But, if they do not understand, they get frustrated. Another word for this is "disequilibration." That is like the feeling one gets from trying the figure drawing and the door puzzle. These feelings make a person think more to solve a problem. If they solve it by making a thought change, then it's called "accommodation."

After their restatement it is encouraging to shyer students if you probe with some questions such as, "How did you react to that idea?" or "I'm not so sure I agree with that . . . do you?"

It is possible that students' restatements will reveal they have skipped over or misunderstood parts of the material. If their retelling reveals this, ask more specific questions such as, "What do you think the author was getting at here?" (if they seemed to have missed the gist of the paragraph) or "What examples or details does the author include to support his main idea?" (if they remembered only the gist and failed to see any details). If students have missed or misunderstood an important vocabulary word, ask specifically, "What do you think is meant by (the word) as it is used in this paragraph?"

As a matter of fact, *it is almost always more profitable to talk about new vocabulary as it comes up naturally in the readings* than to help students with vocabulary out of context. For this reason, memorizing new terms directly from the glossary or word lists in isolation is to be discouraged. Discuss new terms as you and students run across them in the simultaneous reading. Once you feel sure they can talk about the term intelligently in their own words, it is fine to encourage them to use a flash card or other system as a study tool. But, students who make up flash cards from long word lists out of context are headed for a lot of memorizing with very little understanding to accompany it.

During the retelling period, you may feel that progress is slow and think you need to rush students to get through the material so as to be ready for the test or class recitation. If you feel impatient, try to keep in mind that you are modeling for the student the intelligent, thoughtful approach to reading.

Even for skilled readers, academic reading is generally more profitable if done in small chunks which are digested and discussed. As students get better at this method of reading, they can ask themselves the questions you have been asking and retell passages to themselves, becoming more independent readers. Even so, many weeks may pass before you see much progress. So, accept a slow pace and give students plenty of time to think and to respond to your probing questions. Many students put things in their own words rather slowly at first, so do not assume that a slow response necessarily means lack of understanding. It may only be that they are unused to the retelling process.

If students express impatience, emphasize how well they seem to be understanding the material by the retelling method and acknowledge that academic reading is slower than pleasure reading. Of course, no one would read a popular novel or the funny papers in this fashion. But then, most people do not have to take tests on popular novels or *Garfield* either!

Nonreaders

Many tutors find that they are comfortable quite soon with the retelling method. Even though they are tutors who usually specialize in social science, natural science, business or other fields, they realize that no student who has weak reading skills can make much progress in any subject area. And, it is becoming more and more an educational verity that teaching reading or study skills in isolation from subject matter is an approach which has limited value. So, even though you are "out of your field" in tutoring reading-in-sociology, reading-in-history, reading-in-business management, and so on, you are helping students to access the important concepts of the subject area in the most efficient manner possible for them at their skill level.

Occasionally, however, you will encounter students who are unable or unwilling to try the retelling method. Some students are unusually sensitive about their reading skills and feel deeply uncomfortable about exposing any reading deficiencies. So, they may be unwilling even to try. Or, they may try the method but be unable to retell *anything* at all, no matter how hard they struggle. For students such as these, the retelling method will obviously not be successful. So, when you encounter a situation such as this, consult your supervisor, who can put you in touch with a tutor majoring in reading or a reading expert at your school, a neighboring campus or adult education center in your town. It will likely be necessary for you to refer the student for extra help. (See Chapter 7 for methods of referrals.)

Guidelines for Tutors Majoring in Reading/Education

Tutors who have background knowledge in teaching reading to children can adapt for adults several of the techniques with which they are familiar. One of these is "guided reading," * a technique related to the simultaneous reading explained on pages 105-106 of this chapter. Most adult students who are experiencing severe reading deficiencies respond positively to reading experiences guided by a reading tutor. To implement this technique, it is advantageous for you as the reading tutor to obtain copies of students' texts in order to read the assignments and to create study guidelines prior to meeting with students. Three approaches may be used:

(a) Read the chapter (or assignment) before the tutoring session. Circle all new vocabulary words pertinent to the subject. Many texts will place these terms in italics, boldface, pre-chapter lists or in text margins. In texts which do not provide this convenience, you will have to find the words yourself. Check the glossary, a dictionary or context to ascertain the meaning of any words you do not know. Write the terms in a list in the order in which they occur in the assignment. When you meet with students, discuss all the words in the list with them before they attempt to read the chapter. Ask students about their

---

*Russell G. Stauffer, *Directing The Reading-Thinking Process* (New York: Harper & Row, 1969), pp. 3-72.

current understanding of each term. Some of the terms may be familiar to them. Unfamiliar words should be handled in the following way: flip to the section containing the term. Ask students to read the one or two sentences preceding the term, the sentence in which the term appears and the one or two sentences following. From the context, help the student guess the correct meaning of the term. If they do so, they may write the definition in the book margin or on vocabulary cards. If they guess incorrectly, tell them the correct definition so they may write it down or, if time permits, let them look up the term in the glossary or a dictionary. Discuss the meaning of the term with students until they can paraphrase the meaning in their own words. Then allow them to read the assignment independently. When they are finished, ask them to paraphrase the most important sections. In this way, they are helped to review and you can check their comprehension.

(b) Read the assignment previous to meeting with students. Using sub-titles (if provided) or the main idea sentences of each paragraph, make up questions which are pertinent to main ideas or important terms, facts or details. Type or print out the questions following the order of the text. When meeting with students, read through the question list with them first and then let them independently read the assignment in order to find the answers to the questions. Ideally, they should write out the answers. When they are finished, check over their answers quickly and help them locate the information for any questions they were unable to answer. Remind them to keep their questions and answers for review time prior to exams.

(c) Preview the chapter with the student. First, model aloud the practice of initially reading chapter titles, subtitles, boldface headings, italics, captions, vocabulary lists, questions at chapters' ends, summary and introductory paragraphs. (If these aids are not provided, this method is not advised for severely deficient readers.) Then, model aloud the way you would go about turning subtitles, etc., into questions.

Finally, ask students to try making up their own questions. If they seem to have mastered the process, allow them to make up the rest of the set of questions. Then proceed as in 'b' above.

Although all three techniques have been shown effective, they are time-consuming. For this reason, some deficient readers would be better advised to find a textbook dealing with their subject on a more elementary level and read the easier textbook as a substitute for the regular one. If such a textbook can be found, it may cover much of the same material but in simpler terms. You will need to cross-check carefully to be sure the students are verbally filled in on those concepts not found in the more elementary text.

In working with deficient readers, you should make use of any reading specialists available to you. The specialist may be able to suggest other equally effective techniques. Additionally, if dropping a course or taking an incomplete is an option available to students, the specialist (not you as the tutor) can suggest the appropriate alternative to them.

In addition to being called upon to assist students with their study or reading skills in a content area, you may be called upon to help students write papers for courses in your tutoring field. Section e, which follows, will suggest techniques for successful tutoring in writing.

TUTORING IN WRITING (e)

Even if you are not an English tutor, you may at some time in your tutoring career be asked to help a student with writing.

Although you may feel that writing is not your specialty, as a content area tutor, you can assist your students with many pre-writing activities. In fact, you are the best qualified person to help students refine topics for papers and generate ideas about the topics. Of course, if you are an English major, you will spend much of your time assisting students with writing tasks. Therefore, the objective of this section of Chapter 6 is twofold: to help content area tutors assist students with pre-writing activities and to assist writing tutors in refining their tutoring skills in the areas of pre-writing, writing and editing.

One of the most important things you can do to ready yourself for tutoring writing skills is to recall your own experience in fulfilling writing assignments or assignments in art, poetry, drama, speech, dance and other performing or studio arts. Although writing a theme or book review may seem very different from an assignment to draw a still life or to perform a dramatic part, important similarities exist. Just as in the performing arts, writing calls for a considerable investment of time and personality. Especially in the completion of a personal essay or short story, the author is required to draw on much of him/herself that is unique and sometimes confidential. For this reason, most writers make an emotional investment in their writing and have more difficulty in accepting and using criticism here than they would in math or chemistry classes.

If this rationale seems implausible to you, try to recall your own feelings when you were criticized for one of your writing efforts, especially one on which you had expended much effort. These are the deflated and sometimes defensive feelings that are common for writers to experience when someone points out flaws in their work. Although these feelings are not rational (but what feelings are?), they are very real. For this reason, the most valuable trait for a tutor to exhibit in this realm is kindness. Make criticisms gently; do not over-criticize by mentioning every weak verb and unclear sentence you see on the paper and always spend time on pointing out the portions of the writer's work which have been done well (even if very little is up to your standards). This does not mean that giving false praise is advised. Rather, the tutor must sometimes make a point of praising effort, honesty or a "unique approach" in a paper which has little else to recommend it.

Above, you were asked to recall briefly your experiences in fulfilling writing assignments of your own. Continue now with this review in order to clarify the steps you have used to write essays or term papers. Try to separate the process into a series of steps as much as possible in the order they truly occurred. Write the series of steps in the ten blanks below. If you need more room, continue on a sheet of paper. Be sure to include your "pre-writing" activities of selecting a topic, narrowing it, getting organized, etc., as part of the step-by-step list.

1.

2.

3.

4.

5.

6.

7.

8.

9.

10.

As you completed your list, you probably sorted through dozens of separate tasks which make up the writing process. Many of the early steps include talking, organizing, brainstorming and discarding ideas as much as they do writing. In these "pre-writing" steps, any tutor can do a great deal to start the student off well.

Pre-writing Activities:

The following activities have proved helpful in assisting students with the writing process:

1. Help students clarify the directions for the assignment and its purpose. Many students attempt to complete writing assignments without understanding exactly what the instructor wants. Listen carefully to their restatement of the directions. If mimeographed instructions were handed out, ask students to interpret them for you within the context of the course. If the directions are clear to both of you, go on to the purpose of the assignment. Often the purpose of the assignment is not articulated by the instructor. In some cases, the purpose can be inferred from the directions or from students' descriptions of the course as a whole. If the purpose is obscure to you and to students, visit the instructors' offices with students before proceeding further.

2. If the directions provided by the instructor do not give a specific topic or give a very general topic, help the students narrow the topic. For example, a history instructor, Dr. Barns, may have assigned a 5- to 7-page paper dealing with causes of the Industrial Revolution in Britain. The assignment calls for the reading of one book and one journal article dealing with the topic. Students are to "compare and contrast the two sources." A student, Henry, suggests that he will write about the causes he can think of, perhaps as many as twenty-five. You as the history tutor might respond by suggesting that Henry generate a list of the causes. As he mentions the causes you can write them in a list as below:

- working class conditions unequal
- classes — landowners, manufacturers, petty gentry, working people

- steam engine invented
- unequal distribution of wealth
- wages low
- housing poor
- Darwin's ideas about the healthiness of competition
- etc.

From this list, you should encourage Henry to select only one to three items as a focus for his comparison/contrast paper. Obviously, thoroughly covering all seven of the items he originally thought of can hardly be done in only five to seven pages. Thus, you have discouraged Henry from attempting to cover too much material superficially, which is one of the most common problems in the papers of inexperienced writers.

By the process above, you have assisted Henry with the content considerations of the paper. Now Henry can independently start on his first draft if he feels confident enough to do so.

If, however, Henry feels too unsure to proceed on his own, you can consider referring Henry to a writing tutor, assuming that your situation provides such an opportunity. From the content you and Henry generated, a writing tutor could continue with the organizational and mechanical considerations of the paper. (Chapter 7 deals with referrals in more detail.)

Suggestions for the Writing Tutor*

Just as some students with high school diplomas read very poorly, other students are graduated with very poor writing skills. As a writing tutor, many of the students with whom you work will fall into this category. As you may know, a common fault of these inexperienced writers is rushing into the writing process without thinking. In their anxiety or haste to complete an unwanted chore, many beginning composition students ignore the essential pre-writing activities that more experienced writers carry out religiously. Therefore, the pre-writing activities of (a) clarification of assignment; (b) determining a source of information,

---

*This section of the chapter concentrates on techniques appropriate for tutors whose specialty is writing.

i.e. personal experience or library research; (c) brainstorming for ideas; and (d) organizing information (chunking) are discussed in the following paragraphs.

For example, Dr. Everett, a composition teacher, has assigned the class to describe in about 700 words a familiar object or emotion, without naming the object or emotion. The student, Cheryl, decides to write on New York City or the Bowery. You as the writing tutor should remind her that the assignment called for an "object" or "emotion," while both of the present choices are ordinarily referred to as places and may not be what the instructor had in mind. On second thought, Cheryl decides to write on "jealousy." Since there is no doubt that this is an emotion, you encourage Cheryl to try to develop the idea.

As Cheryl thinks aloud her choice of topics, you notice that she is mentioning a number of films and TV episodes that concerned jealousy. When you point out that Cheryl should include some personal examples, she says, "Well, I guess I don't know very much about it. I'm not the jealous type and neither is my partner." You might remind Cheryl that the purpose of the assignment is to develop a detailed description. If she doesn't know much about jealousy, the paper will be difficult to write second hand.

By influencing the choice of topic in this way, you have helped Cheryl avoid two common mistakes: following directions imprecisely and attempting to write on an unfamiliar topic.

You can then encourage Cheryl to brainstorm in order to generate as many ideas (or details) as possible for her paper. At this point, neither you nor Cheryl should concern yourselves with judging or ordering ideas (or details), just gathering them. Cheryl should do most of the talking, so you can make an occasional suggestion and keep a written "grocery" list of the ideas (or details) as they emerge.

Regardless of the topic of the paper, many students have trouble eliminating unrelated ideas and arranging the ideas they would like to include. Even though you suspect that some of the items in the "grocery list" are only loosely related to the topic, it is easier to eliminate unrelated items after students have attempted to arrange them into groups or blocks. Some instructors recommend outlining as the ideal way of grouping items for a paper.

Most beginning writers, however, have great difficulty in building a formal outline. Therefore, it is easier for them to "chunk" related items together by drawing balloons, boxes or connecting arrows on the list. You may need to draw the first balloon and let Cheryl deal with the rest of the list independently. If she discovers that two or three of the items simply cannot be made to fit anywhere, you could encourage their deletion.

Finally, you can talk to Cheryl about the appropriate ordering of the "chunks," letting her take the lead. Your main goal in this regard is to help Cheryl see and verbalize the innate connections between the chunks. (If students have advanced a bit beyond beginning writing, these connections will emerge in the final draft as transitional devices such as "first, . . . second, . . . finally," " . . . if, . . . then, . . . as a result," ". . . a reason, . . . another reason, . . . most important," . . . and so forth.) Right now, it is enough if she can explain how the chunks are related.

Suppose Cheryl ultimately decides to write a 700-word description of a ruler (without naming it, as the assignment dictated). Figure 1 shows how her list may have emerged from the "chunking" session. (See Figure 1.)

In addition to the "grocery list" method for generating ideas, you can also use "directed free writing," as presented in *The Developing Writer.** "Directed Free Writing" (DFW) can help students generate ideas for papers they must write. DFW can be used to help students start actual papers or as warm-up exercises prior to writing papers. At first, you direct the DFW, but later students can use the method on their own. In DFW, request students to write *nonstop* for three to ten minutes on the topic area assigned by the instructor, or on any topic area in which they are interested if the instructor has left the topic open. Even though students cry "I don't know what to say!" encourage them strongly to start writing and keep on writing uninterruptedly even though they may have to write meaningless phrases or simply write their name over and over until their minds get "in gear." They should not stop even momentarily to edit, rethink, cross out or ponder over

---

*Martin McKoski and Lynn Hahn, *The Developing Writer: A Guide To Basic Skills* (New York: John Wiley, 1981), pp. 3-46.

"Directed Free Writing" is the authors' term for McKoski's process.

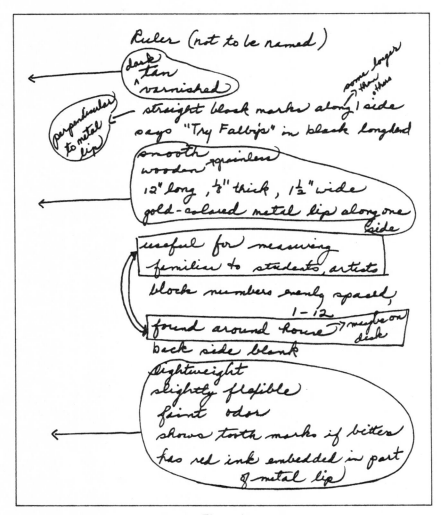

Figure 1

spelling. Correct spelling, punctuation, complete sentences and good organization are not needed here. Warn students that the process may seem pressured and even anti-intellectual, but this is a normal reaction.

The purpose of DFW is to free the mind of worry about spelling, punctuation, organization, or editing and to allow the kernels of ideas to float to the mind's surface. When the free writing is over, it may look something like Figure 2.

Topic: School Memories

lots of hot rooms in grade school -
Mrs. Cokes the teacher - she
didn't like the way I used to
talk and giggle. Mrs. Blank too.
there's a clock on the wall lots
of boys making fun of my pony-
tail and the fact that I'm
too tall. I always was too tall,
too skinny, too smart
boys never like smart
girls teachers either Mrs. Edie
didnt either. big boys pushing
me down or chasing me - Always
the littlest one there until I
got tall quick - not fair.
took bear Timmy to school
scared a lot of both teachers
and students - esp. Mrs. Book-
meyer how I hated her - used
to compare me unfavorably with my
darling ?! sister Karen

Figure 2

Now that the DFW is completed to this point, ask the student to review it with you to survey the ideas presented. Ask students to look for and circle any shreds of thought which they are especially interested in talking about at greater length or which summarize some of the other ideas. In this sample, students might circle "boys never like smart girls" or perhaps "scared a lot of both teachers and students." On the topics of these two kernel ideas, students can write two more separate DFW's for three to ten minutes apiece. From these two writings, students can (as before) select one or two kernels that interest them or which represent summary-type ideas and complete a third writing.

By this time, the student is probably ready to start on a first draft. Quite appropriately, both tutor and student have spent a good deal of time on pre-writing activities. This is the approach to model for students, many of whom rush straight into their first drafts without thinking, planning, listing or free-writing. With continued practice, students will be able to carry out pre-writing activities when tutors are not present to direct them. This is one of the most important steps to becoming an independent writer.

Helping Students During the Writing Process

Most students prefer to write their first drafts alone. But, some prefer to do so when they are in the tutoring center. If they wish to write with tutors nearby for the sake of moral support, you can help other students, checking back at intervals with the student who is developing a draft. This allows you to make full use of your time and gives students "elbow room."

Generally, respond only to questions when students come to you with a developing draft. Refrain from making comments about the draft on points which students have not mentioned. This allows them to feel that the draft is indeed theirs and that they are in charge.

If, on the other hand, students approach you with a partial draft, saying, "What do you think of it so far?" or "Would you help me with this?" you should respond about the basic features only, i.e. the appropriateness and clarity of ideas, the ordering of ideas, the continuity, the general mood and tone, etc.* *For the moment*, you can ignore such things as spelling, punctuation, capitalization conventions, pronoun agreement, sentence grace and economy, etc. These features will become important when the paper is in the finished draft, but they are the "frosting" which should be attended to only after the "pastry" is properly baked.

Ask students questions in order to make subtle suggestions. You might say, "How could you add to the description here?" ... "How could you make the jump from X to Y more obvious?" ... "If the reader is not accustomed to this object, do you think he could actually reproduce one like it from the description?" ... and the like. You should let students respond as they think fit; the paper must be their work, not yours!

It is important to note that up to this point you as the tutor have written not one word on the paper and used a writing implement only to illustrate the drawing of the balloons on the grocery list. In order to keep the work truly in students' own words, many writing lab instructors recommend that tutors not even carry pencils or pens of their own. This helps to curb the inevitable impulse to "fix" the papers of students with a polished sentence or two. Needless to say, it would be easier for you to write an interesting and precise description of the ruler. But, the goal is to make students independent writers rather than dependent ones who approach the writing tutor to polish every composition.

Helping Students with Completed First Drafts

In ideal situations, students come for writing tutoring before they have started on their draft, so that tutors may assist them

---

Mood and *tone* refer to the attitudes of the writer. Mood refers to the attitude the writer projects toward the subject. The mood could be humorous, satiric, serious, formal, colloquial or other. Tone refers to the attitude writers project toward the audience they imagine will be reading the piece of writing. Tone could be patronizing and condescending, seductive and manipulative, straightforward and respectful, etc. Writers alter mood and tone mostly by their choices of words. Many beginning writers err by failing to think about mood and tone before they start writing. With a tutor's help, every student should be able to decide on a mood for a composition. Deciding on tone, however, is sometimes more difficult. It is often a problem to decide on just who is the audience for a piece of writing. Unless the professor specifies otherwise, it is usually safe to assume that the audience is either the professor him/herself or that the students' peers (the other students in the class) are the "hypothetical" audience.

with productive pre-writing activities. Many times, however, students will attempt their first draft alone and come to the tutoring center only for tutors to look over the draft and make comments. This situation is not ideal but can nevertheless be profitable.

As discussed earlier, writing tutors should ask students to paraphrase the assignment and its purpose. If an assignment sheet was handed out, you should read it too. If the assignment called for other "paraphernalia," ask to see it also. For example, the paper may be a review of another book or a comparative review of two or more periodical articles. You will need these items on hand also in order to make helpful suggestions about the draft.

When you are sure you understand what the instructor assigned and have all the material at hand, request to see the draft. Then ask students which parts they like the best, which the worst and why. In this way, students can begin to verbalize their *intentions* for the draft, which may or may not have come through in the written version. You can then read silently through the draft with students reading along with you, making comments as you go along, or waiting until you have finished the whole draft. Finally, point out specifically the parts in which students are on the mark with their verbalized intentions and also look for these primary features:

(a) Is the meaning clear?

- Is there a *thesis or main idea statement* near the beginning of the paper?
- Is there a topic sentence or main idea statement in most of the paragraphs? Topic sentences usually start paragraphs, but this is not always so. Sometimes they are implied or are more effective as final or middle sentences.
- Are the sentences clear? Does each sentence make sense by itself? Does it make sense within the context of the paragraph? Is it a complete sentence or a fragment?
- Are all the parts of the composition about the same subject, or are parts only tangential to the subject?

(b) Does the paper have substance?

- Are the topic sentences supported with details, examples, illustrations, facts and figures or arguments, or are the topic sentences just plopped down on the paper with the expectation that the gullible reader will believe anything?
- If the paper is an argumentative or persuasive one, does it contain substantive arguments? Are obvious arguments omitted?

(c) Does it flow?

- Are there sudden switchbacks and changes of directions in the paper? Do parts of the paper seem to be going directly against the main point?
- Are any "signposts" present, such as the transitional words and phrases, e.g. "first, then, later, if, then, on the other hand," or "for example," etc.?
- Do some sections seem out of order?

(d) Are the mood and tone appropriate?

- Has the audience been considered by the writer?
- Has the writer settled on a consistent attitude toward the topic?

If any of these features needs alteration, you can suggest that students make changes.

If time allows, you may ask students to return with a second draft so you can review any changes and look at the "frosting" features: spelling, punctuation, capitalization, margins, etc. If time does not allow this, you may have to make comments now on these features. If you must use a pen or pencil, use it only to circle features that need correction, explaining the needed correction as you proceed. Students should make the corrections themselves at that time, or later at leisure. Finally, before the student leaves, you can summarize those substantive comments made previously, so that the basic impression left is one which emphasizes content, meaning and clarity, not spelling and capitalization.

Helping Students with Completed Papers

Occasionally a student will bring to the tutoring center a paper which is in final form and ready to turn in to the instructor that day, perhaps the very next hour. In this case, the recommendations of many tutoring centers differ. Some centers prefer not to assist students with papers which are essentially finished on the premise that there is no time for the student to make changes anyway. Some centers may allow tutors to make changes in the paper, but since some centers consider the latter practice to be less than completely honest, check with your supervisor before making changes in a completed paper authored by someone else.

Helping Students with the Mechanics

Poor mechanics* are difficult to remediate in a short time. For this reason, students with whom a writing tutor works only once or twice will benefit little from recommendations in this area. All you can do is to circle troublesome items, explain why they need alteration, and leave students to correct on their own with a handbook or stylesheet. The trouble with handbooks and stylesheets (and dictionaries too) is that the linguistically unskilled person has much difficulty manipulating them and extracting useful information from them. Students with weak writing skills often find using handbooks just one more headache in the writing process.

For this reason, you should encourage students who come for help with mechanical points in writing to become a "regular," i.e. someone who comes to the tutoring center for several months on a consistent basis. This continuing contact will give you the opportunity to start students on a program of exercises and sample worksheets which may help them alter years-old habits of misspellings and mispunctuations. These old habits die hard, so repetition and practice are great helps. The correct forms must come to sound right and look right to students' ears and eyes in order for them to incorporate correct forms into their own writing.

---

*For our purposes, "mechanics" includes points of standard grammar and usage, punctuation, spelling, and considerations such as legibility and neatness.

When working with a student who shows many problems in mechanics, you may wish to consult your supervisor in order to locate materials which contain practice exercises and spelling drills. Progress in this area can be quite slow; many students find it less interesting than brainstorming for ideas and working on their own papers. You may need to be especially patient and not try to change too many old habits at once. For example, students may have general spelling problems, may use pronouns irregularly, and may sometimes write fragments in place of complete sentences. These problems indicate unfamiliarity with written forms in general and a lack of experience in reading and writing for school assignments. Therefore, you could concentrate on one or two improvements at a time until students have mastered them. Then, you could go on to another weak point. However, do not expect dramatic changes too soon.

Occasionally, you will encounter students who are so bored with doing grammar and spelling exercises that they make no progress at all. For students such as these, using their own compositions as the basis of practice material can perk up their interest. From the students' old composition and essay tests, you can extract misspelled words as the basis of spelling drills and quizzes. You can also isolate sentences which contain problems in mechanics, help students to correct the sentences and explain the reason for the corrections. At a subsequent session, ask students to correct the original sentences again independently and explain to you the reason for the changes. Although this process takes more time than relying on an exercise book or a speller, it can keep students' interest higher.

Even more rarely, you may encounter students with whom none of the techniques above is successful. In cases such as these, consult your supervisor, who can assist you or put you in touch with the writing laboratory director or other writing specialists at your school or in your city.

In your tutoring, you will discover that not all problems exhibited by students are study/reading/writing related. Some barriers to effective study are caused by personal problems in students' lives. Chapter 7 discusses the role of the tutor in this realm.

RECOMMENDED READING

Elbow, Peter. *Writing Without Teachers.* London: Oxford University Press, 1973.
    The first chapter of Elbow's book contains helpful information on freewriting.

Chapter 7

DEALING WITH PERSONAL PROBLEMS

IN the last chapter, you dealt with the common tutoring situations of weaknesses in students' study techniques or in reading and writing skills. This chapter will focus on the recognition and remediation/referral of problems that are not specific to the academic setting but can interfere with study efficiency. These interferences may be social, emotional, psychological or medical in origin.

Whatever their origin, these interferences surface fairly often in tutoring. Many teachers and professors see these problems only distantly, due to the impersonality of large classes and the subsequent submerging of personal problems. However, from their relatively intimate standpoint, tutors often observe or are told by students about personal problems: divorces, family disagreements, brushes with the law or bill collectors, illness, alcoholism, low self-esteem, excessive shyness, overwhelming fear of professors, test anxiety and so on. The objectives of this chapter are to (1) explore the supportive resources available in your tutoring situation and (2) learn to identify the personal problems that interfere with academic success. Many of these problems stand far outside the tutoring situation. For this reason, (3) learning to make appropriate referrals to the professional staff at your institution, your college or in your city will occupy a portion of the chapter.

Most college campuses have in place a number of supportive services, e.g. counseling and health center, housing service and financial aid offices for their students, and occasionally even for prospective students. Some small campuses may lack some services or offer services under umbrella areas such as Student Services. To complete this part of the chapter, make a survey of your campus in order to ascertain what kind of supportive services exist and where they are located. This may be as simple as obtaining a brochure from the student information office (should your campus have one), or it may involve considerable leg work on your part in asking questions of various college personnel and in walking about campus to locate various services and buildings.

If your tutoring situation is not on a college campus, you face an even greater challenge. If, for instance, you are tutoring in an adult education center or in a private tutoring situation, you will have to consider the entire city as your "campus" and find those services open to the public and to which you could refer a student who is too anxious, ill, or financially or emotionally troubled to benefit from your assistance as a tutor.

SUPPORTIVE SERVICES

Check to see if you can find a supportive service in each of the areas listed below. Write in the name and room (and building) and/or address of the support area in the space provided.

Financial:

Personal (Emotional or psychological):

Medical:

Family Crisis:

Legal:

,Other:

If you cannot find services available in each of the areas, check with your supervisor for help. As you go about your search, actually visit the service areas themselves. This activity serves two purposes. The superficial purpose is to pick up several copies of any literature available at the service department to keep with your other tutoring materials. These can help you refresh your memory and also can be given to students who need information about campus or city services. A more important reason, however, is to give you current and personal experience with the service area itself. You may never have occasion to visit the service department yourself, but being able to give first-hand directions to potential users of the service can be a great encourager to timid students who may be reluctant to seek professional help. Once you have visited the service department yourself, you do not have to say something impersonal like, "Just follow the map," or "The brochure says it's on the third floor." Instead, you can say something more reassuring such as, "The Counseling Center is in the middle of the hall on the second floor. Watch for the door with the Peanuts® poster on it. Once you get there, look for Jackie, the receptionist. She's very helpful, or at least she has been when I talked with her. She'll help you make an appointment with the right counselor. It's not usually busy in the mornings." After you have actually visited the service areas, keep any notes about the locations, names of receptionists, etc., in the spaces above.

IDENTIFYING PERSONAL PROBLEMS

Below, you will find the profiles of six students, taken from the actual tutor logs of number of students who visited a tutoring center. Peruse each case in order to determine (a) what nonacademic difficulty (personal problem) the case history seems to indicate. After each case, space is provided for you to analyze the situation and to explain (b) what evidence indicates the nature of the problem. Also record in the space (c) whether you would feel it is appropriate to assist the student with the difficulty yourself or refer the student to a professional for more skilled help. If you elect the former, (d) sketch briefly what steps you would take to assist the student yourself. If you elect the latter, (e) state to what person or facility on your campus or in your city you might logically refer the student for assistance.

Situation 1

Luetta was a middle-aged woman who came to the tutoring center for assistance in algebra. This was the beginning of her second year at the school, and she had not taken any math so far. She was only taking six to nine hours each term, and her grade average so far was a B minus. To me, Luetta seemed a bit apprehensive, and she continued to frown a little almost all the time I was with her. I was wondering if she was tired or worried, or if she just did not like me personally. Then I wondered if she did not perhaps dislike me because I must seem like a "young whippersnapper" to her.

This term she was taking only six hours, three in biology and three in math. Her biology course involved a three times weekly lecture, with an optional no-credit lab and brush-up period with the teaching assistant. She said she always attended the no-credit lab, and she felt confident about biology. She explained, "Whenever I don't quite get something during the lecture, I ask Barbara (the lab assistant) about it, and she helps me with it in lab." However, there was no lab period or teaching assistant connected with the math class, and Luetta said she was averaging only 60 percent to 65 percent on most of her daily quizzes. She said that Dr. Riggs was especially hard to follow even though she sat in the front row. I could not imagine Luetta missing much of anything because she was so extremely attentive during all of our conversations. In fact, she seemed to hang on every word I said, leaning toward me and watching my face until it made me feel a little self-conscious.

As she rose to leave one day, I saw her eyeglass case sitting on the table. I ran after her and spoke her name loudly when I was just two steps behind her. But, she kept right on going. At first I could not understand her behavior.

Consider the following factors in your analysis:

(a) what nonacademic difficulty is manifested?

(b) what evidence do you have that this is the problem?

(c) would you assist or refer the student?

(d) if you would assist, what steps would you take?

(e) if you would refer, to whom?

Situation 2

Caroline came to the tutoring center almost in tears. It was the seventh week of her second term. She said she was "doing badly" in all her five subjects and was very worried about her college career. She was taking English 102, Psych 102, Soc 102, Anthro 102, and Math 101. She had been graduated from high school two years before. She said she was on financial aid. She said she had "not much to do but study" because she was single and school was very important to her. She said she thought she spent lots of time studying but still did not get "good enough grades." She said she thought she ought to be able to remember more when she read and wished she did not have to review so much to get sufficiently prepared for her tests. Finally she said her GPA was 2.25 (on a 4 point scale). She said "That's why I'm so upset. If I fall below 2.20, I lose my financial aid. If that happens, I'll have to drop out of school and get a full-time job. I'm so upset, I just can't concentrate."

Consider the following factors in your analysis:

    (a) what nonacademic difficulty is manifested?

    (b) what evidence do you have that this is the problem?

    (c) would you assist or refer the student?

    (d) if you would assist, what steps would you take?

    (e) if you would refer, to whom?

Situation 3

When Paula came to the tutoring center (she smoked two cig-arettes in the hall before coming in), she timidly said she was failing one of her three subjects and barely passing another. It was six weeks into the semester. Her English grade was an A, the speech grade an F, and the sociology grade a C. She had taken all the subjects before in high school and done "ok" in them. Her cook's job required fifteen hours per week. It was an evening job, and she liked it because she did not have to talk to customers. She usually studied her sociology and wrote her speeches on campus during the day and wrote her English papers after work. Her creating of the ideas for English papers she left for weekends. The sociology grades were based on three quizzes, the English grades on three compositions, and her speech grades were a combination of the content grade followed by the performance grade, e.g., A/B. Her grades were B/D, A/F, and B/F. Attendance also counted in the speech class. She admitted she had already cut the three allowed times. She said that the other speech students were all much better than she was and that she had asked to have one of her speeches postponed because of a headache. The teacher agreed. Even so, her grade was A/F.

Consider the following factors in your analysis:

(a) what nonacademic difficulty is manifested?

(b) what evidence do you have that this is the problem?

(c) would you assist or refer the student?

(d) if you would assist, what steps would you take?

(e) if you would refer, to whom?

Situation 4

George came into the tutoring center for a refresher on his math skills. He had not actually enrolled at the school but intended to do so the next term. He was a retired veteran with a family. Both of his children were in high school. His wife was a legal secretary. He spent time selling real estate and golfing. College was a new experience to him. He seemed very enthusiastic and anxious to start. I asked him to take the pre-test in the arithmetic kit. He did pretty well on all but the ratios. He also took the algebra pretest. After about four questions, he said, "I don't even know what they're talking about here. I never took algebra at my high school." So, I excused him from finishing and figured he would have to start at the beginning anyway.

At our next session, George seemed very distracted. He looked away a lot and seemed to be thinking hard. He avoided eye contact and could not restate what I had said to him. I was very surprised at the change in behavior. At the end of the session, he said he would do the next chapter on ratios for the upcoming week.

The next week, he had all the exercises done correctly. I asked him to summarize the things he had learned from the homework, but he seemed reluctant to do so. He looked listless and depressed. His shoulders, usually very military-straight, were slumped. He said, "Actually, I don't even remember; I did it four days ago, and I've been kind of busy since then . . . my wife and I are thinking about a divorce. Seems kind of funny after twenty-three years . . . I moved out of the house on Wednesday."

Consider the following factors in your analysis:

- (a) what nonacademic difficulty is manifested?
- (b) what evidence do you have that this is the problem?
- (c) would you assist or refer the student?
- (d) if you would assist, what steps would you take?
- (e) if you would refer, to whom?

Situation 5

When Tom came to his tutoring session, I noticed that his eyes were puffy and he looked exhausted. For the last two weeks, he had been preparing diligently for his sociology mid-term, scheduled for the following week. I asked him how his reviewing was going. He said he had reviewed chapters one to four, but he had yet to even look at chapter five, which was to be included in the test. Tom explained angrily, "I had set aside last night to do this fifth chapter, and then my roommate decided to have a party in our room. Three of his friends invited themselves and brought a case of beer. They turned the stereo so loud, I couldn't hear myself think. When I asked them to turn it down, we got into a big argument. It's happening more and more often lately. He's really turning into a partier. Maybe he doesn't need to study, but I do. I'm getting awfully tired of his immature attitude." Tom hurried on, "Well, I was so mad after fighting with Earl that I couldn't study last night, so maybe you could just fill me in on chapter 5 . . . you did take the course, didn't you . . . ?"

Consider the following factors in your analysis:
- (a) what nonacademic difficulty is manifested?
- (b) what evidence do you have that this is the problem?
- (c) would you assist or refer the student?
- (d) if you would assist, what steps would you take?
- (e) if you would refer, to whom?

Situation 6

Robertha came to the study center to get help with a beginning history course. It was close to finals time. This was her first semester at college. Her first history test grade at midterm was a 58 percent. It was a multiple choice and short answer test. She said she had studied hard and was very nervous about doing badly on the final. She felt she had to do extremely well to bring up the 58 percent and to avoid her friend's teasing her about failing. I looked at her test paper, text and notebook. All were well-organized and appropriately underlined. She also had some short notes in the book margins which were summaries of some of the important concepts. I looked back at the test paper. On several of the short answers, the teacher had written "good" and "exactly!" Many of the answers counted wrong were left blank. A few of the blanks were the very ideas I had noticed in Robertha's handwriting in the book margins.

I quizzed her on those points, and surprisingly, she knew the answers to all the questions I asked her, even though they were blank on the test. I was puzzled until I pointed out to Robertha that if she were to take the test right now, she'd do much better. She said, "Oh, but sitting here talking to you is nothing like taking a test. I feel relaxed now. I was so nervous when I took this awful test the first time that I forgot everything. My mind was actually a blank. I don't even remember walking to my car afterward. I knew I'd done a terrible job on it." She laughed, "Then I was so mad at myself, because I remembered it all later."

Consider the following factors in your analysis:

    (a) what nonacademic difficulty is manifested?

    (b) what evidence do you have that this is the problem?

    (c) would you assist or refer the student?

    (d) if you would assist, what steps would you take?

    (e) if you would refer, to whom?

When you have finished your analyses, find another tutor who has completed the exercise up to this point. With this partner, discuss your respective answers. Try to come to a consensus about the appropriate steps, if any, for the tutor to take in each of the six cases. When you and your partner have discussed your own answers you may wish to consider the suggested analyses of the cases on page 141. These are not the *right* answers, but they do represent the combined answers of two experienced tutors.

REFERRING STUDENTS FOR ASSISTANCE

Many tutors have rather ambivalent feelings about referring a student to another department or person for assistance. Tutors who feel this way sometimes remark that they feel as if referring a student is shirking responsibility or abandoning a friend in need. Other tutors realize limitations in their skills and refer students with whom they are working in a content area to another tutor for in-depth assistance in reading or writing skills. In other cases, tutors can refer students who experience personal problems to the appropriate professionals such as counselors or psychologists. The vital point is to be honest about your feelings with yourself and with the student. If you feel it is inappropriate for you to discuss personal matters with students, it is your right to say so. Of course, you should make every effort to say so in a courteous and tactful fashion, so as not to jeopardize your tutoring relationship with hurt feelings.

For example, it is perfectly acceptable to say, "I feel a little uncomfortable, Judy, when you talk about your husband to me. I'm not married, you know, and I don't know much about married people's problems." This sort of remark, *about yourself and your preferences, not a remark about Judy*, can let the student know how you feel without being rejecting or unkind. After all, it is very uncomfortable to be "imprisoned" in a conversation which you feel to be embarrassing, inappropriate or compromising. Do not let yourself become the "victim" of someone's confidences *unless you want to and feel it is appropriate for you to engage in the conversation.*

If you feel you are qualified to discuss students' personal problems with them, it is occasionally acceptable for you to do so with two important cautions kept carefully in mind. (1) Do not confuse the tutoring role with the role of the psychologist, financial counselor or physician. Many problems with which you would like to help the student may simply be beyond your, and most persons', reach. Problems such as alcoholism, drug addictions, deafness, stuttering, brain dysfunction, stroke damage, chronic test anxiety, etc., are too complex except for the highly and specifically trained professional. Other problems, such as finances, legal matters or marital problems are simply inappropriate for tutors to handle. (2) Avoid giving advice. Naturally, when you are in your role as spouse, parent, family member and so forth, you are often asked for and probably give advice to others, without fear of consequences. This is your option when you play these roles. However, when you make the decision to discuss personal issues with students, it is wisest to help students by discussing choices with them but *letting them make the choice.* Students often say to tutors such things as, "What would you do if you were me? . . . I know you were in X position; what did you do? . . . I'm going to do X, Y, Z; don't you think I should?" It is always safest for you and ultimately more useful to students to help them brainstorm all the options and think through all the consequences which accompany each option. You might respond to a request for advice by saying, "You're the one who will have to live with the decision, not me, and I'd hate to give you the wrong advice. As I see it, you have at least two options, X and Z. What other possibilities do you see?" From this point, you can continue to discuss the possible consequences with students until they have made a decision. This prevents the all too common occurrence of giving advice and then having it thrown up in the advice-giver's face with the angry remark, "If I hadn't listened to you, I wouldn't be in this awful mess!"

STEPS IN THE REFERRAL PROCESS

Once you have identified that students are suffering with personal problems which are definitely interfering with their academic progress, it is up to you to decide if you can deal with the problem yourself. If you decide that the problem is too embarrassing, too complex, too far-reaching or inappropriate for you to handle, then a referral is in order. (Naturally, if students are experiencing nonacademic problems which do not interfere with study progress, it is not incumbent upon you to do anything about it unless they specifically request help.) Use the following suggestions as a guideline only. Of course, your own good sense and tact will be your best guide.

1. When students bring up problems (which they may do), or when you have decided that the problem can no longer be circumvented without damage to students, bring up the problem to them during your regular tutoring session, in the most delicate and nonconfrontive way you can think of. Before carrying out this step, many tutors discuss the opening remarks with their supervisor or with another more experienced tutor to see how they will sound.

2. If students react in a highly defensive, insulted or other negative way, do not press the issue. Drop it and consult later with your supervisor about the next step. Do not attempt to proceed further without back-up from the professional staff.

3. If students agree that there are problems, proceed with the referral. In order to insure that they carry through with what they may consider unpleasant (think how unpleasant it is for you to make your own appointments at the dentist, doctor, divorce lawyer, etc.), either accompany students to the office of referral to introduce them or, in their presence, discreetly phone ahead and tell the receptionist that they are on their way. If you call to the department of referral, you can say something like, "This is Mary Smith in the tutoring center. I'm talking with Mr. Brown, and he has mentioned that he'd like to meet with someone in your office. May I send him right over to make an appointment?" When students think that someone is expecting them, they generally are less anxious about taking the first step.

4. The next time you see students whom you have referred, inquire casually about their reaction to the service department. Be interested and encouraging, but do not badger or probe for confidential details. If the student failed to make the initial appointment, try once again to make an appointment. If the second attempt fails, consult your supervisor. Do not make a third attempt to set up an appointment without further guidance.

If, on the other hand, students make appointments, but fail to keep them or attend once and then discontinue, try to discover the reason they had so little persistence. If they resist discussion, drop the matter and consult with your supervisor. If a small obstacle was in the way, such as difficulty finding the right office or catching the bus on time, make another appointment by phone, while they listen to your end of the conversation. If, however, students state a more serious objection to the service area, such as, "I could tell as soon as I walked in that they don't like women, gays, blacks, foreign students, and so on there," or some other serious reason, try to help them think of alternative ways to deal with their problems. Maybe students can visit at another hour or day of the week when conditions may be more favorable. Or, perhaps they can utilize a similar service elsewhere.

Whenever you work with nonacademic problems and subsequent referrals, remember that you can only do your best. Some students may not wish to be helped *now*, or they may see the problem differently from the way you see it. All you can do is your best to be of assistance. The rest is up to them.

SUGGESTED ANSWERS TO THE SIX SITUATIONS

Situation 1

    (a) What nonacademic difficulty is manifested?

          Hearing loss seems to be the problem.

    (b) What evidence do you have that this is the problem?

          Luetta apparently failed to hear the tutor when he spoke from behind her. She also stared at his face quite steadily and sits in the front row of classes.

    (c) Would you assist or refer the student?

          Since Luetta's hearing loss is obviously affecting her math class, it may jeopardize her performance in all her lecture classes. Therefore, it is appropriate for the tutor to suggest a referral.

(d) If you would assist, what steps would you take?

Not applicable

(e) If you would refer, to whom?

Luetta should be referred to a health center or speech and hearing clinic.

Situation 2

(a) What nonacademic difficulty is manifested?

The problem is financial and study-related.

(b) What evidence do you have that this is the problem?

Caroline states her problem. She is jeopardizing her financial aid by her low grades.

(c) Would you assist or refer the student?

The tutor could assist her.

(d) If you would assist, what steps would you take?

The tutor could help Caroline with SQ3R or test taking preparation.

(e) If you would refer, to whom?

If Caroline is unsure of her current financial aid status, the tutor could refer her to a financial aid counselor.

Situation 3

(a) What nonacademic difficulty is manifested?

The problem appears to be shyness or lack of self-confidence.

(b) What evidence do you have that this is the problem?

Paula likes her job partly because she does not have to meet the public. She also must perform poorly when she gives speeches because her performance grades are so much lower than her content grades. She also states that she believes all the other students are better speech makers than she.

(c) Would you assist or refer the student?

> It is not appropriate for the tutor to handle such a chronic problem.

(d) If you would assist, what steps would you take?

> Not applicable

(e) If you would refer, to whom?

> Since Paula's shyness will probably cause her to fail her speech class, the tutor could refer Paula to a personal problem counselor, if she is receptive.

Situation 4

(a) What nonacademic difficulty is manifested?

> George has a marital problem, i.e. a divorce, which seems to absorb all his energy.

(b) What evidence do you have that this is the problem?

> George's behavior changes suddenly for the worse, then he states the problem openly.

(c) Would you assist or refer the student?

> Unless George's academic performance is damaged, it is not necessary that the tutor do anything. The tutor could reflect George's feelings if they continue to affect tutoring. If George's feelings grow to make tutoring ineffective, the tutor will have to consider referral.

(d) If you would assist, what steps would you take?

> Not applicable

(e) If you would refer, to whom?

> He could be referred to a personal problem counselor.

Situation 5

(a) What nonacademic difficulty is manifested?

> The problem superficially appears to be the insensitive roommate. On a deeper level, the

problem is that Tom has not thought of alternate places he can go to study.

(b) What evidence do you have that this is the problem?

Although Tom sees only the superficial problem, an astute tutor would reason that Tom needs to consider other quieter study places.

(c) Would you assist or refer the student?

Yes, the tutor can assist Tom here.

(d) If you would assist, what steps would you take?

The tutor might agree to assist Tom in previewing and making up questions for chapter five. At a later session, he could discuss with him alternate study places.

Situation 6

(a) What nonacademic difficulty is manifested?

Robertha appears to suffer from test anxiety.

(b) What evidence do you have that this is the problem?

After the test Robertha is able to recall information that was asked for on the exam but that she could not recall during the test.

(c) Would you assist or refer the student?

If her anxiety is a persistent problem, the tutor should probably refer Robertha since her anxiety will undoubtedly affect her whole academic performance.

(d) If you would assist, what steps would you take?

Not applicable

(e) If you would refer, to whom?

The tutor could refer Robertha to a study skills specialist or personal problem counselor, depending on the resources on the campus or in the city.

Chapters 2 through 7 have presented or facilitated the formation of many concepts and techniques which the authors hope will be helpful to you as you tutor. The next chapter, "Tutoring Applied," presents some basic guidelines for tutoring on a day-to-day basis and shows the application to everyday tutoring of some of the concepts discussed at length elsewhere in the text. Chapter 8 will be of most use to you as a quick refresher or a brass tacks guide just before you start on your tutoring career.

Chapter 8

TUTORING APPLIED

THIS chapter is intended to serve as a selected summary of several of the main ideas covered elsewhere in the text. It is also a quick practical guide to some of the everyday issues of tutoring. If you have never tutored before, use this chapter as a last brush-up or as an applied guide to give you confidence just before you start your tutoring responsibilities. In order to serve as a quick guide, this chapter has been constructed almost as a list of do's and don'ts. If you have completed the remainder of the text, the reasons for all the guidelines suggested here should be clear to you.

RESPECTING FELLOW LEARNERS

As a successful tutor, make it clear by your behavior that you *respect* the students with whom you work. Treating other learners with disrespect can destroy the effect of any knowledge you may have about the topic or about the process of tutoring. Therefore, being on time for appointments, looking students in the eye, paying close attention when they speak and sitting close to them are important factors. Sitting close to students is most effective if the chairs are placed side by side, as if for a conversation, rather than across a table or facing each other in a confrontive fashion. Furthermore, standing over other persons or turning your back on them (for example to write on the chalkboard) is as rude in the tutoring situation as it would be at a dinner party. Other ways to show respect for fellow learners is to accept their studying and thinking tempo; it may be slower than yours, but restrain your impatience. Respect can also be conveyed by showing regard for

146

students' speech habits. Unless you are working on speeches with students, do not correct their oral grammar. To do so is as rude in tutoring as it would be in any conversation. Finally, never break confidentiality with a student. Confidentiality can be respected if you remember not to talk nonchalantly with other tutors or with friends about students whom you are tutoring. Tutoring is a private "conversation," so repeating in public the content of tutoring sessions is a violation of the tutor/student relationship. Of course, you will at one time or another wish to get other tutors' or your supervisor's opinions on particular students to improve your tutoring. In these cases, preserve confidentiality by concealing students' names, or, if you must reveal names make sure the listener understands the conversation is confidential.

Equally important is your attitude as a tutor. It is essential to convey a caring attitude toward the student. Part of caring is being patient and nonjudgmental, i.e. withholding negative judgments about students as individuals or as learners. It is, after all, unnecessary to tell them that you do not like their clothes, hair or choice of classes, nor is it appropriate to comment aloud on students' slowness of reading or comprehension. Keep these thoughts to yourself.

Keep the focus of the tutoring session away from yourself. Do not waste energy on worrying about your own performance. The focus of the tutoring session should be on students' *learning*. Of course, it is all right to like students for themselves, but it is vital that you *care about students' academic successes*. If you do not consider tutoring important and serious, students will know and act accordingly.

SETTING GOALS FOR TUTORING SESSIONS

As in any other activity, have a goal in mind for each tutoring session. It is not enough to say, "Today we'll work on botany," or "Let's look at your test from last week." Goals need to be more specific. For example, a goal might be: "To learn the difference between xylem and phloem," or "To review the teacher's comments on the questions you missed on the test and see what you could have answered differently." Without goals, tutoring sessions can become "gab fests" or sessions during which students transfer to you all of their complaints, worries and problems. Equally dangerous, without goals, neither you nor students can measure progress and feel you are getting somewhere. Keep sessions about one hour in length; few people can concentrate hard for more than sixty minutes.

TUTORING TECHNIQUES

One of the challenges of tutoring is developing techniques which allow you to present material without actually doing the work for students. After all, the easiest and fastest way to get students' homework done is to do it for them. You already know the answer, in some cases, or can figure it out faster than students can. But, needless to say, doing work for students is not only dishonest, but also self-defeating. What you want to do is to work yourself out of a job. You want students eventually to be able to do the work without your assistance.

Developing a facility in a variety of tutoring techniques is one way to help students become independent learners. Any effective technique makes use of the material at hand. If students have a text and a notebook for notes, or a first draft of a speech, use these materials as the basis of the session. It is very difficult to work in a vacuum. If students do not bring any material with them, remind them to do so next time.

As you employ any tutoring technique, realize that your behaviors carry a certain weight with students, and for this reason, they may copy your behaviors when studying alone. Therefore, do not model behaviors you wish students to avoid (for example, overreliance on answer keys and resource books at the expense of thinking and understanding).

Question/Answer

One popular tutoring technique (sometimes called "Socratic") is simply asking students questions in order to provoke them into thinking their way toward understanding. Everyone uses this technique in everyday situations, so it will probably be easy for you to bring to your tutoring. This technique tests the students' knowledge without your having to recite mountains of material to them.

Demonstration

One demonstration is worth a thousand explanations. Showing a process is often easier than explaining it over and over. If students are having difficulties understanding cell division, make use of the diagrams in the book. If there are none, draw the process on a piece of paper. Make it real. Acting out many processes can be helpful. For example, you can sometimes act out "positive body language" or "compulsive behavior" much more quickly than explain them.

Illustration, Example and Analogy

Examples and analogies are as valuable as demonstration. In using examples, make them concrete or visual to increase their effectiveness. To illustrate fractions (rather than to use abstract numbers only), ask students to draw a pie with pieces cut, or some other familiar *real* object. Or, to illustrate the concept of a clutch in an automobile suggest that the clutch is two furry dinner plates, which when pressed face together, drag on each other, thus engaging the power of the motor to the drive shaft.

Induction and Deduction

Both these processes are valuable and can be used with most students. However, some students prefer one process to the other and understand it more easily. If you know which approach makes the most sense to a particular student, capitalize on that approach. Induction appeals to students who like to have the parts or details of a process or principle first and from them figure out the principle or the whole process. Students who prefer deduction want to have the principle clearly stated first or to see the whole process laid out before they hear about or discuss the details or parts. This is illustrated by the way people learn to play cards. Some people like to be told initially, "The object of the game is . . ." (thus hearing the overall principle guiding play) while others say, "Just start playing, and I'll pick it up" (thus gathering up the details as the play proceeds and discovering the basic principle of the game later).

ENCOURAGING THINKING

Tutors can best encourage thinking by modeling it. As you tutor, *think aloud* so the students can hear your reasoning process, and correct yourself aloud. For example, suppose that students have been assigned by the physics professor to write an explanation of why some objects will float on water and others will not. The professor has said, "Do not consult any references to write your explanation. Try to figure out the principle." First, ask students to advance any theories or ideas they have to explain the phenomenon. Keep probing and encouraging students to talk. Do not be critical. If students cannot state the principle, you may help by thinking aloud. As you mull the problem over, think aloud so the students can hear what thought processes are going on in your head. Say under your breath, "Well, there must be a difference in weight between those objects which float and those which do not . . . but, wait a minute, huge ships float, and they must weigh a lot, . . . so, weight must not be the key factor. If weight is not the factor, then maybe it's surface area, . . . now what could be an illustration of that? . . ." Go on in this fashion, and encourage the students to do so in any situation which calls for considerable thought.

POSITIVE REINFORCEMENT

During tutoring, attempt to find opportunities for positive reinforcement. This means complimenting or praising behaviors you think students should continue, for example, working hard, paying attention, asking questions, staying late to work or being active in the tutoring process. Of course, it is easy to praise someone for getting the right answers, but those students who seldom get answers right must be encouraged for their efforts, nonetheless. It is perfectly permissible to praise students for trying hard and getting some part of the answer correct even if they miss the whole answer. Some understanding is better than none, and complete understanding is fully as valuable as "the right answer."

Although these are not the only guidelines to keep in mind as you begin to tutor, they are some of the most basic ones. The authors hope they will lend you a feeling of confidence and readiness so that you enter tutoring sessions with a positive feeling about yourself and with high expectations for the students with whom you work. Enjoy your tutoring experiences! They may be some of the most rewarding and memorable you will ever have.

Chapters 1 through 8 have discussed many ideas for tutoring. One last idea yet to be considered is the evaluation of tutoring. It is placed as a last chapter in this text because evaluation is generally the final step of the tutoring session. Chapter 9 presents several basic approaches to evaluation of tutoring.

Chapter 9

EVALUATING THE TUTORING PROCESS

TUTOR SELF-EVALUATION

AS you tutor, you will naturally want to assess the effects of your tutoring and to make an improvement in your performance, just as teachers and students do. Although it is difficult to see yourself as others see you, there are several areas in which it is possible for you to evaluate your own performance by setting tutoring objectives, meeting those objectives and selecting tutoring materials.

In this chapter you will deal with three *facets* of evaluation: self-evaluation, evaluation by supervisors and evaluation by students. Many tutoring centers have daily log forms which you would fill out after you tutor. Forms such as these provide you the opportunity to record tutoring activities session by session for a particular student. The form on page 154 has been included as an example of the log. Notice that the form asks for the student's name, the date and the type of tutoring session, e.g. introductory, study skills help or tutoring in a specific subject, etc.

The most important part of the form has been left blank for the narrative comments composed by you. In this section, you should include:

a. the learning objective(s) set for the session
b. materials which were used during the session (student texts, students' notebooks, dictionaries, glossaries, etc.)
c. a summary of what occurred
d. objectives (if any) set for the upcoming session

The most effective way to make use of the form is to respond to items a, b, c and d above in your own words as soon as possible after the tutoring session. After you complete the form, you should compare the summary of activities to the objectives set before the session. Do they match? In other words, did you accomplish what you set out to do as the session started? Although this sounds simplistic, you may find that this technique helps you to focus on the tutoring activity at hand without wandering on to other topics.

LOG FORM

Student Name _____   Date _____

Type of session:

               _____ Introductory Session

               _____ Specific Subject Tutoring

               _____ Study Skills Tutoring

               _____ Reading Tutoring

               _____ Writing Tutoring

Summary of Tutoring Session:

Approximate length of contact _____

_____

                                 Tutor signature

Tutor self-evaluation forms serve several additional purposes. For example, if you are sick and unable to meet with a student on your regular schedule, another tutor could locate your log forms, read the summaries and be apprised of the activities you have undertaken with the student. In this way, continuity of tutoring can be maintained in your absence. Also, if the student you are tutoring should return in a subsequent semester after you are no longer with the tutoring center, another tutor could get permission to access the tutoring center's files and consult the logs.

Finally, logs can be used to provide feedback to teachers who have referred a student for tutoring. The teacher can see at a glance what has been covered during the tutoring.

Copies of the tutor self-evaluation log have been completed by several tutors and included as an illustration on pages 157, 158, and 159. They may give you a clearer idea of what to include in a self-evaluation.

EVALUATION BY TUTOR SUPERVISOR

While there are some facets of tutoring that you can best evaluate yourself, other aspects can best be evaluated by someone who assumes the role of observer. In most centers, this is the tutor supervisor, the teacher in charge of the tutoring program or the director of the Adult Basic Education Program. Most supervisors prefer to observe their tutoring staff regularly during the school term. The authors have included forms on pages 160 and 161 as a basis of observation sessions, and for feedback to you about the more subtle aspects of your tutoring performance.

Notice that one form lists a number of specific behaviors and attitudes for the observer to note. This list represents important concepts from the text. The other form provides for comments on the interaction between you and the student, and for general comments by the observer. Your center may have an observation form already in use, or your supervisor may wish to use the forms from this text.

EVALUATION BY STUDENTS

Finally, another important aspect of evaluation of tutoring can be provided by students. Feedback from students who have used the services can be obtained in many ways: some centers mail forms to students; others ask them to fill in evaluation forms in the center and put them in a drop box; others spot-interview students to obtain anecdotal feedback. Check with your supervisor to find what type of student-authored evaluation is to be used. Whatever the method of collecting information, it is a vital part of evaluation, because students are the consumers of the service. Again, the responses given by students can provide very useful information for improving your tutoring.

LOG FORM

Student Name _____ George Sanchez _____ Date _____ 3/2 _____

Type of session:

                  _____ Introductory Session

                  __✓__ Specific Subject Tutoring

                  _____ Study Skills Tutoring

                  _____ Reading Tutoring

                  _____ Writing Tutoring

George came to the tutoring center because he had failed his first accounting exam (it was given the second week of class). He was very apprehensive about failing the course and was thinking of dropping. This is our third session since George failed the first test. Today we focused on George's understanding of the terms debit and credit and on which side of the ledger they belong and why. We spent the hour going over the text explanation of the terms, and on thinking up memory tricks to remember the differences. Then, George filled out a sample ledger sheet in his accounting workbook while I looked on. He did fine without any additional help but is not always sure why items go on the right or left side. Before the next test (in a week) there are several things we have to go over from the old test: the different types of accounts and balances, financial statements, and the *reasons* they are recorded as they are.

Approximate length of contact _____ *one hour* _____

_____ *Alice Ward* _____
                           Tutor signature

LOG FORM

Student Name _____ Sharon West _____ Date _____ May 1 _____

Type of session:

            _____ Introductory Session
            _____ Specific Subject Tutoring
            _✓_ Study Skills Tutoring
            _____ Reading Tutoring
            _____ Writing Tutoring

This is our tenth session. Today we're supposed to be checking Sharon's notes from her lecture class in sociology. She has been practicing the Cornell notetaking system which she read about in the Pauk book from our library. She's still having trouble with picking the wrong key word to write in the recall column, and then can't recite her notes accurately. I'm not sure why the problem is occurring — either she's having trouble picking the main idea of paragraphs, or she is getting the main idea but then picks the wrong key word to represent the idea. Next time, I have asked her to take her notes, but to wait until she's in front of me to fill out the recall column. I think she'll remember because our sessions are right after the soc. class lets out. I'm going to ask her to think out loud in front of me so I can see her reasoning.

Approximate length of contact_____ 40 min. _____

_____ Chas Meyers _____
Tutor signature

LOG FORM

Student Name _____ Marvine Walton _____ Date _____ 9/22 _____

Type of session:

         __✓__ Introductory Session

         _____ Specific Subject Tutoring

         _____ Study Skills Tutoring

         _____ Reading Tutoring

         _____ Writing Tutoring

This was our first session. Marvine was assigned to me because she was having trouble in her Geology I class. I used the hour to get an idea of her study habits. (I already looked at the registration form she filled out and noted her work obligations, her other study obligations and the fact that she'd marked "work schedule conflicts" and "attending classes" as problem areas.) During the session she appeared to be very tired and distracted. She told me that she worked as a security guard until 1 a.m. each weeknight and had all early and mid morning classes, three days a week. As a result, she had missed her allowable maximum in all her classes, and it was only the fourth week of the term. She was reluctant even to think about dropping anything because her employer wanted her to complete 15 hours of law enforcement training before she would be eligible for a promotion or raise. She was so upset that we didn't get to talk about much else. For the next time, I gave her a blank schedule form and asked her to fill it out with her work, home and school obligations.

Approximate length of contact_____ 50 mins. _____

_____ Harlow Mills _____
                                   Tutor signature

OBSERVATION CHECKLIST FOR TUTOR SKILLS

Date_____

Tutor_____ Subject _____

Observer_____ Type of Session   _____ one-to-one
                                              _____ drop-in
Length of Obsrv._____   _____ small group
                                              _____ regular
Tutee (optional)_____   _____ other

Directions: Please indicate your response for as many of the following as apply.

Shows concern for the student	Good____ Average____ Poor____ NA____
Arranges physical setting	Good____ Average ____ Poor____ NA____
Picks up cues of strengths and weaknesses in content areas	Good____ Average____ Poor____ NA____
Asks open-ended questions	Good____ Average____ Poor ____ NA____
Listens	Good ____ Average____ Poor____ NA____
Sets goals	Good____ Average____ Poor ____ NA____
Provides positive reinforcement	Good____ Average____ Poor____ NA____
Shows patience	Good ____ Average____ Poor ____ NA____
Has eye contact	Good ____ Average ____ Poor ____ NA____
Maintains good physical posture	Good ____ Average____ Poor____ NA____
Reflects feeling	Good____ Average ____ Poor ____ NA____
Paraphrases	Good____ Average____ Poor ____ NA____
Recognizes study problem	Good____ Average____ Poor____ NA____
Encourages use of problem-solving/thinking skills	Good____ Average____ Poor____ NA____
Provides examples	Good____ Average____ Poor____ NA____
Clarifies	Good____ Average ____ Poor____ NA ____
Synthesizes	Good____ Average____ Poor ____ NA____
Summarizes	Good____ Average____ Poor ____ NA____
Makes referrals, if appropriate	Good____ Average____ Poor____ NA____

Instructional technique(s): Check all that apply

____ *Demonstration* - Explanation or expansion of a concept of operation using examples and actually modeling underlying thought processes.

____ *Illustration* - Clarification of a concept or operation using aides such as diagrams, pictures, graphs and/or any concrete instances of abstract ideas.

____ *Question-answer* - Questioning students to be sure they have fully processed the concept rather than simply passively receiving it. Incomplete understanding as well as misconceptions can be revealed in this way.

____ *Inductive teaching* - Proceeding from parts-to-whole; i.e. having students discover principles through observation and exploration of carefully selected examples.

____ *Deductive teaching* - Proceeding from whole-to-parts; i.e. traditional lecture methods where learners are expected actively to integrate material they have been told.

TUTOR/STUDENT INTERACTIONS

Comments:_____

_____

_____

_____

_____

_____

_____

Feedback session_____ Date_____
Length of Session_____
Comments:

INDEX

A
Age-oriented attitudes, 50-60
Auditory learning, 41, 42

C
Cultural attitudes, 50-60

D
Deduction, 43, 54
Directed free writing, 117-120

E
Emotional problems
  see "Dealing with Personal Problems"
  Chapter 7, 127-145
Evaluation of tutoring,
  self, 152-4, 157-159
  by student, 156
  by supervisor, 155, 160, 161

F
Financial problems
  see "Dealing with Personal
  Problems" Chapter 7, 127-145

G
Goals, setting of, 90, 91, 100, 147, 148
Grammar, 117, 118, 119, 121

I
Induction, 43, 45

K
Kinesthetic learning, 41, 42

L
Learning
  models of, 33
  modes of, 41, 44, 45
Lecture notetaking, 80-83, 86-91
Linguistic attitudes, 47, 48, 49, 50
Listening
  for facts and feelings, 21-23
  paraphrasing, 27-29
  reflecting feelings 23-27
Log, tutoring, 152, 153, 154, 158, 159

M
Medical problems
  see "Dealing with Personal Problems"
  Chapter 7, 127-145

N
Notetaking
  during lectures, 80-83, 86-91
  from texts, 78-80
  Cornell system, 79

P
Personal problems
  identifying, 129-138
  referral to professionals, 138-145
  resources for, 127-129
Piaget
  accommodation, 42, 43, 44
  assimilation, 42, 43, 44
  equilibration, 42, 43, 44
  model of learning, 33, 36, 37
  self-regulation, 42

163

Pre-writing, 114, 115
Psychological problems
    see "Dealing with Personal Problems"
    Chapter 7, 127-145

Q

Questions in textbooks, 86
Questioning
    open-ended questions, 18-21, 87
    use of in diagnosis of students, 38,
    39, 85, 86, 121, 122, 148
Questions
    student construction of, 110, 111
    tutor construction of, 110, 111
    use in SQ3R, 73, 74, 76

R

Reading
    serious problems in, 104-111
    SQ3R, 73-78
    textbooks, 71-73, 97-100, 104-111

S

Sex-oriented attitudes, 50-60
Spelling, 117, 118, 119, 121, 125
SQ3R, 73-78, 88, 99, 104
Study Skills, 68-111
    informal diagnosis of, 61-68, 84-88
    self-diagnosis, 68-83
    strengthening of 84-100

T

Test anxiety
    see "Dealing with Personal Problems"
    Chapter 7, 127-145
Test taking, 86-88, 91-95
Textbook skills, 71-80, 83, 86-88, 97-
    100, 104-111
Thinking

inductive and deductive, 43, 44, 45
Time scheduling, 86-88, 95-97
Tutor
    role of, 7-17
Tutoring, attitudes, 7-10
    toward language, 47-50
    toward cultural differences, 50-60
    toward differences, 50-60
    toward sexual differences, 50-60
    towards students, 146, 147
Tutoring, behaviors and, 8-10
    positive reinforcement, 150, 151
Tutoring, definition of, 3, 4
Tutoring, evaluation of, 152-161
Tutoring, goalsetting for, 147, 148, 90,
    91, 100
Tutoring, guidelines for, 7-10
Tutoring, logs for, 152, 153, 154, 158,
    159
Tutoring techniques, 148-149
    deduction, 149
    demonstration, 149
    encouraging thinking, 150
    illustration/example/analogy, 149
    induction, 149
    question/answer, 148, 149

V

Visual Learning, 41, 42

W

Writing
    directed free-writing, 117-120
    drafts, 120-123
    grammar, 117, 118, 119, 121, 124, 125
    mechanics, 124-125
    pre-writing, 114-115
    spelling, 117, 118, 119, 121, 125
    tutoring in, 111-126

Reviews of Note
from colleagues and professionals

"BRINGS THE ISSUES OF CHRONIC PAIN AND AGING INTO FOCUS. . . . While giving the reader an overview of the present state of knowledge and treatment, the book also raises questions to be addressed. Readers interested in research may find plenty of potential pathways worthy of pursuit. . . . Should appeal to gerontologists, nurses, social workers, and indeed all clinicians who have elderly patients burdened with chronic pain and who wish to decrease disability and improve quality of life for their patients."

—Dr. Pamela S. Melding, MB, ChB, FFARCS, FRANZCP, Consultant in Old Age Psychiatry, Mental Health Services for Older People, Waitemata Health, Auckland, New Zealand

"Should be required reading for geriatric physicians (and even pediatricians), geriatric psychologists, dentists, physical therapists, nurses, and social workers involved in diagnosis and treatment of chronic pain. . . . I HIGHLY RECOMMEND THIS TO ALL CONCERNED WITH EITHER GERIATRICS, GERONTOLOGY, OR PAIN."

—Stephen W. Harkins, PhD, Professor, Departments of Gerontology, Psychiatry, Psychology, and Biomedical Engineering, Virginia Commonwealth University

"PROVIDES AN EFFECTIVE REVIEW OF CURRENT KNOWLEDGE REGARDING PAIN IN OLDER PEOPLE. . . . This book will be especially useful to researchers and practitioners in areas where it is essential to be able to locate pain-relevant information without searching through large amounts of literature."

—M. Powell Lawton, PhD, Senior Research Scientist, Philadelphia Geriatric Center

Older Women
with Chronic Pain

Older Women
with Chronic Pain

Karen A. Roberto, PhD
Editor

Older Women with Chronic Pain, edited by Karen A. Roberto, PhD, was simultaneously issued by The Haworth Press, Inc., under the same title, as a special issue of *Journal of Women & Aging,* Volume 6, Number 4, 1994, J. Dianne Garner, Journal Editor.

The Harrington Park Press
An Imprint of
The Haworth Press, Inc.
New York • London • Norwood (Australia)

1-56023-061-4

Published by

Harrington Park Press, 10 Alice Street, Binghamton, NY 13904-1580 USA

Harrington Park Press is an imprint of the Haworth Press, Inc., 10 Alice Street, Binghamton, NY 13904-1580 USA.

Older Women with Chronic Pain has also been published as *Journal of Women & Aging*, Volume 6, Number 4 1994.

The development, preparation, and publication of this work has been undertaken with great care. However, the publisher, employees, editors, and agents of The Haworth Press and all imprints of The Haworth Press, Inc., including The Haworth Medical Press and Pharmaceutical Products Press, are not responsible for any errors contained herein or for consequences that may ensue from use of materials or information contained in this work. Opinions expressed by the author(s) are not necessarily those of The Haworth Press, Inc.

The Haworth Press, Inc., 10 Alice Street, Binghamton, NY 13904-1580, USA

Library of Congress Cataloging-in-Publication Data

Older women with chronic pain / Karen A. Roberto, editor.
     p.   cm:
    Also published as Journal of women & aging, v. 6, no. 4, 1994.
    Includes bibliographical references and index.
    ISBN 1-56024-706-1 (alk. paper)–ISBN 1-56023-061-4 (hpp : alk. paper)
    1. Chronic pain. 2. Aged women–Diseases. I. Roberto, Karen A. [DNLM: 1. Pain–in old age. 2. Pain–therapy. 3. Chronic Disease–in old age. 4. Women. W1 J0972H v. 6 no. 4 1994 / WL 704 044 1994]
RB127.034 1994
616'.0472'0846–dc20   *TOC*
DNLM/DLC   94-27471
for Library of Congress   CIP

INDEXING & ABSTRACTING

Contributions to this publication are selectively indexed or abstracted in print, electronic, online, or CD-ROM version(s) of the reference tools and information services listed below. This list is current as of the copyright date of this publication. See the end of this section for additional notes.

- *Abstracts in Anthropology*, Baywood Publishing Company, 26 Austin Avenue, P.O. Box 337, Amityville, NY 11701

- *Abstracts in Social Gerontology: Current Literature on Aging*, National Council on the Aging, Library, 409 Third Street SW, 2nd Floor, Washington, DC 20024

- *Abstracts of Research in Pastoral Care & Counseling*, Loyola College, 7135 Minstrel Way, Suite 101, Columbia, MD 21045

- *Academic Index (on-line)*, Information Access Company, 362 Lakeside Drive, Foster City, CA 94404

- *AgeLine Database*, American Association of Retired Persons, 601 E Street NW, Washington DC 20049

- *Behavioral Medicine Abstracts*, The Society of Behavioral Medicine, 103 South Adams Street, Rockville, MD 20850

- *Cambridge Scientific Abstracts*, *Risk Abstracts*, Cambridge Information Group, 7200 Wisconsin Avenue #601, Bethesda, MD 20814

- *Feminist Periodicals: A Current Listing of Contents*, Women's Studies Librarian-at-Large, 728 State Street, 430 Memorial Library, Madison, WI 53706

- *Guide to Social Science & Religion in Periodical Literature*, National Periodical Library, P.O. Box 3278, Clearwater, FL 34630

- *Human Resources Abstracts (HRA)*, Sage Publications, Inc., 2455 Teller Road, Newbury Park, CA 91320

- *Index to Periodical Articles Related to Law*, University of Texas, 727 East 26th Street, Austin, TX 78705

(continued)

- *Inventory of Marriage and Family Literature (online and hard copy)*, National Council on Family Relations, 3989 Central Avenue NE, Suite 550, Minneapolis, MN 55421

- *Mental Health Abstracts (online through DIALOG)*, IFI/Plenum Data Company, 3202 Kirkwood Highway, Wilmington, DE 19808

- *Periodical Abstracts, Research II* (broad coverage indexing & abstracting data-base from University Microfilms International (UMI) 300 North Zeeb Road, P.O. Box 1346, Ann Arbor, MI 48106-1346), UMI Data Courier, P.O. Box 32770, Louisville, KY 40232-2770

- *Periodical Abstracts Select* (abstracting & indexing service covering most frequently requested journals in general reference, plus journals requested in libraries serving undergraduate programs, available from University Microfilms International (UMI), 300 North Zeeb Road, P.O. Box 1346, Ann Arbor, MI 48106-1346), UMI Data Courier, Attn: Library Services, Box 34660, Louisville, KY 40232

- *SilverPlatter Information, Inc.* "**CD-ROM/online,**" Information Resources Group, P.O. Box 50550, Pasadena, CA 91115-0550

- *Social Planning/Policy & Development Abstracts (SOPODA)*, Sociological Abstracts, Inc., P.O. Box 22206, San Diego, CA 92192-0206

- *Social Work Abstracts*, National Association of Social Workers, 750 First Street NW, 8th Floor, Washington, DC 20002

- *Sociological Abstracts (SA)*, Sociological Abstracts, Inc., P.O. Box 22206, San Diego, CA 92192-0206

- *Studies on Women Abstracts*, Carfax Publishing Company, P.O. Box 25, Abingdon, Oxfordshire OX14 3UE, United Kingdom

- *Women Studies Abstracts,* Rush Publishing Company, P.O. Box 1, Rush, NY 14543

- *Women's Studies Index (indexed comprehensively)*, G.K. Hall & Co., 866 Third Avenue, New York, NY 10022

(continued)

SPECIAL BIBLIOGRAPHIC NOTES

related to special journal issues (separates)
and indexing/abstracting

☐ indexing/abstracting services in this list will also cover material in the "separate" that is co-published simultaneously with Haworth's special thematic journal issue or DocuSerial. Indexing/abstracting usually covers material at the article/chapter level.

☐ monographic co-editions are intended for either non-subscribers or libraries which intend to purchase a second copy for their circulating collections.

☐ monographic co-editions are reported to all jobbers/wholesalers/approval plans. The source journal is listed as the "series" to assist the prevention of duplicate purchasing in the same manner utilized for books-in-series.

☐ to facilitate user/access services all indexing/abstracting services are encouraged to utilize the co-indexing entry note indicated at the bottom of the first page of each article/chapter/contribution.

☐ this is intended to assist a library user of any reference tool (whether print, electronic, online, or CD-ROM) to locate the monographic version if the library has purchased this version but not a subscription to the source journal.

☐ individual articles/chapters in any Haworth publication are also available through the Haworth Document Delivery Services (HDDS).

CONTENTS

Preface   xv

The Study of Chronic Pain in Later Life: Where Are
the Women?   1
    Karen A. Roberto, PhD

The Physiology and Biomedical Aspects of Chronic Pain
in Later Life   9
    Charlene Edwards Morris, MD
    Veeraindar Goli, MD

Assessment of Older Women with Chronic Pain   25
    Dennis C. Turk, PhD
    Akiko Okifuji, MA
    Lisa Scharff, MA

Chronic Musculoskeletal Pain: Older Women
and Their Coping Strategies   43
    Deborah T. Gold, PhD

Current Concepts and Management of Cancer Pain
in Older Women   59
    Anita C. All, RN, PhD

Influence of Chronic Pain on the Family Relations
of Older Women   73
    Ranjan Roy, ADV, DIP, SW

Nonpharmacologic Interventions for the Management
of Chronic Pain in Older Women   89
    Paula R. Mobily, PhD, RN

Chronic Pain and Older Women: An Agenda
for Research and Practice   111
    Karen A. Roberto, PhD

Index   117

ABOUT THE EDITOR

Karen A. Roberto, PhD, is Professor and Coordinator of the Gerontology Program at the University of Northern Colorado. Her research focuses on family and friend relationships in later life and the influences of chronic illness on the lives of older women. She has published extensively on the psychosocial issue and concerns of older women with osteoporosis, and older women's recovery from hip fracture. She serves on the editorial board and is Book Review Editor for the *Journal of Women & Aging.*

Older Women
with Chronic Pain

Preface

Chronic pain often accompanies the predominant non-fatal chronic conditions experienced by older women (e.g., arthritis, osteoporosis). Living with chronic pain can limit the older woman's ability to care for herself, influences the way she feels about herself, and restricts her activities with family and friends. Most of the chronic pain literature, however, does not pay explicit attention to the older population and virtually ignores the possibility that there is a large proportion of older women living with chronic pain.

The authors who contributed to this special volume begin to fill this void by exploring the issues confronting older individuals suffering from chronic pain. Drawing upon the existing pain literature, their knowledge of aging, and recognition of the health issues facing older women, they bring to our attention the particulars of chronic pain in later life in relationship to its etiology, assessment, consequences, and management.

In the first article, I address some of the reasons why chronic pain is an issue for older women. In addition, a brief overview of the literature in relationship to the physical, psychological, and social aspects of chronic pain in later life is provided.

Drs. Charlene Edwards Morris and Veeraindar Goli address the physical and biomedical aspects of chronic pain in later life. They explore different theories and pathways of pain in relationship to changes in the pain perceptions of older adults. In addition, they describe painful conditions commonly found in elderly women.

[Haworth co-indexing entry note]: "Preface." Roberto, Karen A. Co-published simultaneously in *Journal of Women & Aging* (The Haworth Press, Inc.) Vol. 6, No. 4, 1994, pp. xv-xvii; and: *Older Women with Chronic Pain* (ed: Karen A. Roberto) The Haworth Press, Inc., 1994, pp. xv-xvii. Multiple copies of this article/chapter may be purchased from The Haworth Document Delivery Center [1-800-3-HAWORTH; 9:00 a.m. - 5:00 p.m. (EST)].

xv

The importance of using a comprehensive strategy for assessing chronic pain in older women is discussed by Dr. Dennis Turk and his colleagues, Akiko Okifuji and Lisa Scharff. They recommend a multiaxial model of assessment that includes physical, psychosocial, functional, and behavioral assessments of pain, distress, and suffering.

Dr. Deborah Gold focuses her attention on the coping strategies used by older women with chronic musculoskeletal pain. Diseases of the musculoskeletal system generate high disability levels among older women and a frequent consequence of these conditions is chronic pain. She describes pharmacologic, physical, and psychosocial management strategies that older women use to cope with their pain.

Pain is the most common symptom associated with cancer. Dr. Anita All describes the problems associated with cancer pain and pain management in later life including the effect of pain on the personal outlook of older cancer patients.

The influence of chronic pain on the family relationships of older women is addressed by Dr. Ranjan Roy. He uses case studies to illustrate the direct and indirect effects of chronic pain in later life on families. He recommends that an exploration of interpersonal issues and adoption of psychological interventions become routine when working with older persons with pain problems.

Dr. Paula Mobily describes several nonpharmacologic interventions for the management of chronic pain in older women. She suggests that the use of nonpharmacologic interventions, used concomitantly with pharmacologic approaches, will result in more effective pain control.

In the final paper, I present suggestions for future research in the area of women and chronic pain. Implications for health care and human service providers working with this group of older women also are highlighted.

As editor of this collection, it is my hope that we will draw to the attention of researchers, clinicians, and practitioners the importance of understanding the causes and consequences of living with chronic pain in later life. Chronic pain is not, and should not be treated as part of the natural aging process. I would like to thank each of the contributors to this volume for working so diligently to provide the groundwork for future research and practice concerning chronic pain among older adults, and older women in particular.

Karen A. Roberto, PhD

The Study of Chronic Pain in Later Life: Where Are the Women?

Karen A. Roberto, PhD

SUMMARY. Chronic pain often accompanies the predominant non-fatal chronic conditions experienced by older women. Population estimates suggest that 25-50% of community-dwelling older adults suffer as a result of chronic pain problems. Despite the prevalence of chronic pain among older adults, very little attention has been given to the consequences associated with living with chronic pain in later life. Within the limited geriatric pain literature, virtually no attention has been directed towards chronic pain among older women.

In 1990, of the 31.1 million Americans 65 years of age and older, nearly 19 million were women (U.S. Bureau of the Census, 1992). The differences between the number of older men and women grow with advancing age. Women between the ages of 65 and 74 comprise approximately 56% of the young-old population. In the "old-old" age group (i.e., individuals 75 to 84 years of age), women constitute nearly 63% of the population. Among individuals 85 years of age and older (i.e., the "oldest-old"), 72% are women.

The longer life expectancy of women often puts them at a disadvantage with respect to their physical health and well-being. As both men and women age, the probability of having multiple chron-

Karen A. Roberto is Professor and Coordinator, Gerontology Program, University of Northern Colorado, Greeley, CO 80639.

[Haworth co-indexing entry note]: "The Study of Chronic Pain in Later Life: Where Are the Women?" Roberto, Karen A. Co-published simultaneously in *Journal of Women & Aging* (The Haworth Press, Inc.) Vol. 6, No. 4, 1994, pp. 1-7; and: *Older Women with Chronic Pain* (ed: Karen A. Roberto) The Haworth Press, Inc., 1994, pp. 1-7. Multiple copies of this article/chapter may be purchased from The Haworth Document Delivery Center [1-800-3-HAWORTH; 9:00 a.m. - 5:00 p.m. (EST)].

ic illnesses increases. Older women, however, are more likely than their male counterparts to experience prolonged chronic health problems. "Whereas men's lives are shortened by higher rates of fatal illnesses, women's lives are filled with bothersome symptoms of nonfatal ones, due possibly to higher chances of developing conditions at a given age (incidence) and certainly to more total years enduring their progression (duration)" (Verbrugge, 1989, p. 41).

Chronic pain often accompanies the predominant non-fatal chronic conditions experienced by older women (e.g., arthritis and other musculoskeletal and orthopedic conditions) and contributes to their functional limitations. Overall pain, fatigue, and tension are frequent symptoms that pervade the daily lives of older men and women with chronic health problems (Verbrugge, 1989). For example, 80% of individuals over 65 report aches and pains in their joints which limit their mobility and dexterity (Davis, 1988). Personal care tasks, such as bathing, eating, and dressing, may be difficult to complete when burdened with persistent pain. In addition, the older woman's ability to perform instrumental activities of daily living (e.g., shopping, housekeeping, preparing meals) and participate in social activities also may be restricted as a result of the pain that accompanies her primary health condition (Roberto, 1990).

In addition to its relationship to chronic disease, pain may be viewed as a chronic condition in itself. Chronic pain is typically defined as having a duration of more than three months. "It has no autonomic signs, is usually out of proportion to the immediate danger, and is associated with long-standing functional and psychological impairment" (Ferrell, 1991, p. 66). Chronic pain syndromes affect approximately 11% of the adult population (Merskey, 1988). Population-based studies estimate that 25 to 50% of community-dwelling older adults suffer as a result of chronic pain problems (Brattberg, Mats, & Anders, 1989; Crook, Rideout, & Browne, 1984). Among nursing home residents, where women predominate, the prevalence of pain appears to be even higher. Researchers estimate that from 45 to 80% of nursing home residents experience chronic pain (Ferrell, Ferrell & Osterweil, 1990; Roy & Michael, 1986).

Despite the prevalence of chronic pain among older adults, very little attention has been given to the global causes and consequences associated with living with chronic pain in later life. Although a small proportion of individuals over the age of 65 are often included in the samples used to study pain phenomenon, in over 4000 papers published on pain each year, less than one percent focus specifically on the chronic pain experiences of older adults (Melding, 1991). Within the limited geriatric pain literature, virtually no direct attention is given to chronic pain among older women.

PAIN RESEARCH AND OLDER ADULTS

Perhaps one of the reasons for the limited attention given to chronic pain in later life is the lack of a clear consensus among pain experts as to the causes, consequences and treatment of chronic pain within the general adult population. Part of the reason for the disparity arises because researchers cannot identify a psychophysiological reason for chronic pain. Unlike acute pain which provides a warning sign that there is some physical abnormality, chronic pain serves no comparable purpose (Davis, 1989). Therefore, chronic pain itself emerges as a distinct multi-faceted condition to be managed and endured.

Pain researchers who focus on the pain itself tend to examine the pathophysiological mechanisms of pain. There is a commonly held belief that elderly individuals are less sensitive to pain than their younger counterparts. Age-related changes associated with a decline in visual and auditory perception may result in changes in central coding for pain with advancing age. There also is suppression of the immune response following an inflammatory process that may change the clinical presentation of pain. Researchers report conflicting findings, however, suggesting that a consensus does not exist regarding the relationship between pain sensitivity and age (Ferrell, 1991; Harkins & Price, 1992; Sorkin, Rudy, Hanlon, Turk, & Stieg, 1990). Similarities and differences between pain perceptions of older men and women have not been examined.

Researchers who have examined the psychological aspects of chronic pain typically describe how the person's perceptions and beliefs influence, or are influenced by, chronic pain. "What the patient believes to be the cause and probable outcome of the pain experience will define the meaning of the experience for the individual" (DeGood, 1988, p. 5). For older adults, responses to pain also may be influenced by their social history and cultural expectations (Harkins & Price, 1992). Living with recurrent or persistent pain is often viewed as an expected consequence of aging and therefore, elderly individuals may have little inclination to report pain. In addition, older patients may not report pain so as not to displease their doctor or detract from receiving a "cure" for the cause of their pain (Forman & Stratton, 1991).

Psychological problems are frequently associated with chronic pain conditions. For example, estimates of depression in chronic pain populations range from 7 to 52% (Doan & Wadden, 1989). Researchers have only recently turned their attention to the relationship between depression and pain in later life (Moss, Lawton, & Glicksman, 1991; Roy, 1986; Parmelee, Katz, & Lawton, 1991; Sorkin et al., 1990). The outcomes of these studies suggest that depression, as well as other psychological consequences of pain (e.g., loneliness, sleep disturbances) are prevalent among geriatric pain patients. Gender differences with respect to the psychological outcomes of pain in later life have not been explored.

Limited research has been published that examines the impact of chronic pain on the individual's social relationships. What has been written focuses specifically on the relationships between chronic pain patients and their spouses. Positive psychological functioning of pain patients has been associated with the perception of spousal support for their pain problems (Jamison & Vitti, 1990; Kerns & Turk, 1984). Variables associated with pain patients' marital satisfaction include the amount of solicitousness patients perceive from their spouses and the spouses' own marital satisfaction (Flor, Kerns, & Turk, 1987). Individuals whose spouses show a greater empathetic response to their pain expressions also report higher levels of marital satisfaction (Block, 1981). However, greater expressions of marital dissatisfaction have been reported by the spouses than by the pain patients themselves (Flor et al., 1987; Maruta, Osbourne, Swanson, & Hallwig, 1981). As in other areas of pain research, these studies are primarily based on young and middle-aged samples. It is not known if the problems facing these couples (i.e., marital difficulties and personal distress) are similar for older couples in which one member of the marital dyad is experiencing chronic pain.

The literature on pain management is voluminous. Treatment approaches include both pharmacologic and nonpharmacologic regimes. Although commonly prescribed, the use of drug therapy for older individuals with pain is complicated by their elevated risks of experiencing adverse side effects (e.g., tissue inflammation, dizziness, confusion, nausea, gastritis, depression) (Forman & Stratton, 1991; Harkins & Price, 1992). Despite the fact that pharmacologic pain management may entail special problems for older adults, limited information is available as to the implementation and effectiveness of nonpharmacologic strategies with older individuals. When management strategies for older adults are studied, it is typically with respect to specific conditions such as back pain (Mobily & Herr, 1992), fibromyalgia (Wolfe, 1988), headaches (Rappoport, Sheftell, & Baskin, 1983), and neck pain (Moskovich, 1988). In general, the findings of these studies suggest that nonpharmacologic treatment strategies such as the application of heat or cold, relaxation therapy, ergonomics, and transcutaneous electrical nerve stimulation (TENS) are effective in managing specific chronic pain conditions in later life.

There has been growing recognition of the effectiveness of multi-disciplinary treatment programs for persons with chronic pain. These programs use both physical and psychological treatment modalities and report success rates of between 60 to 75% (Guck, Skultety, Meilman, & Dowd, 1985; Painter, Seres, & Newman, 1980). Older adults are seldom referred to these types of programs despite their increasing availability.

CONCLUSIONS

There has been limited focus on the issues facing individuals with chronic pain in later life. The lack of attention given to this population in general, and older women in particular, is disturbing. Although women live longer then men, they do not necessarily live better as they typically confront their later years with one or more non-fatal, but chronic health conditions. As no cure is in sight for most of these diseases, the lifestyles of both current and future cohorts of older women are challenged by the pain associated with their health problems. Research that focuses on chronic pain problems in later life is necessary if we are to ensure a satisfying quality of life for women as they age. We must broaden our understanding of the issues and concerns facing these women and use this information to develop effective management strategies and techniques.

REFERENCES

Block, A. (1981). Behavioral treatment of chronic pain: The spouse as a discriminative cue for pain behavior. *Psychosomatic Medicine, 43*, 415-422.

Brattberg, G., Mats, T., & Anders, W. (1989). The prevalence of pain in a general population: The results of a postal survey in a county of Sweden. *Pain, 37*, 215-222.

Crook, J., Rideout, E., & Browne, G. (1984). The prevalence of pain complaints among a general population. *Pain, 18*, 299-314.

Davis, G. (1989). Measurement of the chronic pain experience: Development of an instrument. *Research in Nursing and Health, 12*, 221-227.

Davis, M.A. (1988). Epidemiology of osteoarthritis. *Clinical Geriatric Medicine, 4*, 241-255.

DeGood, D. (1988). A rationale and format for psychosocial evaluation. In N.T. Lynch & S. Vasudevan (Eds.), *Persistent pain: Psychosocial assessment and intervention* (pp. 1-22). Boston: Kluwer.

Doan, B., & Wadden, N. (1989). Relationships between depressive symptoms and descriptions of chronic pain. *Pain, 36*, 75-84.

Ferrell, B. (1991). Pain management in elderly people. *Journal of the American Geriatrics Society, 39*, 64-73.

Ferrell, B., Ferrell, B., & Osterweil, D. (1990). Pain in the nursing home. *Journal of the American Geriatric Society, 38*, 409-414.

Flor, H., Kerns, R., & Turk, D. (1987). The role of spouse reinforcement, perceived pain, and activity levels of chronic pain patients. *Journal of Psychosomatic Research, 31*, 251-259.

Forman, W., & Stratton, M. (1991). Current approaches to chronic pain in older patients. *Geriatrics, 46*, 47-52.

Guck, T., Skultety, F., Meilman, P., & Dowd, E. (1985). Multidisciplinary pain center follow-up: Evaluation with no-treatment control group. *Pain, 21*, 295-306.

Harkins, S.W., & Price, D.D. (1992). Assessment of pain in the elderly. In D. Turk & R. Melzack (Eds.), *Handbook of pain assessment* (pp. 315-331). New York: The Guilford Press.

Jamison, R. & Vitti, K. (1990). The influence of family support on chronic pain. *Behaviour Research and Therapy, 28*, 283-287.

Kerns, R., & Turk, D. (1984). Depression and chronic pain: The mediating role of the spouse. *Journal of Marriage and the Family, 46,* 845-852.

Maruta, T., Osbourne, D., Swanson, D., & Hallwig, J. (1981). Chronic pain patients and spouses: Marital and sexual adjustment. *Mayo Clinical Proctor, 56,* 307-310.

Melding, P. (1991). Is there such a thing as geriatric pain. *Pain, 46,* 119-121.

Merskey, H. (1988). Forward. In R.D. France & K.R. Krishnan (Eds.), *Chronic pain* (p. xvii). Washington, DC: American Psychiatric Press.

Mobily, P., & Herr, K. (1992). Back pain in the elderly. *Geriatric Nursing, 13,* 110-116.

Moskovich, R. (1988). Neck pain in the elderly: Common causes and management. *Geriatrics, 43,* 65-92.

Moss, M., Lawton, M.P., & Glicksman, A. (1991). The role of pain in the last year of life of older persons. *Journal of Gerontology: Psychological Sciences, 46,* P51-P57.

Painter, J., Seres, J., & Newman, R. (1980). Assessing benefits of pain centers: Why some patients regress. *Pain, 8,* 101-113.

Parmelee, P., Katz, I., & Lawton, M.P. (1991). The relation of pain to depression among institutionalized aged. *Journal of Gerontology: Psychological Sciences, 46,* P15-P21.

Rappoport, A., Sheftell, F., & Baskin, S. (1983). Geriatric headaches. *Geriatrics, 38,* 81-87.

Roberto, K. (1990). Adjusting to chronic disease: The osteoporotic woman. *Journal of Women & Aging, 1,* 33-47.

Roy, R. (1986). A psychosocial perspective on chronic pain and depression in the elderly. *Social Work in Health Care, 12*(12), 27-36.

Roy, R., & Michael, T. (1986). A survey of chronic pain in an elderly population. *Canadian Family Physician, 32,* 513-516.

Sorkin, B., Rudy, T., Hanlon, R., Turk, D., & Stieg, R. (1990). Chronic pain in old and young patients: Differences appear less important than similarities. *Journal of Gerontology: Psychological Sciences, 45,* P64-P68.

U.S. Bureau of the Census (1992). *Sixty-five plus in America* (Current Population Reports, Special Studies, P23-178). Washington, DC: U.S. Government Printing Office.

Wolfe, F. (1988). Fibromyalgia in the elderly: Differential diagnosis and treatment. *Geriatrics, 43,* 57-68.

Verbrugge, L. (1989). Gender, aging, and health. In K. Markides (Ed.), *Aging and health: Perspectives on gender, race, ethnicity, and class* (pp. 23-78). Newbury Park: Sage.

The Physiology and Biomedical Aspects of Chronic Pain in Later Life

Charlene Edwards Morris, MD
Veeraindar Goli, MD

SUMMARY. Pain is a complex phenomenon. In order to understand pain perception one must attempt to understand pain physiology and how certain physiologic and biomedical changes associated with aging may influence the elderly person's pain perception. Understanding the varied changes that occur with aging is very important in diagnosing and managing pain in the elderly population.

Pain is a complex multifactorial phenomenon. It is perceived as an unpleasant sensory and emotional experience and is commonly associated with injury or threat of injury to body tissues. The very mechanisms involved in acute pain which serve a protective function may prolong suffering in chronic pain.

Of community dwelling elderly people, 25 to 50% have pain related problems (Ferrell, 1991). Moreover, 45 to 80% of nursing home residents have documented pain syndromes. According to a Swedish study by Brattberg and colleagues (1989), the population group between 45 to 64 years of age complains of pain more than

Charlene Edwards Morris is Chronic Pain Fellow, Department of Anesthesiology, Duke University Medical Center, Durham, NC 27710.

Veeraindar Goli is Director, Pain Evaluation and Treatment Service, Department of Psychiatry, Duke University Medical Center, Durham, NC 27710.

[Haworth co-indexing entry note]: "The Physiology and Biomedical Aspects of Chronic Pain in Later Life." Morris, Charlene Edwards, and Veeraindar Goli. Co-published simultaneously in *Journal of Women & Aging* (The Haworth Press, Inc.) Vol. 6, No. 4, 1994, pp. 9-24; and: *Older Women with Chronic Pain* (ed: Karen A. Roberto) The Haworth Press, Inc., 1994, pp. 9-24. Multiple copies of this article/chapter may be purchased from The Haworth Document Delivery Center [1-800-3-HAWORTH; 9:00 a.m. - 5:00 p.m. (EST)].

any other age group. Butler found that over 85% of elderly adults suffered from a chronic illness of which pain is a significant component (cited in Witte, 1989).

Despite overwhelming evidence of the magnitude of pain-related problems experienced by elderly individuals, little attention has been focused on this issue. This is even more unfortunate when considering that this population is going to double in the next twenty years. In the year 1900, the age group 65 years and older comprised only 4% of the population, while at the present time it comprises more than 12%. It is projected that this number will reach 20% by the early twenty-first century when the post World War II baby boomers reach the age of 65 years (Besdine, 1980). Thus, prevention and management of pain in the elderly population is an important and large component of geriatric care.

DEFINITION AND THEORIES OF PAIN

The most commonly used definition of pain was given by the taxonomy committee of the International Association for the Study of Pain in 1979. The committee described pain as "An unpleasant sensory and emotional experience associated with actual or potential tissue damage . . ." (Wall, 1984, p. 1). Melzack (1975) emphasized that "to describe pain solely in terms of intensity is like specifying the visual world only in terms of light flux without regard to pattern, colour, texture, and the many other dimensions of visual experience" (p. 278).

Pain Theories

Various theoretical models of pain have been constructed to rationalize the clinical approach to pain management. The *Specificity Theory* dates back to Descartes in 1644 and was reintroduced into modern medicine by von Frey (Melzack, 1973). In this theory, pain was considered to be a sensory event arising from damage to tissues transduced by receptors and transmitted via the nerves and spinal cord to the brain. Thus, the model involves a straight-through transmission from the periphery to the central nervous system (Figure 1).

Limitations of the specificity model (e.g., explaining phantom limb pain where there is absence of peripheral receptors and divided

FIGURE 1. Descartes' (1644) concept of the pain pathway. He writes: 'If for example fire (A) comes near the foot (B), the minute particles of this fire, which as you know move with great velocity, have the power to set in motion the spot of the skin of the foot which they touch, and by this means pulling upon the delicate thread (cc) which is attached to the spot of the skin, they open up at the same instant the pore (d e) against which the delicate thread ends, just as by pulling at one end of a rope one makes to strike at the same instant a bell which hangs at the other end'(Melzack, 1973)

nerve transmission) brought forth the *Pattern Theory* by Gold-scheider in the late 19th century (Melzack, 1973; Nathan, 1976). This theory states that various discharge firing patterns of nerve fibers result in the various sensations we experience. Pain is produced not only by excessive peripheral stimulation but also by spatio-temporal summation of afferent impulses in the central nervous system. Thus, pain is dependent on the pattern of nerve impulses. The pattern theory does not label peripheral nerve fibers according to a specific sensation.

From the pattern theory developed the *Gate Control Theory* by Melzack and Wall (1965). The authors of this theory propose that there are mechanisms in the dorsal horn of the spinal cord where peripheral sensations and pain information enter that act like a gate. They allow increases or decreases in the flow of nerve impulses to the higher centers. The gating mechanism is influenced by ascending sensory information entering the spinal cord, that is, large fiber impulses inhibit small pain fiber impulse transmission, and by descending impulses from central brain centers (Kelly, 1985). While not completely proven, the Gate Control Theory has been universally accepted.

The *Learning Theory* of pain focuses on psychological aspects of pain and differentiates nociception from pain behaviors (Fordyce, 1976). Nociception is the neurophysiological process which becomes conscious as pain. Persistent pain may depend on the absence or presence of positive reinforcement of pain behavior (Sternbach, 1989). Fordyce postulates that continuous operant pain behaviors may explain the complaints of pain despite adequate healing of the original tissue damage. Moreover, how one processes pain information and experiences is integrally related to past pain experiences (Fordyce, 1986).

Although the theoretical perspectives of pain differ in their approach and orientation, most pain researchers agree with the description of pain put forth by Mountcastle (1975):

> Sensations are set by the encoding functions of sensory nerve endings, and by the integrating neural mechanics of the central nervous system. Afferent nerve fibers are not high-fidelity recorders, for they accentuate certain stimulus features, neglect others. The central neuron is a story-teller with regard to the nerve fibers, and it is never completely trustworthy, allowing distortions of quality and measure. (p. 109)

PHYSIOLOGY OF PAIN

Neuroanatomy

Nociceptors are sense organs for tissue damage and are situated at the end of a sensory nerve (Perl, 1984; Zimmermann, 1979). They transduce pain information into nerve impulses which travel in the afferent limb of the nerve to the spinal cord where they synapse with a transmission neuron. Nociceptors can be high threshold mechano-receptors or polymodal nociceptors. High threshold mechano-receptors are connected primarily to thin myelinated A-delta fibers (Bonica, 1977). Polymodal nociceptors are most likely free nerve endings (C fibers) responding to noxious heat, pressure, and chemical irritants.

There are two major ascending systems that convey somatic sensory information from the spinal cord to the cerebral cortex (Martin, 1991) (see Figure 2). The dorsal column-medial lemniscal system relays information chiefly concerning position sense and crosses in the medulla to the other side of the brain. The anterolateral system crosses at entry in the spinal cord to the other side following synapse with the second or transmission neuron.

The anterolateral system is subdivided into three systems which are distinguished by their termination sites. As shown in Figure 3, they are the (a) the spinothalamic (or neospinothalamic) tract, (b) the spinoreticular (or paleospinothalamic) tract, and (c) the spinotectal tract (Bonica, 1977). Most of the paleospinothalamic anterolateral fibers synapse are at the level of the brainstem below the thalamus and predominately in the reticular formation. However, the neospinothalamic neurons terminate in the three nuclei of the posterior thalamus (Smukler, 1985). The last neuron of any of the tracts projects to the sensory cortex. Many propose that the reticular system provides the emotional and motivational component of pain often described as "persistent," "burning" pain (Casey, 1979).

Neurophysiology

Specific neurotransmitters have been identified to play an active role in pain transmission. They may act at any point in the nervous system. Their function in modulating pain perception is quite complex and elaborate. Neurotransmitters may inhibit or enhance pain information (Ferrell, 1991). Examples of neurochemical mediators are presented in Table 1. Important chemicals for pain transmission are opiates and endogenous opioid substances. They have been found to bind with receptors located particularly in the dorsal horn of the spinal cord and periaqueductal and periventricular regions of

FIGURE 2. The hierarchical and parallel organization of sensory systems is demonstrated by two ascending parallel pathways: the main pathway for tactile sensations is termed the dorsal column–medial lemniscal system **(solid line)**; and a circuit whose main function is to mediate pain and, to a much lesser extent, tactile sensations is termed the anterolateral system **(broken line)**. Only when the dorsal column–medial lemniscal pathway becomes damaged, as in certain degenerative neurological disorders, does the anterolateral pathway assume an important role in mediating tactile sensations (Martin, 1991). This figure appeared in *Principles of Neural Science,* Third Edition, edited by Eric R. Kandel, James H. Schwartz, and Thomas M. Jassell, Appelton & Lange, Norwalk, CT.

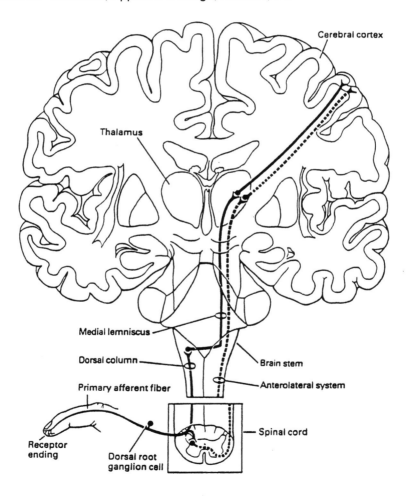

FIGURE 3. A, B, and C, Afferent (ascending) systems in neuraxis. Reprinted with permission, this figure previously appeared in *Archives of Surgery,* Vol. 112: 750-761; June 1977. Copyright 1977 American Medical Association.

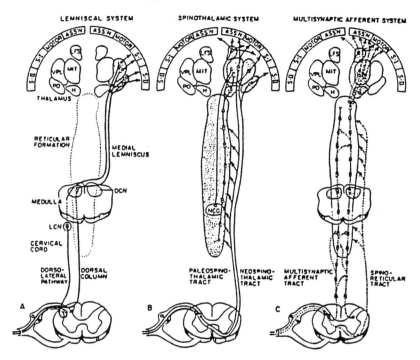

the brain (Mayer, 1979). They inhibit pain impulses directly by both pre- and post-synaptic inhibition of transmission in the dorsal horn and indirectly by stimulating descending inhibitory pathways. Endogenous opioid mediators also have affects on central nervous center excitement, euphoria, and narcosis.

PAIN AND AGE ASSOCIATED CHANGES

Physiological and biomedical changes in older adults have a significant impact on pain perception. Aging occurs in most cells with the exception of those undergoing malignant transformation. Its cause is unknown. Some theories argue that RNA and DNA

TABLE 1. Neurochemical Mediators Identified in Pain Mechanisms. Reprinted with permission of the American Geriatrics Society, "Pain Management in Elderly People, Table 1," by Bruce A. Ferrell, MD, *Journal of the American Geriatrics Society*, Vol. 39(1), p. 65, 1991.

Ascending pathway (dorsal horn neurons). ·
   Substance P
   Neurotensin
   Cholecystokinin
   Somatostatin
Descending pathway (midbrain and spinal cord)
   Serotonin
   Norepinephrine
   Gamma aminobutyric acid (GABA)
   Glycine
   Acetylcholine
Assorted areas (brain, cord, nerves and ganglia)
   Opiate receptors (5 types)
   Endogenous Opioids
      Endorphins
      Enkephalins
      Dynorphins

cumulative errors result in aging (Hazzard, 1987). Others focus on the role of CNS neurotransmitters in the aging process. Most of the studies attempting to support one or the other of these theories have been done in vitro making in vivo correlation speculative. There are age related changes in every organ in the body resulting in declining physiological function. For example, visual and hearing acuity decline with age which may affect the older adult's ability to process and interpret pain.

Past studies have documented decreased pain sensitivity in elderly individuals (Chapman & Jones, 1944). Studies analyzing thermal pain thresholds usually involve heat beamed onto a area of the skin by a projection lamp. The intensity and exposure is controlled. Pain is defined as a point at which there is a sharp pricking or stinging sensation from the light beam. The elderly participants in these studies tolerated stronger light heat longer than younger controls (Chapman & Jones, 1944). Harkins and Chapman (1976) studied the ability of young and elderly men to discriminate various levels of electrical stimulation of the tooth pulp and found no age related changes in pain threshold. Elderly patients, however, were found to be less apt to report electrical stimulation as painful. The findings of this study were substantiated using elderly women (Harkins & Chapman, 1977). Many researchers feel that elderly people are less apt to label a mild noxious stimulus as painful. In radiant heat studies by Procacci, it was thought that increased pain thresholds in elderly individuals could be accounted for by aging skin changes resulting in increased thermal energy dispersion and skin receptor changes at the painful stimulation site (cited in Harkins & Chapman, 1976). Moreover, there is a decrease in the number of Meissner's corpuscles and skin receptors as a function of age. Other reasons for altered pain sensation in older adults include degenerative nerve diseases associated with numbness (e.g., diabetic peripheral neuropathy). In these cases, pain sensitivity changes may be more secondary to peripheral than to centrally mediated changes.

Many researchers feel that the difference in pain threshold in older adults may also be due to attitudinal bias and cautiousness (Harkins & Chapman, 1976). Other investigators cite decreased confidence in judgement and/or difficulty in processing sensory information as biasing report of pain. Some support that elderly individuals may delay their reaction time to a painful stimulus secondary to the extra time needed to make the "right" response. There also may be cognitive and mental deficits that impair the ability to assess pain.

In terms of gender difference, pain seems more commonly reported by women (Crook, Rideout, & Browne, 1984). However, at present, only very few studies support gender differences in pain threshold.

Treatment Issues with Older Pain Patients

Physiological changes in elderly individuals may influence treatment outcomes. Elderly individuals have decreased rates of drug metabolism compared to their younger counterparts (Crooks, O'Mauley & Stevenson, 1976; Richey & Bender, 1977). Age related decreases in kidney function account for most altered drug excretion. In addition, serum albumin levels decrease in elderly persons causing increased free unbound drug, which is usually the active component (Vestal, 1978). A decrease in intestinal motility may elevate drug serum levels as well (Bender, 1968). Other alterations include: decreased intestinal blood flow, gastric secretion, and active transport mechanisms resulting in decreased absorption of orally administered drugs. All of the above mechanisms may result in different blood levels of active medication and, thus, altered response to pain.

Elderly individuals are more sensitive to analgesic medication than their younger counterparts (Bellville, Forrest, Miller, & Brown, 1971). This must be taken into account in addition when treating painful conditions. Thus, elderly patients may require lower narcotic doses. For instance, there is an inverse relationship between the effective opioid epidural dose and age. That is, older individuals need less of the narcotic for equal effect (Ready, Chadwick, & Ross, 1987).

Elderly patients have twice the risk of significant adverse drug reactions precipitating more frequent hospitalizations. Interestingly, women appear to be at a greater risk since they are apt to take twice as many drugs as men (Ready et al., 1987). Polypharmacy is usually the reason for multiple adverse drug reactions. Most elderly Americans receive more than 10 different prescription drugs per year. Hospitalizations resulting from adverse drug reactions are 50% higher in elderly patients than those less than 60 years of age (Rowe, 1977).

COMMON PAINFUL CONDITIONS EXPERIENCED BY ELDERLY WOMEN

There are various physiological changes to the body that occur with aging (Hazzard, 1987). As a result of these changes, older adults, and in some cases older women in particular, are likely to experience at least one chronic disease that has as its accomplice, chronic pain. For example, with age muscle strength, lean body mass, bone mineral content, and bone formation are decreased placing older women at high risk for osteoporosis. Postmenopausal, caucasian women have an increased propensity for developing osteoporosis and by the age of 80, there is an estimated loss of 50% of bone mass (Odom, Carr, & MacDonald, 1990). Chronic pain is a frequent outcome of osteoporosis.

Osteomalacia may develop resulting in greater propensity for bone fractures. Fractures occur mostly in the hip and vertebral bones (Bush, Miller, Criqui, & Barrett-Conner, 1990). Women are twice as likely to fall as men. In the U.S. about 250,000 people suffer hip fractures each year, 90% of whom are women over 70 years of age (Ali & Bennett, 1992). Hip fractures are associated with a 5-20% mortality in the first year following the fracture and often result in long-term pain and disability (Arnaud et al., 1987).

Osteoarthritis is the most prevalent arthritic disease in the U.S.; it effects elderly individuals disproportionately (Portenoy & Farkash, 1988). Data from the National Health and Nutrition Evaluation found that 8% of men and 18% of women were afflicted with osteoarthritis. It may lead to disabling joint pain. The knee joint is the most commonly affected.

Chronic lower back pain often is associated with osteoarthritis. It plagues elderly Americans disproportionately but is also a major health problem in younger age groups. In 1980, after examining over ten thousand back injury/compensation cases for the year 1977, Loeser (1990) reported that over 63 million dollars were paid out. Lumbar disc degeneration was found in 75% of patients between the age of 35-45 in one study. It can be found as early as in the second decade of life (Ritchie & Fahri, 1970). However, no correlation exists between lumbar degeneration and back pain.

There are many other vascular, immune-related, and connective tissue diseases that affect older adults more than the young. Rheumatoid arthritis is particularly worth discussing. Its prevalence is 1 to 2% in the U.S. Peak incidence occurs in the third and fourth decade of life (Csuka & Goodwin, 1990). Women are affected three times more often than men. While prevalence increases, the gender differences decrease with age. There are no decisive diagnostic tests. In fact, many times the diagnosis only comes about after multiple doctor visits, examinations, and laboratory studies stretching over several months (Ehrlich, Katz, & Cohen, 1970). The wrist joint is commonly involved.

Chronic facial pain commonly affects elderly individuals. According to Bonica (1990), over 5 million Americans are affected and treatment expenses approach 4 billion dollars. The etiology may be psychogenic, musculoskeletal, vascular, or neuropathic in origin. Trigeminal, occipital, and post-therapeutic neuralgias are examples of neuropathic head pain.

Trigeminal neuralgia (tic douloureux) involves the fifth cranial nerve (Jannetta, 1973). Patients describe the pain usually as sudden lancinating sensation in the face and or buccal mucosa (Loeser, 1990). Chewing or yawning may exacerbate the pain. Many times there is a trigger zone. The neurological examination is normal. It mostly affects patients over sixty years of age; 60% of the patients are women.

Occipital neuralgia presents with pain in the suboccipital region. Pain is usually described as constant aching and throbbing that radiates to the cervico-occipital junction to the posterior and lateral scalp. Post-therapeutic neuralgia of the face gives rise to burning pain associated with pruritus, dysesthesia, numbness, and paresthesia in the skin of the affected area. If the first division of the trigeminal nerve is affected, ulcerations of the cornea may occur. Atypical facial pain denotes pain without known etiology. The patient is almost always female; there is no age predominance.

Chronic pelvic pain is another devastating disease of women. According to data from the National Center for Health Statistics for 1986, eleven million women experienced pelvic disorders causing over 60 million lost work days costing billions of dollars (Guzinski, Bonica, & MacDonald, 1990). Diagnosable and treatable causes of chronic pelvic pain include pelvic inflammatory disease, neoplasm, uterine prolapse, vascular disorders, developmental abnormalities, and urinary tract abnormalities (Bonica, 1990). Ovarian cancer is the fourth leading cause of cancer death in American women and is the leading cause of death from gynecologic malignancy (Clarke-Pearson & Cressman, 1986). Unfortunately, in the early stages of ovarian cancer patients are often asymptomatic. Pain is uncommon but may occur with twisting of the pelvic organs. Patients with advancing ovarian cancer pain may complain of pelvic pressure and abdominal fullness. Gynecologic malignant tumors comprise 16% of all new cancers (Clarke-Pearson & Cressman, 1986). In many cases of chronic pelvic pain, no obvious pathology can be found.

Malignancy affects the geriatric population disproportionately. Approximately 66% of the patients with the advanced cancer have significant pain syndromes. Pain may be caused by direct tumor action, distant tumor action, by consequences of therapy, or only be indirectly related to the tumor. More than one pain cause may be present at any given time. There may be tumor recurrence, metastases, or new cancers (Ferrell, 1991).

Breast cancer is the leading cause of death in middle-aged women (Cuschieri, 1986). Some patients following mastectomy for breast cancer develop post-mastectomy pain syndrome (Granek, Ashikari, & Foley, 1984). Post-mastectomy pain syndrome is thought to be secondary to intercostobrachial nerve entrapment. Patients usually describe burning pain associated with sensory loss in the anterior chest wall, axilla, and posterior aspect of the upper arm. Fortunately, severe pain from breast cancer is uncommon; if it occurs it is usually secondary to metastases, brachial plexus neuropathy, or of psychogenic origin (Watson & Evans, 1982).

In many cases chronic pain states may be concurrent with major depression (Turner & Romano, 1981). Patients find it despairing that they not only have to deal with chronic pain but also live a disabling lifestyle. Depression may follow pain but pain may also follow depression. Somatic complaints as a manifestation of major depression are quite common among elderly persons. Unfortunately many elderly chronic pain sufferers become prescription drug abusers thus complicating treatment options. Moreover, chronic pain is associated with sleep and appetite disturbances resulting in fatigue and morbidity. In addition, often psychological factors may influence the presentation of pain.

CONCLUSIONS AND IMPLICATIONS

The myth that chronic debilitating pain is an inevitable part of aging still plagues the medical profession. In addition, in many cases elderly patients choose not to report or to under-report even severe pain states. They feel that getting old is synonymous with "ill feelings" and pain. Given the physical and emotional changes that occur with aging, the astute and responsible practitioner should be able to either eradicate the cause of pain or adequately treat pain symptoms to assure an acceptable quality of life (Sturgis, Dolce, & Dickerson, 1987).

REFERENCES

Ali, N.S., & Bennett S.J. (1992). Postmenopausal Women: Factors in osteoporosis preventive behaviors. *Journal of Gerontological Nursing, 18*(12), 23-32.

Arnaud C.D., Christiansen C., Cummings, S., Fleisch, H., Gennari, C., Kanis J., Ledingham J., MacIntyre I., Martin, T.J., Peck, W., Riis, P., Samsioe, G., & Shulman, L. (1987). Consensus Development Conference: Prophylaxis and treatment of osteoporosis. *British Medical Journal, 295,* 914-915.

Bellville, J.W., Forrest, W.H., Miller, E., & Brown, B.W. (1971). The influence of age on pain relief from analgesics: A study of postoperative patients. *Journal of the American Medical Association, 217,* 1835-1841.

Bender, A.D. (1968). Effect of age on intestinal absorption: Implications for drug absorption in the elderly. *Journal of the American Geriatrics Society, 16,* 1331-1339.

Besdine, R.W. (1980). Geriatric Medicine: An overview. In C. Eisdorfer (Ed.), *Annual review of gerontology and geriatrics: Vol. 1* (pp. 135-153). New York: Springer.

Brattberg, G., Thorslund, M., & Wikman, A. (1989). The prevalence of pain in a general population: The results of a postal survey in a county of Sweden. *Pain, 37,* 215-222.

Bonica, J.J. (1990). General considerations of pain in the pelvis and perineum. In J.J. Bonica, J.D. Loeser, C.R. Chapman, & W.E. Fordyce (Eds.), *The management of pain* (pp. 1283-1313). Philadelphia: Lea and Febiger.

Bonica, J.J. (1977). Neurophysiologic and pathologic aspects of acute and chronic pain. *Archives of Surgery, 112,* 750-761.

Bush, T.L., Miller, S.R., Criqui, M.H., & Barrett-Conner, E. (1990). Risk factors for morbidity and mortality in the older population: An epidemiologic approach. In W.R. Hazzard, E.L. Bierman, J. Blass, W. Ettinger, J.B. Halter (Eds.), *Principles of geriatric medicine and gerontology* (pp. 125-137). New York: McGraw Hill.

Casey, K.L. (1979). Supraspinal mechanisms. In H.W. Kosterlitz & L.Y. Terenius (Eds.), *Pain: The reticular formation in pain and society* (pp. 183-200). Weinheim: Verlag-Chemie.

Chapman, W.P., & Jones, C.M. (1944). Variations in cutaneous and visceral pain sensitivity in normal subjects. *Journal Clinical Investigation, 23,* 81-91.

Clarke-Pearson, D.L., & Cressman, W.T. (1986). Ovarian cancer. In A.R. Moossa, M. Robson, & S. Schimpff (Eds.), *The comprehensive textbook of oncology* (pp. 845-854). Baltimore: Williams & Wilkins.

Crook, J., Rideout, E., & Browne, G. (1984). The prevalence of pain complaints in a general population. *Pain, 18,* 299-314.

Crooks, J., O'Mauley, K., & Stevenson, I. (1976). Pharmacokinetics in the elderly. *Clinical Pharmacokinetics, 1,* 280-296

Csuka, M.E., & Goodwin, J.S. (1990). Rheumatoid arthritis. In W.R. Hazzard, E.L. Bierman, J. Blass, W. Ettinger, J.B. Halter (Eds.), *Principles of geriatric medicine and gerontology* (pp. 869-879). New York: McGraw Hill.

Cuschieri, A. (1986). Tumors of the breast: An overview. In A.R. Moossa, M.

Robson, & S. Schimpff (Eds.), *The comprehensive textbook of oncology* (pp. 959-967). Baltimore: Williams & Wilkins.

Ehrlich, G.E., Katz, W.A., & Cohen, S.H. (1970). Rheumatoid arthritis in the aged. *Geriatrics, 25*, 103-113.

Ferrell, B. (1991). Pain management in elderly people. *Journal of the American Geriatric Society, 39* 64-73.

Fordyce, W.E. (1976). *Behavioral methods for chronic pain and illness.* St. Louis, MO: C. V. Mosby.

Fordyce W.E. (1986). Learning processes in pain. In R.A. Sternbach (Ed.), *The psychology of pain* (pp. 49-65). New York: Raven Press.

Granek, I., Ashikari, R., & Foley, K. (1984). The post-mastectomy pain syndrome: Clinical and anatomical correlates. *Proceedings of the American Society of Clinical Oncology, 3*, 122.

Guzinski, G.M., Bonica, J.J., & MacDonald, J.S. (1990). Gynecologic pain. In J.J. Bonica, J.D. Loeser, C.R. Chapman, & W.E. Fordyce (Eds.), *The management of pain* (pp. 1344-1367). Philadelphia: Lea and Febiger.

Harkins, S.W., & Chapman, C.R. (1976). Detection and decision factors in pain perception in young and elderly men. *Pain, 2*, 253-264.

Harkins, S.W., & Chapman, C.R. (1977). The perception of induced dental pain in young and elderly women. *Journal of Gerontology, 32*, 428-435.

Hazzard, W.R. (1987). Biology of aging. In E. Braunwald, K.J. Isselbacher, R. Peterdorf, D. Wilson, J. Martin, & A.S. Fauci (Eds.), *Harrison's principles of internal medicine* (11th ed.) (pp. 447-454). New York: McGraw-Hill.

Jannetta, P.J. (1973). Pain problems of significance in the head and face, some of which often are misdiagnosed. *Current Problems in Surgery, 2*, 47-53.

Kelly, D. (1985). Central representations of pain and analgesia. In E.R. Kandel & J. H. Schwartz (Eds.), *Principles of neural science* (pp. 331-343). New York: Elsevier.

Loeser, J.D. (1990). Cranial neuralgias. In J.J. Bonica, J.D. Loeser, C.R. Chapman, & W.E. Fordyce (Eds.), *The management of pain* (pp. 676-686). Philadelphia: Lea and Febiger.

Martin, J.H. (1991). Receptor physiology and submodality coding in the somatic sensory system. In E.R. Kandel, T.M. Jassell, & J.H. Schwartz (Eds.), *Principles of neural sciences* (3rd ed.) (p. 333), Norwalk, CT: Appleton & Lange.

Mayer, D.J. (1979). Endogenous analgesia systems: Neural and behavioral mechanisms. In J.J. Bonica, J.C. Liebeskind, & D.G. Albe-Fessard (Eds.), *Advances in pain research and therapy: Vol 3* (pp. 305-410). New York: Raven Press.

Melzack, R. (1973). The evolution of pain theories. In R. Melzack (Ed.), *The puzzle of pain* (pp. 125-152). New York: Basic Books.

Melzack, R. (1975). The McGill Pain Questionnaire: Major properties and scoring methods. *Pain, 1*, 277-299.

Melzack, R., & Wall, P.D. (1965). Pain mechanisms: A new theory. *Science, 150*, 971-979.

Mountcastle, V.B. (1975). The view from within: Pathways to the study of perception. *Johns Hopkins Medical Journal, 36*, 109-131.

Nathan, P.W. (1976). The Gate-Control Theory of Pain: A critical review. *Brain*, *99*, 123-158.

Odom, M.J., Carr, B.R., & MacDonald, P.C. (1990). The menopause and estrogen replacement therapy. In W.R. Hazzard, E.L. Bierman, J. Blass, W. Ettinger, J.B. Halter (Eds.), *Principles of geriatric medicine and gerontology* (pp. 777-788). New York: McGraw Hill.

Perl, E.R. (1984). Characterization of nociceptors and their activation of neurons in the superficial Dorsal Horn: First steps for the sensation of pain. In L. Kruger & J.C. Liebeskind (Eds.), *Advances in pain research and therapy: Vol. 6* (pp. 23-52). New York: Raven Press.

Portenoy, R.K., & Farkash, A. (1988). Practical management of non-malignant pain in the elderly. *Geriatrics*, *43*(5), 29-47.

Ready, L.B., Chadwick, H.S., & Ross, B. (1987). Age predicts effective epidural morphine dose after abdominal hysterectomy. *Anesthesia Analgesia*, *66*, 1215-1218.

Richey, D.P., & Bender, A.D. (1977). Pharmacokinetics consequences of aging. *Annual Review Pharmacological Toxicology*, *17*, 49-65.

Ritchie, J.H., & Fahri, W.H. (1970). Age changes in lumbar intervertebral discs. *Canadian Journal of Surgery*, *13*, 65-71.

Rowe, J.W. (1977). Clinical research on aging: Strategies and directions. *New England Journal of Medicine*, *297*, 1332-1336.

Smukler, N.M. (1985). Pain perception. *Bulletin on the Rheumatic Diseases*, *35*, 1-8.

Sternbach, R.A. (1989). Behaviour therapy. In P.D. Wall & R. Melzack (Eds.), *The textbook of pain* (2nd ed.) (pp. 1015-1020). New York: Churchill Livingston.

Sturgis, E.T., Dolce, J.J., & Dickerson, P.C. (1987). Pain management in the elderly. In L.L. Carstensen & B.A. Edelstein (Eds.), *The handbook of clinical gerontology* (pp. 190-203). New York: Pergamon Press.

Turner, J.A., & Romano, J.M. (1981). Review of prevalence of coexisting chronic pain and depression. In C. Benedetti, C. Chapman, & G. Moricca (Eds.), *Advances in pain research and therapy* (pp. 123-130). New York: Raven Press.

Vestal, R.E. (1978). Drug use in the elderly: A review of problems and special considerations. *Drugs*, *16*, 358-382.

Wall, P. (1984). Introduction. In P. Wall & R. Melzack (Eds.), Textbook of Pain (pp. 1-16). New York: Churchill Livingston.

Watson, C., & Evans, R.J. (1982). Intractable pain with breast cancer. *Canadian Medical Association Journal*, *126*, 263-266.

Witte, M. (1989). Pain control. *Journal of Gerontological Nursing*, *15*(3), 32-37.

Zimmermann, M. (1979). Peripheral and central nervous mechanisms of nociception, pain, and pain therapy: facts and hypotheses. In J.J. Bonica, J.C. Liebeskind, & D.G. Albe-Fessard (Eds.), *Advances in pain research and therapy: Vol 3* (pp. 3-32). New York: Raven Press.

Assessment of Older Women
with Chronic Pain

Dennis C. Turk, PhD
Akiko Okifuji, MA
Lisa Scharff, MA

SUMMARY. Females suffer from a larger number of chronic pain syndromes, live longer with chronic pain and disability, and more often live alone than males. Thus, they should be prime candidates for pain treatment. Yet a number of factors inhibit geriatric patients from receiving rehabilitation for their pain. Chronic pain has been determined to be a complex perceptual event that is influenced by psychosocial, behavioral, and biomedical factors. A comprehensive strategy for assessing chronic pain patients is described. Special attention is given to the association between pain and depression and the important mediation of perceived interference with life, social support, and functional activities as these variables appear to be particularly relevant to a geriatric pain population.

Pain is an extremely pervasive phenomenon. The number of health problems that involve pain is quite extensive and pain is the

Dennis C. Turk is Director, Pain Evaluation and Treatment Institute, University of Pittsburgh School of Medicine, Pittsburgh, PA 15213-1217.

Akiko Okifuji is a doctoral student at State University of New York at Binghamton, Binghamton, NY 13902-6000.

Lisa Scharff is a research assistant, Pain Evaluation and Treatment Institute, University of Pittsburgh School of Medicine, Pittsburgh, PA 15213-1217.

[Haworth co-indexing entry note]: "Assessment of Older Women with Chronic Pain." Turk, Dennis C., Akiko Okifuji, and Lisa Scharff. Co-published simultaneously in *Journal of Women & Aging* (The Haworth Press, Inc.) Vol. 6, No. 4, 1994, pp. 25-42; and: *Older Women with Chronic Pain* (ed: Karen A. Roberto) The Haworth Press, Inc., 1994, pp. 25-42. Multiple copies of this article/chapter may be purchased from The Haworth Document Delivery Center [1-800-3-HAWORTH; 9:00 a.m. - 5:00 p.m. (EST)].

presenting symptom in 80% of all office visits to physicians. The statistics on pain are especially relevant to women. Other than acute pain associated with traumas and post-procedural and post-surgical pain, the most common pain problems include back pain, headaches, temporomandibular jaw pain, fibromyalgia, and arthritis. With few exceptions, the incidence of each of these disorders is higher in females than males (Verbrugge, 1985a,b). In North America, women report a higher incidence of both temporary and persistent pain than men (Crook, Rideout, & Browne, 1984), and more women seek treatment for chronic pain than men (Margolis, Zinny, Miller, & Taylor, 1984).

No consensus exists about gender differences in pain threshold and tolerance. Although some laboratory studies on pain characteristics have shown no gender differences (Bush, Harkins, Harrington, & Price, 1993; Strong, Ashton, & Chant, 1991), others have shown gender differences to exist (Feine, Bushnell, Myron, & Duncan, 1991). These findings may be more reflective of social influences rather than any real differences in pain sensitivity or threshold.

There has been recent evidence of different pain mechanisms in males and females, with estrogen playing an important role in pain sensitivity (Mogil, Sternberg, Kest, Marek, & Liebeskind, 1993). Sex hormones may be involved in pain perception by mediating the release of endorphins (Ginzler, 1980), and estrogen in particular may be involved in both opioid (Ryan & Maier, 1988) and non-opioid analgesia (Touchette, 1993). Pain sensitivity has also been shown to vary with the menstrual cycle, with sensitivity at its highest level when estrogen is at its lowest level (Goolkasian, 1980). Pain in conditions such as chronic migraines has been demonstrated to fluctuate with estrogen levels (Epstein, Hockaday, & Hockaday, 1975). Many women who suffer from migraines report severe headaches during the late luteal phase or within the first three days of menses. When estrogen is given premenstrually, it can delay the onset of these migraines (Somerville, 1971).

If systematic differences exist in how males and females differ in their attributions of meaning to pain problems, this could be expected to be reflected in systematic differences in pain-related suffering and behavior. Physicians may treat women's pain complaints less seriously (Greer, Dickerson, Schneiderman, Atkins, & Bass, 1986). In one study (Armitage, Schneiderman, & Bass, 1979), for example, the proportion of physician ordered work-ups for pain complaints such as back pain and headaches were significantly disproportionate between men and women, with men receiving more extensive works-ups for the same presenting symptoms. Physicians also appear more likely to consider the psychological components of the patient's illness if the patient is female than if the patient is male (Wallen, 1979). Somewhat paradoxically, although medical *testing* is less common in women, medical *treatment* is more common. Women at all ages obtain more prescription medications per year than do men (Verbrugge, 1985a,b), and of the 25 most common operative procedures, 11 are performed only on women (Friedman, 1988).

PAIN AND AGING

The likelihood of suffering from a chronic or disabling medical condition increases rapidly with age. People over age 65 account for one-third of the country's total personal health care expenditures (U.S. Senate Special Committee on Aging, 1987-1988) and more than four out of five people over the age of 65 have at least one chronic medical illness, and many have multiple conditions. It is well documented that age and physical disability have an important relationship (Nagi, 1976). The frequency of disability increases steadily with age from less than 1.5% in individuals under age 25 to nearly 20% in those 65 and older (Wood & Turner, 1985).

Clinical experience tells us that older people suffer from a large number of painful conditions such as osteoporosis, osteoarthritis, rheumatoid arthritis, cervical spondylosis, stroke, intermittent claudication, sympathetic dystrophies, vasculitis, diabetic neuropathies, and herpes zoster. Up to 73% of the elderly population report experiencing some degree of pain on a regular basis (Ferrell, Ferrell, & Osterweil, 1990; Sengstaken & King, 1993). Almost 50% of people over age 65 are estimated to suffer from one painful condition alone, arthritis (National Center for Health Statistics, 1986).

Although mortality is generally higher among men, chronic conditions are more prevalent in women. In a community survey of

240 women over age 65, Heidrich (1993) noted that the most bothersome symptoms included pain, achiness, stiffness and fatigue. Parmelee, Katz, and Lawton (1991) found that geriatric women reported more intense pain and a greater number of localized pain complaints than did geriatric men. This gender effect remained significant even when differential health and functional ability were controlled for.

The consequences of pain are widespread in the elderly population. Decreased socialization, falls, slow rehabilitation, cognitive dysfunction, malnutrition, depression (Dworkin, Von Korff, & LeResche, 1990), sleep disturbance (Roy, 1986), impaired ambulation (Lavsky-Shulan et al., 1985; Roy, 1986) increased health care costs and utilization (Lavsky-Shulan et al., 1985), and polypharmacy have all been associated with the presence of pain among elderly persons.

Pain, Depression, and Aging

Blazer and Williams (1980) reported that almost 15% of a large, stratified sample of older adults in the community had "substantial depressive symptomatology," and in nearly one half of this subgroup, depressive symptoms were judged to be related to medical illnesses. Physical illness can be considered a risk factor for depression at any age, but the link between medical illness and depression may be stronger in the older than in younger age groups. Williamson and Schulz (1992) found that physical illness, functional disability, and pain were correlated with depression in a sample of 228 people over age 55 attending outpatient geriatric clinics. Functional disability (but not physical illness) accounted for differences in reported pain between non-depressed subjects and those at risk for developing clinical depression. Functional disability mediated the relationship between pain and depressed affect.

One of the primary differences between older versus younger chronic pain patients appears to be the role that depression may play in their pain conditions. Depressive symptoms may subsequently affect how women cope with pain (Chrischilles, Lemke, Wallace, & Drube, 1990). Chrischilles et al. found that depressed elderly women in severe pain were more likely to take analgesic medication than were depressed male geriatric patients reporting comparable levels of pain.

In one study, Rudy, Kerns, and Turk (1988) found that the perceived impact of pain on social, recreational, family, and occupational activities along with perceived control over life significantly mediated the relationship between pain and depression. Turk, Okifuji, and Scharff (1993) replicated these findings; however, when the association between pain and depression was examined for older and younger patients, quite a different relationship was identified. For younger patients, the relationship between pain and depression was nonsignificant ($r = .07$), whereas there was a highly significant relationship for older patients ($r = .51$). In addition, for the older patients the perceived life interference of their pain was significantly associated with depression, but this was not the case for the younger patients. These data suggest that additional life interference in people who already may have experienced some reduction in activities due to age has a more profound effect on depression. Williamson and Schulz (1992) also identified the critical role of reduction in activity levels and depression in geriatric patients. However, there may be gender difference in how depression is associated with pain. For example, Haley, Turner, and Romano (1985) have found that depression in men was not associated with pain severity but with day-time inactivity, whereas in women, pain severity and depression were significantly correlated.

One factor that may account for the special relationship between pain and depression in older patient groups is the role of social support. A much larger percentage of older patients, especially older women, live alone, and the availability of social support has been shown to play an important role in depression among chronic pain patients (Turk, Kerns, & Rosenberg, 1992). The results of these studies on depression emphasize the importance of carefully assessing the impact of pain on functional activities and the availability of social support for female geriatric patients.

TREATMENT OF CHRONIC PAIN IN OLDER ADULTS

Despite the fact that a greater percentage of older persons experience chronic or recurrent pain in comparison to younger adults

(Crook et al., 1984; Lavsky-Shulan et al., 1985) they are under-represented in specialty pain clinics (Melding, 1991). In a recent meta-analysis examining the results of 65 studies (including over 3,000 patients) that had evaluated the efficacy of pain clinics, the median age of treated patients was 44.91 with an age range 34-56. None of the studies cited included patients over age 65 (Flor, Fydrich, & Turk, 1992). It would appear that although elderly persons represent a large percentage of those with chronic pain, they are under-referred for pain management (Harkins, 1988; Melding, 1991).

There are several reasons why the elderly pain patient may not be referred to specialty pain clinics most notably clinician bias regarding older persons' need or ability to benefit from rehabilitation programs. Perhaps most importantly, stereotypes of health service providers may inhibit geriatric patients from receiving pain rehabilitation services. These biases may originate in the unfounded skepticism about efficacy of pain rehabilitation for elderly persons (e.g., older individuals do not benefit from multidisciplinary pain rehabilitation programs) or a myth related to pain and aging (e.g., complaints of pain in the aged are a natural part of the aging process, and thus do not require extensive evaluation or treatment).

Another common misconception of many health care providers is that older people exaggerate complaints, and this may lead to half-hearted examination and treatment. "Given the large burden of illness and disabilities . . . complaints of the elderly are remarkably low keyed and valid" (Eckstein, 1978, p. 16). What may be an indication of hypochondriasis in a 30-year old woman may be an accurate self-assessment in a 70-year old.

Older adults themselves may view pain as a normal part of the aging process and therefore do not complain (Ferrell, 1991). Additionally, pain may have persisted for such an extended period that they may not recall a time when symptoms were absent and are thus unable to identify their present symptoms as abnormal or atypical.

Despite the under-representation of geriatric patients at pain clinics, in several studies, age has been shown to be no impediment to successful treatment outcome (Middaugh et al., 1988; Puder, 1988). Older and younger chronic pain patients are reported to employ similar strategies to cope with their pain (Colenda & Dougherty, 1990; Keefe & Williams, 1990). Sorkin and colleagues (1990) reported that older patients were equally likely to accept, to remain in and to benefit from a rehabilitation treatment consisting of psychological as well as physical therapies. Conversely, other researchers (e.g., Guck, Skultety, Meilman, & Dowd, 1985; Holroyd & Penzien, 1986) have reported that older patients do less well in nonmedical pain treatment programs. These conflicting findings may indicate special pain assessment and treatment needs in the elderly population as well as the need to consider some specific accommodations for a geriatric population.

ASSESSMENT OF PERSONS WITH CHRONIC PAIN

Traditionally, assessment of chronic pain was exactly that, attempts by physicians to determine the physical cause of the pain so that it could be blocked pharmacologically or surgically. Extensive physical evaluations as well as laboratory and imaging procedures were performed in an attempt to find the cause of the pain. The assumption was that there should be a close linear relationship between pain severity and physical pathology. Despite major advances in the understanding of the nervous system, in the development of potent analgesic preparations, and in increasingly sophisticated surgical procedures, permanent amelioration of pain has not been achieved. The inadequacy of surgical and pharmacological treatment regimens has frustrated physicians, as well as patients, as many patients continue to report pain despite the disruption or blockage of pain pathways. Further confusion is added when health care professionals observe that patients respond quite differently to ostensibly the same syndrome and note widely varying benefits from identical treatment interventions.

Failure to identify a physical basis for the reported symptom of pain when the determination has been made by a physician that the pain reported was disproportionate to the physical pathology, or when patients fail to respond to "appropriate" treatment often results in a suggestion that either the complaint is caused by psychological factors or motivated by secondary gains such as financial compensation or attention. It is important to note that there is no objective way to determine the severity of an individual's pain, that is, there is no "pain thermometer." The only way to establish the extent of an individual's pain is by attending to what is overtly conveyed, either verbally or through the individual's behavior (e.g., limping, moaning, grimacing). Thus, pain evaluation is based on inference and subjectivity by both the patient and health care provider.

The patient's perspective interacts reciprocally with emotional factors, behavioral responses, and sensory phenomenon. Moreover, the patient's behavior will elicit responses from significant others (family members, friends, health care providers) that can reinforce both maladaptive and adaptive modes of thinking, feeling, behaving and physiological activity that can exacerbate or maintain pain (Turk & Rudy, 1992). Specific types of cognitive experiences relevant to pain perception are thought to include focus of attention, beliefs, attributions, expectations, coping self-statements, images, and problem solving cognitions. These cognitive variables have been demonstrated to be related to motivation for treatment, compliance with treatment recommendations, disability, and successful rehabilitation. Thus, comprehensive assessment should evaluate them and the evaluation information should be incorporated within the treatment.

Multiaxial Assessment of Pain Patients

Assessment of the person, not just the pain, in chronic pain patients requires assessment of their moods, attitudes, coping efforts, resources, responses of family members, and the impact of pain on their lives as well as the sensory (somatic) component. Three central questions involved in pain assessment are: (1) What is the extent of the patient's disease or injury (physical impairment)? (2) What is the magnitude of the illness (i.e., to what extent is the patient suffering, disabled, and unable to enjoy usual activities)? and (3) Does the individual's behavior seem appropriate to the disease process or is there evidence symptoms are amplified for any of a variety of psychosocial or behavioral responses? Due to lack of space we will focus on the two latter questions (see Turk & Melzack, 1993, for a broad coverage of the assessment of physical impairment).

Turk and Rudy (1987, 1988) have proposed a model of pain assessment that they label a Multiaxial Assessment of Pain (MAP) patients. The MAP approach postulates that three axes that coincide with the three questions listed above are essential to appropriately assess people with persistent pain: biomedical, psychosocial, and behavioral. From this perspective, each of these general domains must be assessed with appropriate standardization (e.g., age-specific norms) and psychometrically-sound instruments and procedures. Moreover, the results of the assessment of each axis should be combined into a meaningful taxonomy or classification system that can be of assistance in treatment decision making and planning.

Physical Assessment

Although we will not focus on physical assessment of pain in elderly persons, it is worth noting the physical abnormalities likely to be identified may be the results of age-related changes unrelated to pain that may not require invasive interventions. For example, Swezey (1988) noted that geriatric patients often can present with symptoms of sciatica (pain localized in the lower back radiating down one leg associated with involvement of the sciatic nerve) and have a positive radiograph of the lower back showing spinal stenosis. He demonstrated that the results of conservative treatment in a series of 30 patients with spinal stenosis and acute to subacute radiculopathy was very good, with 10 of the 11 recovered. Sorkin et al. (1990) noted that although older patients presented with a larger number of physical abnormalities, they did not report higher levels of pain or pain-related disability. Thus, clinicians must be cautious not to over-interpret the presence of structural abnormalities or to be overly aggressive in performing invasive interventions.

Psychosocial Assessment

We have noted that depression is a particular concern for all chronic pain patients. Although there are a number of questionnaires available to assess depression, a specific measure–the Geriatric Depression Scale–has been developed for geriatric individuals that includes simple wording, makes use of a yes/no response format, and has available geriatric norms (Yesavage et al., 1983). This questionnaire may be particularly useful for assessing depression in geriatric pain patients.

In an attempt to assess the chronic pain experience in a comprehensive manner, Kerns, Turk, and Rudy (1985) developed the West Haven-Yale Multidimensional Pain Inventory (MPI). This assessment instrument was designed to assess the impact of pain from the patient's perspective. The MPI operationalizes psychological reactions to chronic pain, perceived responses of significant others, and activities interfered with because of pain. The MPI requires only a sixth-grade education; has demonstrated good internal consistency; test-re-test reliability; face, convergent, discriminant validity; and can be computer scored. Moreover, the MPI scales do not appear to differ for different age groups or gender.

Using the MPI, Turk and Rudy (Turk & Rudy, 1988; 1990) empirically identified three subgroups of patients that they labeled "Dysfunctional," characterized by high levels of pain severity, life interference, and affective distress, and lower levels of life control; "Interpersonally Distressed," characterized by low levels of social support; and "Adaptive Copers," characterized by lower levels of pain, life interference, and affective distress, and higher levels of activity and life control. Headache, chronic low back pain, and temporomandibular disorder patients were classified within each of these three subgroups (Turk & Rudy, 1990). These data indicate that certain modal patterns, based on the quantitative integration of psychological assessment data, recur in persistent pain patients irrespective of physical diagnosis. Moreover, these patterns were not associated with gender, socioeconomic status, duration of pain, or number of surgeries. These three subgroups have recently been replicated in a study reported by Talo (1992).

Turk et al. (1993) found that the percentage of pain clinic patients classified within the three subgroups differed by age, with a higher percentage of the younger patients classifiable as dysfunctional and a higher percentage of the older patients classifiable as adaptive copers. Moreover, as noted, the younger patients reported a significantly higher level of affective distress than did the older patients. These results suggest that when patients older than age 70 are referred to specialty pain clinics they may be significantly less psychologically distressed than the younger patients. These results coupled with the evidence suggesting that geriatric patients may do as well, if not better, in pain rehabilitation programs than younger patients (Middaugh et al., 1988; Puder, 1988) support the contention that geriatric pain patients should be referred more often for pain rehabilitation at specialized pain clinics.

The MAP taxonomy proposed should enhance our understanding of chronic pain, assist in the evaluation and the prescription of specific therapeutic interventions, and further our ability to predict treatment outcome. Alternative strategies for combining information might also be considered; however, the important point is that there needs to be a systematic strategy for (1) integrating diverse sets of information acquired from different sources and procedures, and (2) matching patients to treatment on the basis of physical and psychosocial diagnosis, along with functional ability and relevant demographic factors such as age and gender.

Functional Assessment

Traditional physical and laboratory measures are not direct measures of symptoms or function, but only proxies. Commonly used physical tests of muscle strength and range of motion correlate poorly with actual behavior (Mellin, 1987). In contrast, self-report functional status instruments seek to quantify symptoms, function, and behavior more directly. A number of self-report measures have been designed to assess individuals' reports of ability to engage in functional activities such as walking up stairs, sitting for a specific amount of time, lifting specific weights, and performing activities of daily living. These instruments also measure pain severity during activity. Self-report instruments are economical and efficient, enable the assessment of a wide range of relevant behaviors, and permit social and mental functions to be evaluated. Many of the same assessment instruments and procedures originally developed for use with younger populations can be readily used with geriatric patients (Norris, Gallagher, Wilson, & Winograd, 1987).

Use of functional assessment measures should only be undertaken when appropriate norms are available as use of norms developed on younger samples may lead to erroneous conclusions. Although the validity of self-reports of the ability to perform tasks is often questioned, researchers report good correspondence among self-reports, disease characteristics, physicians' or physical therapists' ratings of functional abilities, and objective functional performance (Deyo, 1988).

Behavioral Assessments of Pain, Distress, and Suffering

People display a broad range of reactions–some controllable others not–that are indicative of pain, distress, and suffering. For example, autonomic response activity such as rapid heart rate or perspiration may indicate the presence of acute pain. Over time, however, these physiological signs habituate and their absence cannot rule out pain.

Behavioral manifestations of pain have been labeled "pain behaviors" (e.g., signs, limping, distorted gait, frequent shifting of posture). Pain behaviors and self-report of pain are significantly, although not perfectly correlated. In addition to their association with pain, pain behaviors are significant in their own rights as they are observable and elicit responses from others. Various reinforcements (e.g., attention, avoidance of undesirable activity, financial compensation) may maintain these behaviors.

Pain behaviors may be assessed by having patients keep diaries of their activities. Commonly, patients record the amount of time or the number of times they perform specific activities such as reclining, sitting, standing, walking, and so forth. These activities have a good deal of overlap with functional activities but they are recorded on an ongoing basis using a diary format. Diaries can be compared with reports of typical activity which require an individual to aggregate, average, and than estimate the frequency of the performance of activities over a specified time period (e.g., week, month) or usually, typically, or regularly. Observational procedures have also been developed (Keefe & Block, 1982) where health care providers record the occurrence of specific pain behaviors in either a structured set of conditions (walking, sitting, standing) or during interviews or examinations.

It is worth reiterating our point that with all of the measures described above, consideration must be given to the availability of geriatric norms. In the case of measures of pain behaviors this is especially important as alterations in movements may result from age-related changes and these may be unrelated to pain per se.

CONCLUSIONS AND IMPLICATIONS

Despite the high prevalence of pain problems in elderly individuals, little research has delineated factors specifically relevant to pain assessment for this population in general and geriatric women suffering from chronic pain more specifically. We have emphasized a multidimensional perspective of chronic pain and the importance of biomedical, psychosocial, functional, and behavioral assessment for geriatric as well as all pain patients. Assessment of geriatric chronic pain patients should take into consideration the affects of aging on adjustment. Such areas as memory difficulties, physical limitations, reduced levels of energy, social isolation, and logistic problems are especially worthy of special attention.

Elderly women, in particular, tend to experience unfavorable socioeconomic conditions, partially due to their longer life expectancies and consequent, reduction in social support, as well as limitations of financial resources. These two factors have been associated with increased depression (Turk et al., 1993). The greater association between pain and depression in the elderly compared to younger pain patients suggests that particular attention should be focused on depression for this population. Future research needs to clarify how life conditions of elderly women interact with pain, functional disability, and depression.

Misconceptions and myths regarding pain and aging also need to be addressed. These misconceptions are likely to inhibit physicians from referring elderly patients to specialized pain clinics, and older adults themselves may be inhibited from seeking rehabilitative treatment, despite the fact that a number of previous studies have reported that geriatric pain patients may benefit at least as much as younger pain patients from these treatment programs (Middaugh et al., 1988; Puder, 1988). The overall goals of comprehensive rehabilitation programs are similar for older as well as younger patients, namely, to increase independence, to maximize function and adaptive coping, and to improve quality of life.

It is important to consider the limitations of even the small amount of information we currently have about the different assessment and treatment needs of elderly individuals. Psychosocial factors that have been found to exist may be reflections of a cohort effect as opposed to the aging process itself, and the influences of each are impossible to tease apart (Donaldson & Horn, 1992). It is possible that within a few years a new cohort of aged patients will show completely different characteristics with regard to attitudes toward health care.

It should be emphasized that the research to date on older patients with chronic pain has focused on a group that might be referred to as the "young-old," people between the ages of 65-75. There is minimal information about chronic pain in people ages 76 and older. Differences might increase as people move from the "young-old" to the "old-old" age group; however, data on chronic pain patients over age 76 is currently nonexistent. Thus, it is impossible to know how rehabilitation-oriented treatment for chronic pain might have to be modified to accommodate for age-related changes in physical and mental functioning such as visual and hearing impairments and reductions in short-term memory.

It is important to note that much of the data on older chronic pain patients have focused on those who are referred to specialty pain clinics. This is an atypical set of individuals as only a small subset of people with chronic pain are ever treated at pain clinics. These people tend to have higher rates of psychological distress and more constant pain; they more frequently use opioid medications, and are of lower socioeconomic status than chronic pain patients treated in primary care settings (Crook et al., 1984). Moreover, a relatively small number of geriatric patients are treated at pain clinics and thus are likely to be unrepresentative of the general population of older people with chronic pain. Geriatric patients that are currently seen at pain clinics tend to have lower levels of depression than younger pain patients, while the base rates of depression in the general elderly population are quite high. This indicates that there is a bias to refer more functional elderly to pain clinics, which needs to be taken into account when examining any research regarding geriatric pain assessment and treatment.

Finally, clinicians need to be cautious when selecting instruments for assessing geriatric pain patients. Many commonly used assessment measures were never standardized on older samples and thus the norms available may be inappropriate. If appropriate normative information is unavailable, considerable caution must be made in making inferences and drawing conclusions about geriatric pain patients.

REFERENCES

Armitage, K.J., Schneiderman, L.J., & Bass, R.A. (1979). Response of physicians to medical complaints in women and men. *Journal of the American Medical Association, 241,* 2186-2187.

Blazer, D., & Williams, C. (1980). Epidemiology of dysphoria and depression in an elderly population. *American Journal of Psychiatry, 137,* 439-444.

Bush, F.M., Harkins, S.W., Harrington, W.G., & Price, D.D. (1993). Analysis of gender effects on pain perception and symptom presentation in temporomandibular pain. *Pain, 53,* 73-80.

Colenda, C.C., & Dougherty, L.M. (1990). Positive ego and coping functions in chronic pain and depressed patients. *Journal of Geriatric Psychiatry and Neurology, 3,* 40-44.

Chrischilles, E.A., Lemke, J.H., Wallace, R.B., & Drube, G.A. (1990). Prevalence and characteristics of multiple analgesic drug use in an elderly study group. *Journal of the American Geriatrics Society, 38,* 979-984.

Crook, J., Rideout, E., & Browne, G. (1984). The prevalence of pain complaints in a general population. *Pain, 18,* 299-314.

Deyo, R.A. (1988). Measuring the functional status of patients with low back pain. *Archives of Physical Medicine and Rehabilitation, 69,* 1044-1053.

Donaldson, G., & Horn, J.L. (1992). Age cohort and time developmental muddles: easy in practice, hard in theory. *Experimental Aging Research, 18,* 213-222.

Dworkin, S.F., Von Korff, M., & LeResche, L. (1990). Multiple pain and psychiatric disturbance: An epidemiological investigation. *Archives of General Psychiatry, 47,* 239-244.

Eckstein, D. (1978). Common complaints of the elderly. In W. Reichel (Ed.), *The geriatric patient* (pp. 167-184). New York: HP Publishing.

Epstein, M.T., Hockaday, J.M., & Hockaday, T.R. (1975). Migraine and reproductive hormones throughout the menstrual cycle. *Lancet, i,* 543-547.

Feine, J.S., Bushnell, M.C., Myron, D., & Duncan, G.H. (1991). Sex differences in the perception of noxious heat stimuli. *Pain, 44,* 255-262.

Ferrell, B.A. (1991). Pain management in elderly people. *Journal of the American Geriatrics Society, 39,* 64-73.

Ferrell, B.A., Ferrell, B.R., & Osterweil, D. (1990). Pain in the nursing home. *Journal of the American Geriatric Society, 38,* 409-414.

Flor, H., Fydrich, T., & Turk, D.C. (1992). Efficacy of multidisciplinary pain treatment centers: A meta-analytic review. *Pain, 49,* 221-230.

Friedman, E. (1988, April 25). Changing the ranks of medicine: Women's MD's. *Medical World News,* pp. 57-68.

Ginzler, A.R. (1980). Endorphin-mediated increases in pain threshold during pregnancy. *Science, 210,* 193-195.

Goolkasian, P. (1980). Cyclic changes in pain perception: An ROC analysis. *Perception and Psychophysics, 27,* 499-504.

Greer, S., Dickerson, V.M., Schneiderman, L.J., Atkins, C., & Bass, R. (1986).

Responses of male and female physicians to medical complaints in male and female patients. *Journal of Family Practice, 23*, 49-53.

Guck, T.P., Skultety, F.M., Meilman, P.W., & Dowd, E.T. (1985). Multidisciplinary pain center follow-up study: Evaluation with a no-treatment control. *Pain, 21*, 295-306.

Haley, W.E., Turner, J.A., & Romano, J.M. (1985). Depression in chronic pain patients: Relation to pain, activity, and sex differences. *Pain, 23*, 337-343.

Harkins, S.W. (1988). Pain in the elderly. In R. Dubner, G.F. Gebhart, & M.R. Bond (Eds.), *Pain research and clinical management.* Vol 3. (pp. 355-367). Amsterdam: Elsevier.

Heidrich, S.M. (1993). The relationship between physical health and psychological well-being in elderly women–A developmental perspective. *Research in Nursing & Health, 16*, 123-130.

Holroyd, K.A., & Penzien, D.B. (1986). Client variables and the behavioral treatment of recurrent tension headache: A meta-analytic review. *Journal of Behavioral Medicine, 9*, 515-536.

Keefe, F.J., & Block, A.R. (1982). Development of an observation method for assessing pain behavior in chronic low back pain patients. *Behavior Therapy, 13*, 365-375.

Keefe, F.J., & Williams, D.A. (1990). A comparison of coping strategies in chronic pain patients in different age groups. *Journal of Gerontology: Psychological Sciences, 45*, P161-P165.

Kerns, R.J., Turk, D.C., & Rudy, T.E. (1985). The West Haven-Yale Multidimensional Pain Inventory (WHYMPI). *Pain, 23*, 345-356.

Lavsky-Shulan, M., Wallace, R.B., Kohout, F.J., Lemke, J., Morris, M.C., & Smith, I.M. (1985). Prevalence and functional correlates of low back pain in the elderly: The Iowa 65+ Rural Health Study. *Journal of the American Geriatrics Society, 33*, 23-28.

Margolis, R., Zinny, G., Miller, D., & Taylor, J. (1984). Internists and the chronic pain patient. *Pain, 20*, 151-156.

Melding, P.S. (1991). Is there such a thing as geriatric pain? *Pain, 46*, 119-121.

Mellin, G. (1987). Chronic low back pain in men 54-63 years of age: Correlations of physical measurements with the degree of trouble and progress after treatment. *Spine, 11*, 421-425.

Middaugh, S.J., Levin, R.B., Kee, W.G., Flammetta, D., Barchiesi, D., & Roberts, J.M. (1988). Chronic pain: Its treatment in geriatric and younger patients. *Archives of Physical Medicine and Rehabilitation, 69*, 1021-1026.

Mogil, J.S., Sternberg, W.F., Kest, B., Marek, P., & Liebeskind, J. (1993). Sex differences in the antagonism of swim stress-induced analgesia: Effects of gonadectomy and estrogen replacement. *Pain, 53*, 17-25.

Nagi, S.Z. (1976). An epidemiology of disability among adults in the United States. *Milbank Memorial Fund Quarterly/Health and Society, 54*, 439-467.

National Center for Health Statistics. (1986). Aging in the eighties, age 65 years and over and living alone, contacts with families, friends, and neighbors.

Advance Data from Vital and Health Statistics, 116 (DHHS Publication No. 86-1250). Hyattsville, MD: Public Health Service.

Norris, J.T., Gallagher, D., Wilson, A., & Winograd, C.H. (1987). Assessment of depression in geriatric medical outpatients: The validity of two screening measures. *Journal of the American Geriatrics Society, 35*, 989-995.

Parmelee, P.A., Katz, I.R., & Lawton, M.P. (1991). The relation of pain to depression among institutionalized aged. *Journal of Gerontology: Psychological Sciences, 46*, P15-P21.

Puder, R.S. (1988). Age analysis of cognitive-behavioral therapy for chronic pain outpatients. *Psychology and Aging, 3*, 204-207.

Roy, R. (1986). A psychosocial perspective on chronic pain and depression in the elderly. *Social Work in Health Care, 12*, 27-36.

Rudy, T.E., Kerns, R.J., & Turk, D.C. (1988). Chronic pain and depression: Toward a cognitive-behavioral mediation model. *Pain, 35*, 129-140.

Ryan, S.M., Maier, S.F. (1988). The estrous cycle and estrogen modulates stress-induced analgesia. *Behavioral Neuroscience, 102*, 371-380.

Sengstaken, E.A., & King, S.A. (1993). The problems of pain and its detection among geriatric nursing home residents. *Journal of the American Geriatrics Society, 41*, 541-544.

Somerville, B.W. (1971). The role of progesterone in menstrual migraine. *Neurology, 21*, 853-859.

Sorkin, B.A., Rudy, T.E., Hanlon, R., Turk, D.C., & Stieg, R.L. (1990). Chronic pain in old and young patients: Differences appear less important than similarities. *Journal of Gerontology: Psychological Science, 45*, P64-P68.

Strong, J., Ashton, R., & Chant, D. (1991). Pain intensity measurement in chronic low back pain. *Clinical Journal of Pain, 7*, 209-218.

Swezey, R.L. (1988). Low back pain in the elderly: Practical management concerns. *Geriatrics, 43*, 39-44.

Talo, S. (1992). *Psychological assessment of functioning in chronic low back pain patients.* Turku, Finland: Social Insurance Institution.

Touchette, N. (1993). Estrogen signals a novel route to pain relief. *Journal of National Institute of Health Research, 5*, 53-58.

Turk, D.C., Kerns, R.D., & Rosenberg, R. (1992). Effects of marital interaction on chronic pain and disability: Examining the down-side of social support. *Rehabilitation Psychology, 37*, 259-274.

Turk, D.C., & Melzack, R. (Eds.) (1993). *Handbook of pain assessment.* New York: Guilford.

Turk, D.C., Okifuji, A., & Scharff, L. (1993). *Chronic pain and depression: Role of perceived impact and perceived control in different age cohorts.* Manuscript submitted for publication.

Turk, D.C., & Rudy, T.E. (1987). Toward the comprehensive assessment of chronic pain patients. *Behavior Therapy and Research, 25*, 237-249.

Turk, D.C., & Rudy, T.E. (1988). Toward an empirically derived taxonomy of chronic pain patients: Integration of psychological assessment data. *Journal of Consulting and Clinical Psychology, 56*, 233-238.

Turk, D.C., & Rudy, T.E. (1990). Robustness of an empirically derived taxonomy of chronic pain patients. *Pain, 43,* 27-35.

Turk, D.C., & Rudy, T.E. (1992). Cognitive factors and persistent pain: A glimpse into Pandora's box. *Cognitive Therapy and Research, 16,* 99-122.

U.S. Senate Special Committee on Aging. (1987-1988). *Aging America: Trends and projections.* Washington, DC: U.S. Government Printing Office.

Verbrugge, L.M. (1985a). Gender and health: An update on hypotheses and evidence. *Journal of Health and Social Behavior, 26,* 156-182.

Verbrugge, L.M. (1985b). An epidemiological profile of older women. In M.R. Haug, A.B. Ford, & M. Sheafor (Eds.), *The physical and mental health of aged women* (pp. 41-64). New York: Springer.

Wallen, J. (1979). Physician stereotypes about female health and illness: A study of patient's sex and the information process during medical interviews. *Women & Health, 4,* 135-146.

Williamson, G.M., & Schulz, R. (1992). Pain, activity restriction, and symptoms of depression among community-residing elderly adults. *Journal of Gerontology: Psychological Sciences, 47,* P367-P372.

Wood, W., & Turner, R.J. (1985). The prevalence of physical disability in Southwestern Ontario. *Canadian Journal of Public Health, 26,* 262-265.

Yesavage, J.A., Brink, T.L., Rose, T.L., Lum, O., Huang, V., Adey, M.B., & Leirer, V.O. (1983). Development and validation of a geriatric screening scale: A preliminary report. *Journal of Psychiatric Research, 17,* 37-49.

Chronic Musculoskeletal Pain: Older Women and Their Coping Strategies

Deborah T. Gold, PhD

SUMMARY. Two diseases, osteoporosis and osteoarthritis, are responsible for a majority of the chronic musculoskeletal pain that older women experience. Osteoporosis is the metabolic bone disease most common in older women and is responsible for fractures, kyphosis, and chronic pain. Osteoarthritis, the most commonly diagnosed musculoskeletal problem in older women, causes degeneration of the weight-bearing joints in the body, resulting in limited function and chronic pain. In this paper, these and other common disorders are briefly described and typical coping strategies used by older women in pain are reviewed. In addition, potential multidisciplinary treatment regimens are discussed.

Late life offers many challenges to older women. As women age, their bodies become less flexible and less resilient. Convalescence from acute problems takes older women longer than it takes younger women, and chronic illnesses such as diabetes and hypertension are much more prevalent. Of the physical problems likely to affect large numbers of older women, those of the musculoskeletal system

Deborah T. Gold is affiliated with the Departments of Psychiatry and Sociology, Center for the Study of Aging and Human Development, Duke University Medical Center, Durham, NC 27710.

Work on this manuscript was supported by National Institutes of Health grants HD30442 and AG11268.

[Haworth co-indexing entry note]: "Chronic Musculoskeletal Pain: Older Women and Their Coping Strategies." Gold, Deborah T. Co-published simultaneously in *Journal of Women & Aging* (The Haworth Press, Inc.) Vol. 6, No. 4, 1994, pp. 43-58; and: *Older Women with Chronic Pain* (ed: Karen A. Roberto) The Haworth Press, Inc., 1994, pp. 43-58. Multiple copies of this article/chapter may be purchased from The Haworth Document Delivery Center [1-800-3-HAWORTH; 9:00 a.m. - 5:00 p.m. (EST)].

43

may be the most challenging. These conditions generate high morbidity and disability but rarely are life threatening. The most frequent consequence accompanying chronic musculoskeletal disease is pain. Musculoskeletal pain in elderly women is a serious public health problem, but one that has received relatively little attention from researchers and clinicians. This pain has serious implications for quality of life of older women, yet is very poorly understood.

This paper explores chronic musculoskeletal pain in older women. First, the physiological causes of this pain in older women are reviewed briefly. Next, management strategies are described in three important domains: the pharmacologic, physical, and psychosocial. Finally, the importance of multidisciplinary treatment strategies and areas for future research are noted.

CAUSES OF MUSCULOSKELETAL PAIN IN OLDER WOMEN

Musculoskeletal pain in general and low back pain in particular are common complaints from adults of all ages. Eighty percent of all adults experience some back pain during their lives (Zetterberg, Mannius, Mellstrom, Rundgren, & Astrand, 1990). But back pain without underlying structural causes is most frequent early in adulthood; non-structural back pain in women, for example, occurs most between ages 25 and 55 (de Giriolamo, 1991). During these thirty years, increased age leads to increased risk of low back pain. However, age-related increases last only until age 55 (Deyo, Rainville, & Kent, 1992). After that, non-specific low back pain actually decreases with age (Zetterberg et al., 1990).

This reduction in non-specific low back pain occurs in both men and women. In fact, in young and middle adulthood, men and women have equal risk of back pain. Both have reduced risk of non-specific back pain after age 60, but disease-based back pain in late life is most prevalent in women (Loeser & Volinn, 1991). This gender difference occurs primarily because the diseases that produce back pain in late life tend to be gender related (e.g., osteoporosis).

Just as prevalence and incidence rates of back pain change for older adults, the nature of back pain changes as well. Unlike the back pain of early adult years, musculoskeletal pain in older women stems from four primary causes: (a) degeneration of the spine and its associated structures; (b) metabolic bone disease resulting in deformation or fractures; (c) a form of rheumatic disease; or (d) trauma (Mobily & Herr, 1992). Older women who suffer pain from one of the first three causes often find that their pain is chronic in nature and unresponsive to management techniques effective for younger adults.

Within these categories fall specific diseases that cause musculoskeletal pain in older women. Conditions including spinal stenosis and ankylosing spondylitis, bursitis, sciatica, and herniated disks can cause back pain for women in late life (McCain & Scudds, 1988), but they are relatively rare. Two diseases are primarily responsible for older women's musculoskeletal pain: osteoporosis and arthritis.

Osteoporosis

Osteoporosis, a metabolic bone disease, is most prevalent in post-menopausal women. Bone remodelling problems result in demineralized bone that is susceptible to fracture with little or no trauma (Cummings, 1991). Bone mineral loss starts in adults at age 35; for women, the perimenopausal years are critical because reduced estrogen levels increase bone loss, putting many peri- and post-menopausal women at high risk of osteoporosis (Avioli, 1987). Risk of osteoporosis for both men and women increases with age (Resnick & Greenspan, 1989).

Osteoporosis is typically silent until the first fracture occurs. The most common osteoporotic fracture is the vertebral compression fracture, often occurring with little or no trauma. Other common fractures include the wrist, the ribs, and hip. These fractures usually cause substantial acute pain, worsened by activity; rest does not usually relieve it. In most cases, this pain resolves in four to eight weeks. However, chronic pain is associated with osteoporosis as well (Ettinger et al., 1992). Multiple vertebral fractures result in kyphosis and evolve into pain that appears to be postural in nature (Lyles et al., 1993). These vertebral compression fractures can cause substantial diminution of quality of life (Gold, Bales, Lyles, & Drezner, 1989).

Arthritis

Osteoarthritis, the most commonly diagnosed musculoskeletal problem in older women, affects weight-bearing joints; primary sites include the spine, the knees, and small joints of the hands and feet (Gandy & Payne, 1986). Osteoarthritis causes degenerative changes in these joints, perhaps from wear and tear. Unlike osteoporosis, which changes the mineral composition of bone, osteoarthritis causes pain by stimulating growth of osteophytic spurs which impinge on nerve roots (Mobily & Herr, 1992). Although most adults over age 65 show some evidence of osteoarthritis on x-ray, it is frequently asymptomatic (Svara & Hadler, 1988; Wigley, 1984).

When osteoarthritic pain occurs, it may be felt in a single joint or radiate through the body. Patients usually describe this pain as dull and aching, and it is often accompanied by muscle spasms. Activity exacerbates this pain, while rest relieves it, regardless of the affected region (Wigley, 1984). Older women often report that their osteoarthritis is worst upon awakening and wanes with activity. Weather changes can often intensify pain and stiffness (Gandy & Payne, 1986; Mobily & Herr, 1992).

Rheumatoid arthritis (RA) is a chronic inflammatory joint disease of unknown cause. Researchers suspect that RA has multiple etiologies (van der Heijde et al., 1991). Peak age of onset is typically between 25 and 55 years, although there is an elderly-onset RA that differs somewhat from younger-onset RA (Deal et al., 1985).

Insidious-onset RA is not rare in late life and is characterized by discoloration of and swelling in and around a shoulder, ankle, knee, wrist, or other large joint. In other cases, carpal tunnel syndrome is the first sign of rheumatoid arthritis, with other early symptoms that include weight loss, sweating, muscle pains, and excessive fatigue (van Schaardenburg, Lagaay, Breedveld, Hijmans, & Vandenbroucke, 1993). Severe joint stiffness is also a major problem in elderly-onset RA (Deal et al., 1985).

As the disease progresses, typical symptoms include joint swelling (particularly in the hands and fingers), swelling of the wrist, and weakened grip strength. Deformities and/or rheumatoid nodules, morning stiffness, and substantial pain are also characteristic, as are involvements of the foot and ankle. Further, neck pain stemming from involvement of the cervical spine can be severe and debilitating. Evidence suggests that older women are more likely than older men to survive long periods of disability from rheumatoid arthritis, having to manage deformity, pain, substantial disability, and social role loss (Hart, 1977).

Other Musculoskeletal Conditions

Several other conditions cause substantial musculoskeletal pain in older women. *Fibromyalgia,* first described in 1904, is a nonarticular rheumatism characterized by musculoskeletal aches and pains (Komaroff & Goldenberg, 1989). Although this disease is not well-recognized by the lay public and is difficult to diagnose, it may be an extremely common disorder (Goldenberg, 1987). Symptoms of fibromyalgia include generalized aches and pains, multiple tender points, sleep problems, headaches, and fatigue (Wolfe, 1986). Most research indicates that most fibromyalgia patients are females between 20 and 50 years old (Komaroff & Goldenberg, 1989). In fact, the literature is almost devoid of information about fibromyalgia in older adults. Wolfe (1988) suggests that fibromyalgia may occur in the presence of other musculoskeletal disorders in older people, but he gives no epidemiologic evidence regarding this disorder in people age 65 and older.

Lumbar spinal stenosis is a musculoskeletal disease that manifests itself by a decrease in the volume of the spinal canal (Svara & Hadler, 1988). Although it can be a congenital condition, it is most commonly found in older adults with degenerative changes of the spine. Spinal stenosis can be clinically asymptomatic, making diagnosis difficult (Spengler, 1987). The symptomatic version induces mild to moderate low back pain which frequently radiates to the legs, buttocks, or thighs. Standing still can exacerbate the pain of spinal stenosis, and pain is almost always alleviated by forward flexion at the waist or by sitting or lying down.

Ankylosing spondylitis is one of the few inflammatory rheumatic diseases associated with low back pain. The spondylitic patient almost always is diagnosed before age 30, with pain typically beginning gradually in young adulthood (Calin, 1985). In late life, this pain can become chronic. Exercise may improve the pain somewhat, especially for young adults. However, immobilization may be used with the older spondylitic patient in response to pain.

COPING WITH CHRONIC MUSCULOSKELETAL PAIN

Clearly, musculoskeletal pain in older women has neither a single cause nor a single trajectory. This pain varies by disease and is affected by psychosocial, environmental, and co-morbid factors as well. Yet, regardless of its source, chronic musculoskeletal pain requires management and coping efforts by the individual sufferer.

There is an important distinction between coping approaches that allows us to better differentiate between individuals and their coping styles. Richard Lazarus and his colleagues (e.g., Lazarus & Folkman, 1984; Folkman & Lazarus, 1980) makes this distinction between two coping styles used in everyday life: active and passive coping. People who rely primarily on active coping strategies work despite pain or use strategies that have a direct impact on the pain (e.g., exercise, massage). People who rely primarily on passive coping strategies expect others (e.g., physicians, physical therapists) to control their pain. Multiple studies suggest that individuals may use both strategies at different times to cope with pain (Carver, Scheier, & Weintraub, 1989; Crisson & Keefe, 1988). Active coping strategies are typically more effective in pain management than passive strategies. Active coping occurs within pharmacologic, physical, and psychosocial domains.

Pharmacologic Domain

Medications for pain management are perhaps the best known strategies of all. Pain medication, or analgesics, cannot cure the pain; instead they provide temporary relief. In some instances of acute pain (e.g., after surgery), temporary pain relief is sufficient. As a long-term management strategy for musculoskeletal pain in older women, pharmacologic intervention offers only transient relief at best. However, some chronic conditions of late life have acute episodes for which pain medication can be extremely helpful.

Fracture-based pain in osteoporosis and pain with inflammation in osteoarthritis respond best to the salicylates (aspirin and acetaminophen) and to nonsteroidal anti-inflammatory drugs (NSAIDs). The analgesic effects of these drugs are well established, and side effects are limited. Aspirin and NSAIDs have been extremely helpful in reducing osteoarthritic joint pain as well as the acute pain that accompanies vertebral fracture (Bellville, Forrest, Miller, & Brown, 1981). Muscle relaxants may be prescribed for acute muscle spasms or for chronic muscle pain. Unfortunately, most muscle relaxants including diazepam (Valium) and the benzodiazapenes can be associated with agitation, delirium, depression, or extreme sleepiness, especially in older adults. Further, standard doses of these medications may be excessive for older women. The frail older woman who lives alone should be advised to take these medications only when appropriate monitoring is available. Muscle relaxants use should be limited with older women, especially when medications for other co-morbid conditions may lead to polypharmacy (Svara & Hadler, 1988).

Deyo, Rainville, and Kent (1992) suggest in the *Journal of the American Medical Association* an alternative to analgesics for individuals with chronic pain. They believe that pain may be more effectively treated with anti-depressant rather than analgesic medication. Chronic pain can lead to sleep problems, loss of appetite or weight gain, lethargy, and irritability—in other words, the symptoms of clinical depression. Depression can exacerbate pain and confound traditional therapy. Once such symptoms are reported, treatment with tricyclic antidepressants may be appropriate. Not only do trycyclics have mood-elevating properties, but they also have independent analgesic effects that may reduce pain while easing depression (Watson, Evan, & Reed, 1982; Wolfe, 1988). Unfortunately, side effects of tricyclic medications include dry mouth, orthostatic hypotension, sedation, and delirium. Should any of these symptoms appear, these medications should be limited or discontinued immediately.

Physical Domain

The second arena of pain management, the physical domain, is one in which pain is minimized or eliminated through altering physical effects on the body. Often, the goal of physical domain treatments is to reduce pain while preventing further pathology.

Many physicians and patients alike view bed rest or reduced activity as the first step in the treatment of musculoskeletal pain. No one advocates inactivity on a permanent or long-term basis, but many feel that rest is a necessary concomitant of pain management.

This may be especially true in acute periods of chronic illnesses. For example, fractures or periods of inflammation might signal that bed rest could help (Hallal, 1991; Mobily & Herr, 1992). On the other hand, some experts believe that long periods of rest generate even more problems than they solve (Deyo, 1991; Wigley, 1984). Unfortunately, many older women with musculoskeletal pain choose contorted positions or recline against pillows which may exacerbate the underlying conditions. Extended bed rest can also cause skin breakdown, rapid muscular atrophy, bone mineral loss, and venous thrombosis (Mobily & Herr, 1992).

As an alternative to extended bed rest, carefully monitored combinations of rest and exercise may have better outcomes (Gandy & Payne, 1986; Wigley, 1984). Deyo (1991) recommends brief periods of standing after 3 hours of bed rest. Others (e.g., Hallal, 1991) feel that activity should occur early in the day when the muscle structures are strong, with rest used later to avoid fatigue in the spine and other vulnerable parts of the musculoskeletal system. Regardless of the patterns of rest selected for relieving pain, almost everyone agrees that complete or near complete bed rest should not continue for more than two weeks (Mobily & Herr, 1992).

A second important strategy in the physical domain of chronic musculoskeletal pain in older women is the use of hot and cold compresses (Mobily & Herr, 1992). Typically, cold provides the greatest relief for acute episodes of musculoskeletal pain, but some older women find cold compresses unappealing, especially during winter months. Moist heat seems to be more effective for chronic pain (Gandy & Payne, 1986). Older women and their family members can be taught to administer heat and cold properly. Of course, temperatures can be too extreme, resulting in skin breakdown and burns. But carefully used heat and cold can be extremely useful in chronic musculoskeletal pain management.

Exercise is the third strategy in the physical domain. Many clinicians feel that exercise is an excellent strategy for controlling muscle pain in older women (Hallal, 1991; Lyles et al., 1993). It is important not to exercise in the midst of an acute episode of pain, especially if pain emanates from the muscles that would be exercised. Further, consensus has not yet been reached about the best exercise format to use with older women within the confines of their particular diseases. For example, Wigley (1984) suggests that passive, non-stressful range of motion (ROM) exercises should be used for arthritis. Deyo (1991) delineates exercise options including aerobic fitness exercises, stretching exercises, or strengthening extension exercises. He also identifies isometric flexion exercises (called the Williams exercises) as another option. However, the literature suggests that fractures during exercise are more likely during the Williams exercises than when doing extension exercises (Lyles et al., 1993).

Multiple factors must be considered when designing an exercise program for an older woman with chronic pain. In addition to the patient's musculoskeletal diagnosis and overall conditioning (or deconditioning), practitioners must remember co-morbid disease (especially cardiovascular and pulmonary disease), medications, cognitive ability, and availability of supervision. Exercise, however, can be a potent physical intervention with both long- and short-term positive outcomes.

Finally, assistive devices and joint protection devices offer ways in which stress on the musculoskeletal system can be relieved. Braces and corsets can be prescribed for spine support in women with spinal fractures or other conditions of the lumbar spine (Mobily & Herr, 1992). These supports are often most useful during acute episodes of chronic illnesses, and patients may be told to wear them later in the day as key muscles fatigue (Swezey, 1988). Canes, splints, and shoe inserts may be helpful in reducing strain on specific joints (Wigley, 1984). Education about when to use these devices and how to use them correctly is key. Ergonomic counseling can help older women identify how to use their bodies efficiently in order to avoid strain on compromised joints and muscles (Swezey, 1988). An ergonomics expert can help women identify ways in which their day-to-day activities can be carried out with minimal physical strain.

Other possibilities for physical domain interventions for chronic musculoskeletal pain include acupuncture, massage, chiropractics, ultrasonography, hydrotherapy, traction, TENS (see Mobily, this issue), diathermy, and surgery. Space limitations preclude review of these methods here, and not all of them have proven efficacy. Conservative rather than invasive management techniques should always be the first choice in musculoskeletal pain in older women.

Psychosocial Domain

Efforts in the psychosocial domain of chronic pain management help older women understand and manage their pain more effectively. These approaches are conceptualized in two ways in the psychological literature: (a) coping as a process and (b) coping as a trait (Brown & Nicassio, 1987; Carver, Scheier, & Weintraub 1989). These two approaches differ in their understanding of coping and the relationship between stress and coping.

Coping as process. As previously noted, Lazarus and his colleagues (Lazarus & Folkman, 1984; Folkman & Lazarus, 1980) differentiated between active and passive coping strategies. This important distinction was a major step forward in understanding how individuals manage stressful situations. Lazarus and colleagues also defined coping as an ongoing process rather than as a stable personality trait (Lazarus, 1966; Cohen & Lazarus, 1973). They believed that the nature of coping changes across different stressful situations or even different aspects of the same stressful situation. Because the selection of coping strategies by older women affects both psychosocial functioning and physical well-being (Keefe et al., 1987), it is important to understand how coping strategies are used.

The process of coping includes specific thoughts and behaviors that individuals use to manage pain or to manage their emotional responses to pain (Brown & Nicassio, 1987). As previously mentioned, active coping strategies are more useful and more adaptive to the situation of chronic pain while passive strategies are viewed as maladaptive (Brown & Nicassio, 1987).

Coping as trait. The second coping perspective comes from the theoretical model initially presented by the Wallstons: the health locus of control (HLOC) model (Wallston & Wallston, 1981; 1982). This model emphasizes "trait" rather than "state" issues in its conceptualization of the individual's health-related responsibility. In short, there are believed to be three different HLOC orientations: Internal, Powerful Others, and Chance. In the many research studies using HLOC as a theoretical construct, one of the most typical findings is that individuals with a strong internal HLOC have more positive outcomes (Wallston & Wallston, 1981). Those people feel that they themselves have control over their health outcomes. However, the findings with regard to this have been inconsistent. Nagy and Wolfe (1984) found that compliance with self-management recommendations was more likely in patients with stronger beliefs in control by powerful others. A study of older women with vertebral compression fractures and health locus of control found that there was no relationship between HLOC and psychosocial improvements (Gold et al., 1991). Thus, although HLOC is a popular way in which to conceptualize coping approaches, the findings are often contradictory.

Wallston and Wallston (1981) examined the relationship between HLOC and the "active" and "passive" coping styles. In general, passive coping is associated with low scores on internal HLOC and high scores on external HLOC. In contrast, active approaches to coping are strongly related to high scores on internal HLOC. Given those relationships, it may be that active coping and internal HLOC are not conceptually distinct. Little research on older women in particular has examined the HLOC orientation (Gold et al., 1991).

MULTIDISCIPLINARY TREATMENTS FOR CHRONIC MUSCULOSKELETAL PAIN

Three strategies for managing chronic musculoskeletal pain in older women have been reviewed here. Any of these strategies is presumably better than no coping at all, but contributions from all of these areas and from medical treatment should provide a complete and efficacious pain management program. Much has been written about multidisciplinary treatment for chronic pain (e.g., Crue & Pinsky, 1984; Rosomoff & Rosomoff, 1991; Steele, 1984), and there seems to be general agreement that programs that combine medical, physical therapy, and pharmacologic approaches with behavioral management are particularly successful. Sadly, few of these are directed at older women whose needs may not be compatible with some pain programs (e.g., those in which work-related issues are stressed). In other circumstances, Medicare may not cover these programs, thus severely limiting the number of older women who can afford to participate.

The literature on musculoskeletal pain contains only limited evaluation of programs designed for older women with specific diseases (see, for example, our work on a multidisciplinary program for older women with osteoporosis, Gold et al., 1989; Gold et al., 1993). Yet, disease-specific programs have several advantages. First, sharing participation with other older women who experience the same stresses normalizes the disease process and reduces individuals' feelings of deviance (Gold et al., 1989). Second, health care providers become more successful in managing pain as they learn more about its causes and manifestations. Thus, if a health care team works primarily or solely with patients with a specific disease (e.g., osteoporosis), this team will become more accomplished over time. Third, a multidisciplinary team comes to recognize that the sum of its parts is far greater than the whole. However, not every community can have a multidisciplinary team for every disease. Teams exist in large tertiary care centers which limits general access to them. As noted previously, insurance programs frequently refuse to cover team care, or at least refuse to cover certain components of care (e.g., nutrition, group or individual psychological services). At this time, this type of care is limited both in terms of the diseases treated as well as the geographical areas covered.

CONCLUSIONS AND IMPLICATIONS

Although knowledge of chronic musculoskeletal pain in older women has improved somewhat, this phenomenon is still poorly understood. For example, there is little evidence that coping with the diseases that affect the musculoskeletal system differs between men and women or between younger and older adults. Although older adults have co-morbid conditions which affect decisions about medication, exercise, diet, and other important areas of daily living, it is still not clear how multiple diseases interact. Research efforts might be concentrated on areas where established gender differences exist. For example, epidemiologic studies show that osteoporosis is six times more prevalent in older women than in older men (Cummings, 1991). This substantial difference suggests that research focused on older women and their pain management would have far greater impact than more general studies. In this time of fiscal reform and limited research dollars, it is critical to target studies of pain to those most likely to experience a given disease.

It is also important to recognize that responsibility for health care is not limited to health care providers. Individuals must accept at least partial responsibility for personal health and minimize those noxious influences that increase risk of disease. Changes in lifestyle can be prescribed by a physician; however, the individual is solely responsible for carrying out those changes. Sometimes minor adjustments in daily living, such as adding regular exercise to the daily routine, can serve powerful preventive and therapeutic functions. Add these kinds of adjustments to medical or pharmaceutical treatment regimens, and older women regain substantial control over pain and musculoskeletal disease and improve their quality of life.

REFERENCES

Avioli, L.V. (Ed.) (1987). *The osteoporotic syndrome: Detection, prevention, and treatment* (2nd ed). Orlando, FL: Grune & Stratton.

Bellville, J.W., Forrest, W.J., Miller, E., & Brown, B.W. (1981). Influence of age on pain relief from analgesics. *Journal of the American Medical Association, 217*, 1835-1837.

Brown, G.K., & Nicassio, P.M. (1987). Development of a questionnaire for the assessment of active and passive coping strategies in chronic pain patients. *Pain, 31*, 53-64.

Calin, A. (1985). Ankylosing spondylitis. In W.N. Kelley, E.D. Harris, & S. Ruddy (Eds.), *Textbook of rheumatology* (pp. 993-1031). Philadelphia, W.E. Saunders.

Carver, C.S., Scheier, M.F., & Weintraub, J.K. (1989). Assessing coping strategies: A theoretically based approach. *Journal of Personality and Social Psychology, 56*, 267-283.

Cohen, F., & Lazarus, R.S. (1973). Active coping processes, coping dispositions, and recovery from surgery. *Psychosomatic Medicine, 35*, 375-389.

Crisson, J.E., & Keefe, F.J. (1988). The relationship of locus of control to pain coping strategies and psychological distress in chronic pain patients. *Pain, 35*, 147-154.

Crue, B.L., & Pinsky, J.J. (1984). An approach to chronic pain of non-malignant origin. *Postgraduate Medicine Journal, 60*, 858-864.

Cummings, S.R. (1991). Epidemiologic studies of osteoporotic fractures: Methodologic issues. *Calcified Tissue International, 49*, S15-S20.

Deal, C.L., Meenan, R.F., Goldenberg, D.L., Anderson, J.J., Sack, B., Pastan, R.S., & Cohen, A.S. (1985). The clinical features of elderly-onset rheumatoid arthritis. *Arthritis and Rheumatism, 28*, 987-994.

de Giriolamo, G. (1991). Epidemiology and social costs of low back pain and fibromyalgia. *The Clinical Journal of Pain, 7*, S1-S7.

Deyo, R.A. (1991). Nonsurgical care of low back pain. *Neurosurgery Clinics of North America, 2*, 851-862.

Deyo, R.A., Rainville, J., & Kent, D.L. (1992). What can the history and physical examination tell us about low back pain? *Journal of the American Medical Association, 268*, 760-765.

Ettinger, B., Black, D.M., Nevitt, M.C., Rundle, A.C., Cauley, J.A., Cummings, S.R., Genant, H.K., & Study of Osteoporotic Fractures Research Group. (1992). Contribution of vertebral deformities to chronic back pain and disability. *Journal of Bone and Mineral Research, 7*, 449-456.

Folkman, S., & Lazarus, R.S. (1980). An analysis of coping in a middle-aged community sample. *Journal of Health and Social Behavior, 21*, 219-239.

Gandy, S., & Payne, R. (1986). Back pain in the elderly: Updated diagnosis and management. *Geriatrics, 41*, 59-73.

Gold, D.T., Bales, C.W., Lyles, K.W., & Drezner, M.K. (1989). Treatment of osteoporosis: The psychological impact of a medical education program on older patients. *Journal of the American Geriatrics Society, 37*, 417-422.

Gold, D.T., Stegmaier, K., Bales, C.W., Lyles, K.W., Westlund, R.E., & Drezner, M.K. (1993). Psychological functioning and osteoporosis in late-life: Results of a multidisciplinary intervention. *Journal of Women's Health, 2*, 149-155.

Gold, D.T., Smith, S.D., Bales, C.W., Lyles, K.W., Westlund, R.E., & Drezner, M.K. (1991). Osteoporosis in late life: Does health locus of control affect psychosocial adaptation? *Journal of the American Geriatrics Society, 39*, 670-675.

Goldenberg, D.L. (1987). Fibromyalgia syndrome: An emerging but controversial condition. *Journal of the American Medical Association, 257*, 2782-2787.

Hallal, J.C. (1991). Back pain with postmenopausal osteoporosis and vertebral fractures. *Geriatric Nursing, 6*, 285-287.

Hart, F.D. (1977). Presentation of rheumatoid arthritis and its relation to prognosis. *British Medical Journal, 2*, 621-628.

Keefe, F.J., Caldwell, D.S., Queen, K.T., Gil, K.M., Martinez, S., Crisson, J.E., Ogden, W., & Nunley, J. (1987). Pain coping strategies in osteoarthritis patients. *Journal of Consulting and Clinical Psychology, 55*, 208-212.

Komaroff, A.L., & Goldenberg, D.L. (1989). The chronic fatigue syndrome: Definition, current studies and lessons for fibromyalgia research. *Journal of Rheumatology, 16*, 23-27.

Lazarus, R.S. (1966) *Psychological stress and the coping process.* New York: McGraw Hill.

Lazarus, R.S., & Folkman, S. (1984). *Stress, appraisal, and coping.* New York: Springer.

Loeser, J.D., & Volinn, E. (1991). Epidemiology of low back pain. *Neurosurgery Clinics of North America, 2,* 713-718.

Lyles, K.W., Gold, D.T., Shipp, K.M., Pieper, C.F., Martinez, S., & Mulhausen, P.L. (1993). Association of osteoporotic vertebral compression fractures with impaired functional status. *American Journal of Medicine, 94,* 595-601.

McCain G.A., & Scudds, R.A. (1988). The concept of primary fibromyalgia (fibrositis): Clinical value, relation and significance to other chronic musculo-skeletal pain syndromes. *Pain, 33,* 273-287.

Mobily, P.R., & Herr, K.A. (1992). Back pain in the elderly. *Geriatric Nursing, 2,* 110-116.

Nagy, V.T., & Wolfe, G.R. (1984). Cognitive predictors of compliance in chronic disease patients. *Medical Care, 22,* 912-921.

Resnick, N.M., & Greenspan, S.L. (1989). Senile osteoporosis reconsidered. *Journal of the American Medical Association, 261,* 1025-1029.

Rosomoff, H.L., & Rosomoff, R.S. (1991). Comprehensive multidisciplinary pain center approach to the treatment of low back pain. *Neurosurgery Clinics of North America, 2,* 877-890.

Spengler, D.M. (1987). Degenerative stenosis of the lumbar spine. *Journal of Bone and Joint Surgery, 69A,* 305-314.

Steele, R. (1984). Is the pain program cost effective? *Pain, 2,* 438-443.

Svara, C.J., & Hadler, N.M. (1988). Back pain. *Clinics in Geriatric Medicine, 4,* 395-410.

Swezey, R.L. (1988). Low back pain in the elderly: Practical management concerns. *Geriatrics, 43,* 39-44.

van der Heijde, D., van Riel, P., van Leeuuwen, M.A., van 't Hof, M.A., van Rijswijk, M.H., & van de Putte, L. (1991). Older versus younger onset rheumatoid arthritis: Results at onset and after 2 years of a prospective follow-up study of early rheumatoid arthritis. *The Journal of Rheumatology, 18,* 1285-1289.

van Schaardenburg, D., Lagaay, A.M., Breedveld, F.C., Hijmans, W., & Vanden-broucke, J.P. (1993). Rheumatoid arthritis in a population of persons aged 85 years and over. *British Journal of Rheumatology, 32,* 104-109.

Wallston, K.A., & Wallston, B.S. (1981). Health locus of control scales. In H.M. Lefcourt (Ed.), *Research with the locus of control construct. Volume 1. Assessment methods* (pp. 189-243). New York: Academic Press.

Wallston, K.A., & Wallston, B.S. (1982). Who is responsible for your health? The construct of health locus of control. In G. Sanders & J. Suls (Eds.), *Social psychology of health and illness* (pp. 65-95). Hillsdale, NJ: Erlbaum.

Watson, C.P., Evan, R.J., & Reed, K. (1982). Amitriptyline versus placebo in postherapeutic neuralgia. *Neurology, 32,* 671-673.

Wigley, F.M. (1984). Osteoarthritis: Practical management in older patients. *Geriatrics, 39,* 101-120.

Wolfe, F. (1986). The clinical syndrome of fibromyalgia. *American Journal of Medicine, 81*, 7-14.

Wolfe, F. (1988). Fibromyalgia in the elderly: Differential diagnosis and treatment. *Geriatrics, 43*, 577-68.

Zetterberg, C., Mannius, S., Mellstrom D., Rundgren, A., & Astrand, K. (1990). Osteoporosis and back pain in the elderly: A controlled epidemiologic and radiographic study. *Spine, 15*, 783-786.

Current Concepts and Management of Cancer Pain in Older Women

Anita C. All, RN, PhD

SUMMARY. Pain is the most common symptom associated with cancer. Sixty to eighty-five percent of individuals with advanced cancer have pain either of a severe or a chronic nature. Despite the fact that appropriate pain management exists, cancer pain is often inadequately controlled. Management strategies for older cancer patients must address the physical, psychological, and social concerns of the individual. The special problems of drug management presented by older patients reinforces the importance of implementing nonpharmacologic therapies when possible.

Cancer is a disease that is characterized by uncontrolled growth and spread of abnormal cells. The American Cancer Society has estimated that somewhere around 30% of the population will develop cancer and approximately 3 to 3.5 million Americans are presently living with the disease (Ferrell, 1993; Harmon, 1991). It has been estimated that approximately 90% of individuals who develop cancer could survive if their disease were detected early. In 1993 approximately 1,170,000 new cancer cases were diagnosed (American Cancer Society, 1993).

The death rate for malignant neoplasms per 100,000 residents of the United States is highest in the age group of 85 years or older

---

Anita C. All is Assistant Professor, The Medical College of Georgia, School of Nursing–Adult Health, Augusta, GA 30901.

[Haworth co-indexing entry note]: "Current Concepts and Management of Cancer Pain in Older Women." All, Anita C. Co-published simultaneously in *Journal of Women & Aging* (The Haworth Press, Inc.) Vol. 6, No. 4, 1994, pp. 59-72; and: *Older Women with Chronic Pain* (ed: Karen A. Roberto) The Haworth Press, Inc., 1994, pp. 59-72. Multiple copies of this article/chapter may be purchased from The Haworth Document Delivery Center [1-800-3-HAWORTH; 9:00 a.m. - 5:00 p.m. (EST)].

(United States Department of Health and Human Services, 1993). In 1990 the death rate for all races in the 55 to 64 year old age group was 449.6 per 100,000 individuals. This rate increased to 872.3 in the 65 to 74 year old age group and rose to 1,348.5 in the 75 to 84 year old group. The rate of deaths per 100,000 individuals for all races was 1,752.9 in the 85 year old or older group. When comparing white males to white females, there were 1,883 deaths per 100,000 individuals in the white male group age 75 years to 84 years. White females had a death rate of 1,011.8 in this same age group. Black females of the same age had a rate of death of 1,059.9 per 100,000. In the 85 year old or older group the white male rate was 2,715.1, white females 1,372.3, and a slight increase occurred for black females with a rate of 1,431.3.

Costs that are associated with cancer treatment are extremely dependent upon the setting in which the treatment is provided. The City of Hope Medical Center compared the cost of using intravenous morphine at home versus hospitalization. The differences were dramatic. The average daily cost of home care, including pharmacy and nursing charges was $120 as compared to $1,771 per day for the hospitalized patient (Ferrell, 1993). Individuals experiencing pain often are extremely vulnerable and may blindly agree to any procedures or costs that offer any possibility of relief. Patients are frequently not provided with information on associated costs or alternatives. As care becomes more and more complex they may leave decisions to health care workers who are themselves unaware of the cost of one treatment protocol versus another.

The type of cancer that most affects women is breast cancer. Approximately one out of every nine women will be diagnosed with breast cancer (Contanza, 1992). Age is an additional risk factor for the development of breast cancer. Survival rates are lower for the older woman. Due to the high percentage of women affected and the increased morbidity associated with later diagnosis, special attention needs to be directed at this issue.

BREAST CANCER AND ELDERLY WOMEN

The risk of developing breast cancer has been shown to increase with age. Women who are 65 years old or older represent 14% of the female population, but these women represent 43% of the cases of invasive breast cancer (Contanza, 1992; Contanza et al., 1992; Mor, Pacala, Rakowski, 1992; Satariano, 1992; Zapka & Berkowitz, 1992). Older women initially present with more extensive disease than their younger counterparts and their survival rates are much lower (Clark, 1992). Women 65 or older have a six times higher risk of developing breast cancer and a seven times higher risk of dying from it (Contanza, 1992). Perhaps this happens because older women do not receive complete workups for definitive staging of their breast cancer and are more likely not to receive optimal therapy. Older women are less likely to undergo regular breast examinations, less likely to practice breast self-examination (BSE), and their physicians, usually internists, are less likely to recommend mammography (Annas, 1992). Additionally, older women are less likely to comply with recommended standards of care in relation to breast cancer prevention. Ninety percent of woman over the age of 40 have heard of mammography but only about one half have ever had a mammogram (Mor et al., 1992). As women get older they are even less likely to have had a mammogram. Women age 75 to 84 years of age were one-third less likely to have had a mammogram than women 65 to 74. Non-white women are even less likely to have had a mammogram. Women below the poverty level are one-half to two-thirds less likely to have had a mammogram (Mor et al., 1992). The Public Health service has recommended that the percentage of women age 50 and older who receive a mammogram with a clinical breast examination be increased from 25% to 60% by the year 2000 (Satariano, 1992). It becomes very easy to see that since older women are seen later in the disease process they are less likely to receive the curative benefits of surgery and consequently, deal with the pain issues of advanced disease.

TYPES AND STAGES OF CANCER PAIN

Pain can be defined in different ways depending on the focus. It can be and often is described in terms of tissue damage. This definition of pain is "an unpleasant sensory and emotional experience associated with actual or potential tissue damage or described in terms of such damage" (Levy, 1988 p. 266). A more practical definition is that "pain is what the patient says it is and occurs when he or she says it does" (Levy, 1988, p. 266). Cancer related pain is the type of pain studied to the greatest extent in terminally ill individuals.

Cancer pain is not the same as acute pain or chronic non-cancer pain. Acute pain tells someone to seek out specific therapy which is usually curative, making the pain ultimately reversible. The chronic pain of cancer, particularly advanced cancer, is usually irreversible and related to disease progression. The individual is in a cycle of pain that goes from bad to worse. Cancer pain unlike the pain associated with chronic pain syndrome (CPS) has an organic source. CPS pain often exists without actual or likely tissue damage (International Association for the Study of Pain, 1979; McCaffery, 1979). Pain impairs the desired lifestyle of cancer victims and reminds them constantly of the incurable nature of their disease.

Mathews, Zarro, and Osterhom (1973) described three stages of cancer pain. The first or early stage occurs during the diagnostic phase of the illness. It usually follows surgery for the treatment or diagnosis of the primary lesion. The pain decreases as incisional healing occurs. The stress of awaiting laboratory results may increase this pain. The intermediate or second stage results most often from cancer recurrence. Further diagnostic testing and anxiety may increase the pain that accompanies this stage in the disease progression. Palliative treatment with radiation or chemotherapy may produce significant pain relief. The final stage of cancer pain coincides with the terminal phase of the illness. These patients experience anxiety and depression and become debilitated as death appears to be imminent. The continuous nature of the pain that is present at this point in the illness overwhelms them and rules their lives. It interferes with all their normal activities and prevents them from enjoying the remaining days of their lives.

PSYCHOSOCIAL ISSUES INHERENT TO CANCER PAIN

Even though the stimulus responsible for the pain sensation may be physiological, the experience of pain is believed to be influenced by psychological and social variables. The psychosocial tasks of a terminal illness include the maintenance of a meaningful quality of life with disease and the threat of death, coping with disfigurement and loss of function, confronting existential and spiritual questions, and finally planning for surviving family members and friends. Individuals with cancer are faced with the challenge of trying to continue to function with an unknown future. Family and friends may not understand or be able to accept the severity of the illness and pressure persons to maintain an independence of which they are no longer capable. Fearing the inability to cope with the symptoms and pain of an incurable illness can cause a person with cancer pain to experience intense feelings of helplessness and hopelessness.

Hope and Hopelessness

A feeling of hope is associated with either an increased sense that one can cope or be helped to cope by others. Hope may also be accompanied by actual biological changes that enhance physical as well as mental well-being (Moynihan, Christ, & Silver, 1988). The most striking and recurrent theme faced by those working with individuals with terminal illnesses is the struggle to maintain hope. Hope is believed to be related to many factors. These include: (a) psychiatric status, (b) endocrine function, (c) stress and illness, and (d) susceptibility to infection. Loss of hope is a biopsychosocial interaction that can account for the phenomenon of rapid death from voodoo, evil eye, and belief in hexes. This phenomenon can be seen in the abrupt death of individuals after being told of a fatal prognosis. The central feature of hope is that there is an expectation that something worthwhile lies ahead.

Hope may impact the progression of cancer in early stages. As with depression and distress, hopelessness is experienced by individuals who are diagnosed with cancer. This issue speaks to the importance of early intervention to help newly diagnosed individuals deal with the stresses associated with their disease (Chuang, Devins, Hunsley, & Gill, 1989; Ostrow, et al., 1989; Rabkin, Williams, Neugebauer, Remien, & Goetz, 1990).

Family Issues

Pain effects not only individuals experiencing it but also members of their social network. The importance of including the family of the person with cancer pain in the development and implementation of the treatment plan has been well substantiated (Brockopp & Brockopp, 1990). When family members are included in the planning of care a clear message is given as to their importance in the overall treatment regime. Depression and anxiety are common in the person with cancer and the family can play a vital role in helping a person maintain hope (Sizemore, 1989). Family and friends also must be encouraged, however, to maintain their own lives and they must also face their feelings of abandonment and anger. As it is not socially acceptable to be angry at someone who is dying, the professional must allow the family to ventilate their feelings in a non-judgmental atmosphere (Moynihan, Christ, & Silver, 1988).

PAIN MANAGEMENT

Pain connected with advanced cancer is often inadequately controlled, especially in the period immediately preceding death. Approximately 25% of cancer patients die without satisfactory pain relief (Sizemore, 1989). This inadequate control appears to be related not to a lack of knowledge but the improper use of the current knowledge available concerning pain. Many cancer patients fear dying in pain more than they fear death. Rankin (1990) reported that cancer patients describe their pain as becoming progressively more severe and frequent. The pain finally develops into violent, relentless and intolerable suffering. It demoralizes the person and prevents him or her from eating, resting, or sleeping. It is continuous and produces mental and physical exhaustion. This pain traps the person in a situation where there is no foreseeable end.

Cancer pain responds to appropriate therapy. The most difficult aspect of pain control is the accurate assessment of pain intensity (McGuire, 1984). Comfort measures and therapeutic interventions must be simple enough to be followed by those terminally ill individuals who may have impaired cognitive ability and inconsistent primary care. The hospice movement in Britain has demonstrated that with careful narcotic dosing, pain control and mental clarity can be achieved simultaneously (Mount, Ajemian, & Scott, 1976). Improved function actually allows for an elevation of the pain threshold. Research has shown certain cancer pain syndromes are responsive to specific therapies as alternatives or adjuncts to narcotics. Cancer caused pain accounts for approximately 70% of the pain experienced by these individuals (Levy, 1988). The remainder of pain results from treatment protocols or from coincidental, associated, or unassociated medical problems.

Pain control remains a major problem in the care of individuals with cancer. There must be adequate use of narcotic analgesics. Practitioners must confront their own discomfort in dealing with the issues of dying, and knowledge must be increased concerning the value of adjunctive treatments. The tendency to hold dosing of narcotics until pain is severe must be discontinued (Sizemore, 1989). Pain management requires an interdisciplinary approach. The most effective approaches to pain management utilize the expertise of all professional staff members (Lipman, 1993; Loscalzo & Jacobsen, 1990; Miller & Jay, 1990). Accurate assessment of pain is of utmost importance in its management. Open channels of communication are essential to the patient's well-being. The misconceptions of health care professionals concerning the use of analgesics and accurate assessment of pain have been responsible for the failure to provide adequate pain control (Rankin, 1990). The patient and the family must be a part of the planning. Patients are particularly vulnerable to a loss of autonomy when it comes to pain management. They become desperate for relief.

Until a cure is achieved, living with oncology pain will continue to affect all levels of society. It is a physically, emotionally, and spiritually devastating experience for the patient and his or her family. Many of the clinical issues associated with treating cancer pain have gained considerable attention in recent years. Various strategies possess unique qualities that can benefit the care and management of these individuals and provide a better understanding of the disease (Miller & Jay, 1990). This understanding may lead to enhancing the patient's ability to develop coping mechanisms that could be effective in confronting the pain associated with cancer.

Pharmacological Pain Management

The diagnosis of cancer is synonymous with pain. The greatest immediate concern is fear of unrelieved pain. It must be remembered that not all people with cancer suffer from pain, but for many it can be a serious complication. It occurs most frequently in the later stages of the disease and is associated with recurrence and/or metastasis. The pain is intensified because of the psychological influence of knowing that the disease causing the pain will inevitably cause death.

Analgesics are drugs that are used symptomatically. They act either to reduce the painful stimulus or to reduce the perception of the painful stimulus. The action of a specific drug varies, but primarily all the pharmaceutical action occurs either at the receptor site or in the brain. Many health care professionals have advocated preventing the occurrence of pain if at all possible. This involves medication at regularly scheduled intervals to maintain constant blood levels of the drug, with additional as needed drugs for times of increased pain. Saunders (1981) explained in his work that prompt relief from pain at the beginning reassures patients and they do not increase their pain by fear and tension.

Narcotic analgesics are the main group of medication used for the treatment of patients with cancer. The World Health Organization, as reported by Payne (1989), suggested a step approach to the management of cancer pain. They have suggested starting with nonopiate analgesics, proceeding to weak opiates, and progressing as necessary to strong opiate analgesics. Nonopiate analgesics are represented by drugs such as aspirin and other nonsteroidal anti-inflammatory drugs (NSAIDS). The stronger opiates consist of such drugs as morphine, hydromorphone, and methadone. Research by the British hospice movement has documented that the administration of narcotics around the clock is safe and effective (Mount, Ajemian, & Scott, 1976). Jacox (1979) found a positive relationship between a person's pain and his or her analgesic regime. As-needed dosing regimes do not provide adequate pain control for many persons. Results indicated that pain and distress continue to be in the moderate range with as-needed dosing protocols. Revising this rigid scheduling could alleviate or decrease the amount of pain that patients experience.

Adjuvant drugs may be combined with narcotics to decrease the side effects of the narcotics or to increase their analgesic effects. Nonsteroidal anti-inflammatory drugs (NSAIDS) can increase the effects of narcotics on cancer pain. These drugs must be used cautiously in elderly persons. Most persons with cancer are older adults and they frequently have hematological and renal disorders. The peripheral prostaglandin inhibitors may have more side effects in elderly individuals (Bruera, 1990).

Tricyclic antidepressants are often used in hospice centers. It has been suggested that this category of drugs works by enhancing descending inhibitory pathways and they interact with morphine by increasing its bioavailability. There is no conclusive evidence existing about optimal dosing but it appears lower doses are needed than when the drugs are used strictly for their antidepressant effect (Bruera, 1990). Other drugs that may be valuable are corticosteroid, amphetamine derivatives, phenothiazine, and benzodiazepines. Additionally, there are many nonpharmacological measures that can be useful in reducing or alleviating cancer pain.

Pharmacologic Problems in the Elderly Population

Narcotic or opiate drugs given to older adults have their effects increased and they may remain in the individual's system longer since the drug's half-life may be prolonged. It is frequently necessary to prescribe an anti-nausea drug concurrently for the elderly patient experiencing cancer pain. The usual adult dose of morphine given intravenously in an older person can cause symptoms of severe toxicity. These differences are due to decreased liver and renal functioning, the primary sites for detoxification and excretion. The older person may also have fewer receptor sites and this may produce a more profound drug effect (Henry, 1987). Initial dosing of an elderly person should be started at the low end and carefully monitored.

The treatment of pain in older persons with cancer is difficult due to the presence of multiple pathology, altered clinical presentation of diseases, loss of compensatory reflexes, and altered elimination of drugs. Elderly persons are more likely to suffer from increased and more serious adverse reactions to non-steroidal anti-inflammatory drugs (NSAIDS). Most NSAIDS will cause gastric irritation of one form or the other in older adults. Severe gastric hemorrhage and perforation is the most common cause of death in elderly persons from adverse effects of NSAIDS (Pearson, 1987).

Nonpharmacologic Treatment

Radiation and chemotherapy are important modes of therapy. Most persons with cancer will respond to radiation therapy with significant relief. There is a purpose to radiation and chemotherapy beyond saving or prolonging life (Bruera, 1990). Reduction of the tumor size can reduce pain.

Recent approaches to alleviating, controlling, or teaching individuals to cope with cancer pain have focused on behavioral-oriented treatment and biofeedback. The use of cognitive-oriented muscle relaxation is employed to reduce sensory input. The tensing and relaxing of various muscle groups, combined with deep breathing and cognitive imagery, assist individuals in developing coping skills. This process of focusing is a useful coping strategy. Visual imagery is employed to make the development of conscious control easier (Loscalzo & Jacobsen, 1990; Miller & Jay, 1990). The object is to teach the individual to release tension and to relax, a technique that often increases the pain threshold.

Much of the work done with nonpharmacological approaches to pain control has been done utilizing persons with chronic pain not necessarily related to an organic cause. Stans et al. (1989) reported statistically significant reductions in self-monitoring comparisons of pain. Patients reported having less pain, consuming less medication, and having enhanced activity levels after a short cognitive-behavioral treatment program. They reported improved attitudes, greater resourcefulness, and better coping strategies. The patients who reported improvement were found to have a high correlation between a sense of mastery and integrating the newly learned coping skills into their daily lives.

CONCLUSION AND IMPLICATIONS

Pain afflicts approximately one third of individuals with primary carcinoma. Sixty to eighty-five percent of the individuals with advanced cancer have pain either of a severe nature or a chronic nature that requires some type of pain management (Bruera, 1990; Ferrell, 1993; Levy, 1988; Portenoy, 1990; Spiegel & Sands, 1988). Pain is the rule rather than the exception. It is an everyday companion. The impact of living with cancer pain and the importance of its treatment cannot be underestimated.

Pain invades the entire spectrum of the older person's physical, psychological, and social lives. The affected person must deal with issues of self-concept, independence, interpersonal relationships, and hope in the face of an uncertain future. People who are terminally ill seldom want to deal with the issue of death because they are frequently focusing their energy on the demanding task of daily living. Fears of death are usually exacerbated, however, as the illness progresses and when the individual perceives a loss of function. Older cancer patients and their families need to ventilate their feelings about loss and separation; they must be given the opportunity to grieve.

Feelings of anxiety are often associated with fear of reoccurrence and fear of pain (Mendelsohn, 1990). The best that professionals at this point can offer persons with cancer is information. Elderly patients need to become familiar with all their treatment options. Individuals report feeling strongly reassured by being actively involved in their treatment; they begin to have some control when it seems that they have lost all hope of control (Moynihan et al., 1988).

The response of older individuals to most painful conditions has been found to be similar to that of younger individuals (Ghose, 1987). No documentation exists that pain sensation is altered for older adults. Responses to pain in the older person, however, may be modified by various psychosocial factors that have occurred over their life-time (Kwentus, Harkins, Lignon, & Silverman, 1985). Health and human service providers must take into account the influence of these factors and the role religious faith and upbringing has on the outward expression of pain. Generational variations also may exist in attitudes towards pain and its expression. Individuals working with the older adults must increase their awareness of the varied ways that pain can be expressed.

Progress has been made in the treatment of cancer pain. Pain research has consistently ranked among the top priorities in the National Oncology Nursing Society priorities survey. The topic of cancer pain has increased in the literature since the mid-1960s with comfort becoming firmly established as a goal for treatment of cancer patients. With few exceptions, however, we have ignored the older population, and older women in particular, as sufferers of cancer pain. Many areas of cancer research and the management of cancer pain lend themselves to the study of older adults. The relationship of particular individual characteristics, interpersonal style, and the perceptions of provider-patient interaction are areas that directly relate to adherence. Questions such as physician gender, the beliefs of the person and provider of services concerning health screening, and health practices in relationship to coping with cancer pain are areas that must be addressed in future research with older adults (Zapka & Berkowitz, 1992).

As the numbers of elderly women with breast cancer grow, and if the trend continues that they are seen later in the disease process, effective pain management strategies must be further developed. Older men and women deserve the same management of pain as do other segments of the population. Yet, there is very little in the literature directed at pain management for the older adults. Ferrell (1992) reviewed 11 leading textbooks of geriatric medicine and found that only two devoted chapters to the management of pain. The eight geriatric nursing textbooks reviewed devoted a total of less than 18 pages (out of 5000) to pain relief in later life!

Pain management for older cancer patients must be viewed as a research priority as they are the primary age group for the occurrence of cancer and its associated pain. Being old does not mean cancer pain does not exist or that older adults do not deal with the same issues of despair and fears of dying. Elderly women with cancer often present special concerns, however, that need to be acknowledged when developing management plans. These needs include limited financial and social resources, multiple medical problems, and the challenge of possible multiple drug interactions.

REFERENCES

American Cancer Society (1993). *Cancer Facts & Figures-1993*. Atlanta, Georgia.

Annas, G. (1992). Breast cancer screening in older women: Law and patient rights. *The Journal of Gerontology, 47* [Special Issue], 121-125.

Brockopp, G., & Brockopp, D. (1990). Chronic pain: The family in treatment. In T. Miller (Ed.), *Chronic Pain Vol. 2* (pp. 573-583). Madison, CT: International Universities Press.

Bruera, E. (1990). Symptom control in patients with cancer. *Journal of Psychosocial Oncology, 8*(2/3), 47-73.

Chuang, H., Devins, G., Hunsley, J., & Gill, M. (1989). Psychosocial distress and well-being among gay and bisexual men with human immunodeficiency virus infection. *American Journal of Psychiatry, 146*, 876-880.

Clark, G. (1992). The biology of breast cancer in older women. *The Journal of Gerontology, 47* [Special Issue], 19-23.

Contanza, M., Annas, G., Brown, M., Cassel, C., Champion, V., Cohen, H., Frame, P., Glasse, S., Mor, V., & Pauker, S. (1992). Supporting statements and rationale. *The Journal of Gerontology, 47* [Special Issue], 7-16.

Contanza, M. (1992). Breast cancer screening in older women: Overview. *The Journal of Gerontology, 47* [Special Issue], 1-3.

Ferrell, B. (1992). Building a program of pain research. *Proceedings of the Second National Conference on Cancer Nursing Research.* Baltimore, Maryland: The American Cancer Society.

Ferrell, B. (1993). Cost issues surrounding the treatment of cancer related pain. *Journal of Pharmaceutical Care in Pain & Symptom Control, 1*(1), 9-23.

Ghose, K. (1987). Pain and the elderly. In K. Ghose (Ed.), *Drug Management in the elderly* (pp. 1-7). Boston: MTP Press Limited.

Harmon, M. (1991). The use of group psychotherapy with cancer patients: A review of recent literature. *The Journal for Specialists in Group Work, 16*(1), 86-61.

Henry, J. (1987). Clinical pharmacology of the narcotic analgesics. In K. Ghose (Ed.), *Drug management in the elderly* (pp. 27-37). Boston: MTP Press Limited.

International Association for the Study of Pain (1979). Subcommittee on taxonomy pain terms: A list with definitions and notes of usage. *Pain, 6*, 249-252.

Jacox, A. (1979). Assessing pain. *The American Journal of Nursing, 79*, 895-900.

Kwentus, J. Harkins, S., Lignon, N., & Silverman, J. (1985). Current concepts of geriatric pain and its treatment. *Geriatrics, 40*, 48-57.

Levy, M. (1988). Pain control research in the terminally ill. *OMEGA, 18*(4), 265-279.

Lipman A. (1993). Pain management and pharmaceutical care. *Journal of Pharmaceutical Care in Pain & Symptom Control, 1*(1), 1-3.

Loscalzo, M. & Jacobsen, P. (1990). Practical behavioral approaches to the effective management of pain and distress. *Journal of Psychosocial Oncology, 8*(2/3), 139-167.

Mathews, G., Zarro, V., & Osterhom, J. (1973). Cancer pain and its treatment. *Seminar in Drug Treatment, 3*(1), 45-53.

McCaffery, M. (1979). *Nursing management of the patient with pain,* New York: J. B. Lippincott.

McGuire, D. (1984). The measurement of clinical pain. *Nursing Research, 33*, 152-156.

Mendelsohn, G. (1990). Psychosocial adaptation to illness by women with breast cancer and women with cancer at other sites. *Journal of Psychosocial Oncology, 8*(4), 1-25.

Miller, T., & Jay, L. (1990). Pharmacologic and nonpharmacologic approaches to pain management. In T. Miller (Ed.), *Chronic pain Vol. 2* (pp. 525-571). Madison, CT: International Universities Press.

Mor, V., Pacala, J., & Rakowski, W. (1992). Mammography for older women: Who uses, who benefits? *The Journal of Gerontology, 47* [Special Issue], 43-50.

Mount, B., Ajemian, I., & Scott, J. (1976). Use of Brompton mixture in testing the chronic pain of malignant disease. *Canadian Medical Association Journal, 113*, 112-129.

Moynihan, R., Christ, G., & Silver, L. (1988). AIDS and terminal illness. *Social Casework: The Journal of Contemporary Social Work, 69*, 380-387.

Ostrow, D., Monjan, A., Joseph, J., VanRaden, M., Fox, R., Kingsley, L., Dudley, J., & Phair, J. (1989). HIV-related symptoms and psychological functioning in a cohort of homosexual men. *American Journal of Psychiatry, 146*, 737-742.

Payne, R. (1989). Pharmacologic management of bone pain in the cancer patient. *Clinical Journal of Pain, 5*(suppl. 2), S43-S49.

Pearson, R. (1987). Non-steroidal anti-inflammatory drugs. In K. Ghose (Ed.), *Drug management in the elderly* (pp. 39-44). Boston: MTP Press Limited.

Portenoy, R. (1990). Pharmacologic approaches to the control of cancer pain. *Journal of Psychosocial Oncology, 8*(2/3), 75-107.

Rabkin, J., Williams, J., Neugebauer, R., Remien, R., & Goetz, R. (1990). Maintenance of hope in HIV-spectrum homosexual men. *American Journal of Psychiatry, 147*, 1322-1326.

Rankin, M. (1990). Using drugs for cancer pain. In T. Miller (Ed.), *Chronic pain Vol. 2* (pp. 667-723). Madison, CT: International Universities Press.

Satariano, W. (1992). Comorbidity and functional status in older women with breast cancer: Implications for screening, treatment, and prognosis. *The Journal of Gerontology, 47* [Special Issue], 24-31.

Saunders, C. (1981). Current views on pain relief and terminal care. In M. Swerdlow (Ed.), *The therapy of pain* (215-241). Philadelphia: J. B. Lippincott.

Sizemore, W. (1989). Assessment and treatment of cancer pain. In J. D. Loeser & K. J. Egan (Eds.) *Managing the chronic pain patient* (pp. 179-186). New York: Raven Press.

Spiegel, D., & Sands, S. (1988). Pain management in the cancer patient. *Journal of Psychosocial Oncology, 6*(3/4), 205-216.

Stans, L. Goossens, L., Van Houdenhove, B., Adriaensen, H., Verstraeten, D., Vervaeke, M., & Fannes, V. (1989). Evaluation of a brief chronic pain management program: Effects and limitations. *The Clinical Journal of Pain, 5*, 317-322.

United States Department of Health and Human Services (1993). *Health United States 1992 and Healthy people 2000 review* (DHHS Publication No. PHS 93-1232). Hyattsville, Maryland: U. S. Government Printing Office.

Zapka, J., & Berkowitz, E. (1992). A qualitative study about breast cancer screening in older women: Implications for research. *The Journal of Gerontology, 47* [Special Issue], 93-99.

Influence of Chronic Pain on the Family Relations of Older Women

Ranjan Roy, ADV., DIP., S.W.

SUMMARY. Explorations of family problems in elderly women with problems of chronic pain is an uncharted territory as is the application of family and couple therapy. The interpersonal conflicts encountered by older pain patients are not fundamentally different than their younger counterparts. Several case illustrations are provided to show the impact of chronic pain as it affects older women in their roles as patients and caregivers.

How does chronic pain in an elderly person affect family relationships? This simple question, in turn, begs more questions, such as, are elderly individuals affected differently than their younger counterparts? There is the other side of the question, as well. Does family relationship influence or affect the experience of chronic pain? One fact is clear. There is very little guidance to be had from the relevant literature, because such literature is virtually non-existent. On the other hand, considerable knowledge about the family functioning of younger chronic pain sufferers, whose average age of inception into a pain clinic is about 43 years, has accumulated over the past decade or two. An important point needs to be made at the very outset of this paper: elderly persons with chronic pain are not frequent consumers of pain clinics. One plausible explanation is

---

Ranjan Roy is Professor, Social Work and Psychiatry, University of Manitoba, Winnipeg, Canada R3T 2N2.

[Haworth co-indexing entry note]: "Influence of Chronic Pain on the Family Relations of Older Women." Roy, Ranjan. Co-published simultaneously in *Journal of Women & Aging* (The Haworth Press, Inc.) Vol. 6, No. 4, 1994, pp. 73-88; and: *Older Women with Chronic Pain* (ed: Karen A. Roberto) The Haworth Press, Inc., 1994, pp. 73-88. Multiple copies of this article/chapter may be purchased from The Haworth Document Delivery Center [1-800-3-HAWORTH; 9:00 a.m. - 5:00 p.m. (EST)].

that the pain complaint in most elderly persons has a discernible organic rather than a psychogenic or an elusive cause. The latter two causes are frequently observed in the younger pain clinic patients. Nonetheless, Sorkin and associates (1990) concluded that elderly persons were just as likely to benefit from the standard multidisciplinary treatment of chronic pain as the younger patients.

The truth is, however, that older adults tend to underutilize not only the services of pain clinics, but also mental health services. The principal cause for the former is that pain is viewed as an unavoidable accompaniment of old age and for the latter, a general tendency to normalize loss and depression in old age as well as a belief that elderly persons are less likely to benefit from psychological treatments.

It is noteworthy that several years ago Ouslander (1982) recognized an interesting association between pain and depression in the elderly population, an association explored by Romano and Turner (1985), and urged that psychological and social interventions should be available to older adults as they were vulnerable to loss of function and diminished autonomy. However, Steuer (1982) observed that psychotherapy was a rather unusual treatment for elderly persons. Edinberg (1985) offered several common myths associated with aging that contribute to this state of affairs: (a) loss of productivity; (b) inevitable and irreversible loss of mental ability, sexuality, and capacity for change; (c) emotional fragility; and (d) inability to take care of themselves. This level of stereotyping is remarkable especially in view of the wide range of variability in the health status and abilities found among older adults compared to any other age group.

CHRONIC PAIN AND INTERPERSONAL RELATIONSHIPS

The impact of chronic pain on interpersonal relationship has been demonstrated to be multifarious. A partial list of problems reported in the literature includes: the marriage relationship itself (Ahern, Adams, & Follick, 1985; Feurstein, Sult, & Houle, 1985; Kerns & Turk, 1984; Mohamed, Weisz, & Waring, 1978), drastic reduction in sexual activities (Flor, Turk, & Scholz, 1987; Maruta & Osborne, 1978; Maruta, Osborne, Swanson, & Halling, 1981; Roy 1988,

1989), spousal depression (Ahern et al., 1985; Flor, Turk, & Rudy, 1987; Kerns & Turk, 1984), and increased burden on the well spouse and other members of the family (Rowat & Knafl, 1985; Roy, 1988, 1989).

The impact of chronic pain on the family as a system is one area of relative neglect by researchers. Roy (1988, 1989) found that the overall family functioning of individuals with chronic head and back pain problems was adversely affected. These families were assessed, using the McMaster Model of Family Functioning (Epstein & Bishop, 1981), on six dimensions of family functioning: (a) *Problem-Solving*–the family's ability to resolve its difficulties in a way that allows it to maintain a level of effective family functioning; (b) *Communication*–the exchange of information between or among family members; (c) *Role*–the repetitive patterns of behavior by which individuals fulfil family functions; (d) *Affective Responsiveness*–the family members' ability to respond to a range of stimuli with the appropriate quality and quantity of feelings; (e) *Affective Involvement*–the degree to which the family shows interest in values, activities, and interests of its members; and (f) *Behavior Control*–the pattern the family adopts for handling behaviors in different situations. Both groups were found to be lacking virtually in every aspect of family functioning. The pain sufferers in these studies were in attendance at a pain clinic and thus by definition constituted a rather disabled group. In a more recent study (Roy & Thomas, 1989; Thomas & Roy, 1989), 52 chronic pain patients and their spouses were evaluated for their family functioning using the Family Adaptability and Cohesion Evaluation Scale (Olson, Portnoy & Lavee, 1985). This scale measures families' adaptability in dealing with altered situations as well as the level of cohesion with which families function. The results confirmed clinical observations, as well as earlier findings, that these families encountered problems in all aspects of couple functioning. These problems could be further exacerbated by the presence of clinical depression in the patients. The overall functioning of the subjects was found to be in the mid to extreme range of family problems.

Elderly Families and Chronic Pain

Gender issues, as far as the elderly chronic pain sufferer is concerned, remain an uncharted territory. The problem of chronic pain itself is somewhat of a different proposition in the elderly population. Unlike their younger counterparts, elderly pain sufferers are more likely to have a discernible organic basis for the pain. Their attitude to pain is also likely to be more accepting than what is observed with either pain clinic populations or non-clinical populations. Unfortunately the older population, in general, tends to display a rather fatalistic attitude to pain. Pain is viewed as a 'normal' consequence of old age, although it is not inevitably so (Cook & Roy, in press; Roy & Thomas, 1987 a,b). It is equally true that psychological approaches to the treatment of pain, so commonly available to a general pain clinic population, may not be so readily available to the elderly pain sufferer (Vendendries, in press). In more general terms, psychological and emotional problems in elderly individuals tend to be minimized or even ignored, and significant underutilization of mental health services by older adults is not uncommon (Lasoski, 1986).

In a review of the literature focusing on the use of family therapy with elderly persons, Roy (in press) found the field to be characterized by a paucity of outcome research. Clinical reports abound, but that is only a recent phenomenon. Family or couple therapy with the elderly pain patient is close to non-existent (Roy, 1990).

The literature, limited as it is, is suggestive of wide-ranging interpersonal problems routinely experienced by elderly individuals. These problems are heightened by illness or disability which, unfortunately, is relatively commonplace in this population. In considering the elderly population a simple truth needs reiteration: many elderly persons, and especially women, live in single households. In a study of 205 elderly persons living at home of whom 143 registered pain complaints, the proportions of widowed persons were 49% and 56% respectively in the pain and no-pain groups. Even more striking was the finding that 58% in the pain group and 71% in the no-pain group lived alone. This particular study did not specifically investigate family relations, but examined the extent of social connectedness and found that both groups were extensively involved in a wide range of activities. This population was drawn from a social and recreational organization which undoubtedly influenced the finding (Roy & Thomas, 1987 a,b). In a comparative study of British subjects attending a pain clinic, and Canadian subjects with pain complaints but not attending pain clinics, the pattern of social activities varied to the extent that British subjects spent more time visiting relatives, whereas the Canadians were more prone to socializing with friends and participated more in organized activities. This study also found that single British and Canadian subjects were more vulnerable to depression than were the married subjects (Roy, Thomas, & Berger, 1990).

In a pilot study of couple functioning of nine patients aged 65 years and over, attending a pain clinic, much evidence of discord and unhappiness was found (Roy, unpublished). On the basis of the Family Adaptability and Cohesion Evaluation Scale III, couples were found to be struggling with the problem of adapting to chronic pain. Of the nine couples only three were 'connected' and the rest showed various levels of disconnectedness.

The broader literature addressing the interpersonal conflicts in the aged population is inconclusive. The literature on multi-generational families is unequivocal about the pressures and conflicts engendered by sickness or disability in an elderly parent (Shanas, 1984). The burden on the well spouse of a chronically sick partner is also well documented, especially in relation to partners of Alzheimer's patients (Chenworth & Spencer, 1986; George & Gwyther, 1986; Poulshock & Deimling, 1984). Conversely, researchers report that families of elderly stroke patients returned to normal functioning within a relatively short period, particularly when the stroke itself was of a less damaging kind (Bishop, Epstein, Keitner, Miller & Srinivasan, 1986). In addition, Ratna and Davies' (1984) investigation of referrals to a psychogeriatric clinic found that of 142 patients, evidence of interpersonal conflicts existed in only 14% of the cases.

Interpersonal conflicts do not appear to diminish with age (Hughston, Christopherson & Bonjean, 1989). Perhaps, they change in quality and the causes for their emergence or persistence may also be different. Altered circumstances such as financial hardship may create a whole set of unpredictable problems. Chronic pain may or may not directly contribute to the emergence of those problems.

Sometimes the pain contributes to further exacerbation of an existing problem. Sometimes the extent of suffering with pain is not readily acknowledged by family members for simple or complex reasons, denial not being an uncommon explanation for such behavior (Roy & Thomas, 1987b). At other times, chronic pain and accompanying disability may even resolve some long standing marital conflicts. To put it more simply, the clinical observation of this author is that many of the interpersonal issues for the elderly patients brought on by chronic pain are not that different from those of younger patients. Life issues are indeed different. To state the obvious, retirement, widowhood, fixed and low income for many, declining physical capacity, fear of incapacity and death, and many more transitional issues are relevant to older adults. These changes, in combination with illness and pain, are capable of producing profound changes in their intimate relationships.

CASE ILLUSTRATIONS

Some interpersonal problems are commonly observed in couples when one member has chronic pain. Others are more complex in nature and presence of chronic pain probably helps to exacerbate existing conflicts. Yet another set of problems appears to be a combination of transitional issues and living with pain. A very special category of family relations arises when both partners are victims of pain. Yet another somewhat baffling problem is associated with combined presence of pain and depression or severe anxiety and the incredible pressure that generates on the well partner.

There is no research evidence to suggest distinct age-specific problems within the elderly population, such as greater prevalence of inter-generational (parent-child) conflict in the "old-old"(over the age of 80) category than "young-old" (between the ages of 65 to 70). It is not feasible to provide case illustrations for every kind of relationship issue caused by chronic pain. The purpose of the following illustrations is to reemphasize that old age does not preclude the existence of serious marital and family conflicts only to be worsened by illness and pain. When these interpersonal issues are therapeutically addressed, they are likely to be moderated or even ameliorated. The cases described below were seen by the author at a hospital based pain clinic.

Mrs. A., Age 67 Years: Why Pain Now?

Mrs. A. was referred to the pain clinic following a rather dramatic deterioration of her head and back pain. Neurological and orthopedic investigation failed to account for the exacerbation of her pains. She had a lifelong history of headache with which she had coped very effectively over the years and her back pain also had a 25 year old history. Despite her prolonged history of pain, she described herself as a healthy person. Only recently she had difficulty in coping with her day to day chores. Her headaches were definitely more troublesome which led her to seek the specialized services of a pain clinic. Her headaches had been treated by her family physician by narcotic and pain analgesics as well as anti-migraine agents and amitriptyline. She failed to respond.

Mrs. A along with her husband were seen for routine psychosocial assessment. They had a traditional marriage. Mrs. A was a homemaker. She raised five children, all of whom were grown up and doing well. Mr. A was recently retired. He had had a successful business career and the family was financially secure. Mrs. A described her husband as somewhat peripheral to the family system although in recent years he had grown closer to the children. Mr. A angrily rejected her characterization. He had a very responsible position which prevented him from spending much time with the family. He portrayed his wife as a perfectionist, overbearing and always expecting too much from him. Despite these chronic conflicts, he asserted, they had raised five very fine children who were pursuing various professions. Both of them acknowledged that since his retirement their relationship had deteriorated rather sharply.

Since his retirement, her husband had intruded into her daily life in a wholly unacceptable way. He showed very little regard for her daily routine, sat reading the newspaper for hours on end in the kitchen, did not shave unless he had to and worst of all wore the same underclothes for two or three days in a row. Then there was another development. He claimed that he could not always hear his wife. She would be blasting away at him about this and that and he would sit without as much as moving a muscle. Mrs. A was convinced that he was going deaf. Her headaches took a severe turn which compromised her day-to-day functioning to a rather 'frightening' level. Some days she could not even get out of bed. Mr. A would be a transformed man then. He would be very solicitous, take over the household chores (which he was not very good at it) and 'unendingly' fuss over his wife. Even his hearing seemed to improve. As soon as her headaches improved, he returned to his old 'obnoxious self'.

This case had several interesting clinical features. First, the timing of the onset of the severe pain for Mrs. A was interesting and revealing. It coincided with the retirement of her husband and quickly deteriorated. Roy (1986) observed that exacerbation of pain and the arrival of a patient at the pain clinic was often preceded by recent life changes. The relationship between life-change events and onset of pain, however, has received limited empirical support (Roy, 1992).

The second and a more interesting issue from the interpersonal perspective is the 'message' or the metaphorical aspect of Mrs. A's pain. At its simplest, the pain was a powerful means for expressing her disaffection with her life situation in general and the marital relationship in particular. At a more complex level, pain served the purpose of correcting what the family theorists have described as 'hierarchical incongruity'. This concept is predicated on the assumption that while a symptomatic partner in a marriage assumes a dependent position, symptom also empowers that individual, which in turn corrects the power imbalance in marriage (Madanes, 1981). In short, pain enables the person in the one below position to gain the upper hand. Mr. A, having lost his authority in the business world, virtually destroyed Mrs. A's assumptive world and the control she had exercised over this world all her married life. His desire to be in charge was challenged only when Mrs. A's pain reached a high level of disability. At that point there was somewhat of a reversal of the power relationship. He was forced into a totally unfamiliar nurturing role, and for once Mrs. A was listened to, both literally and figuratively.

This case was chosen to make the point that age alone does not change some basic dynamics of marital relationships. Hierarchical incongruity is a gender and age neutral concept. Nevertheless, in examining the meaning and purpose of pain and illness in older couples, the relevance of this concept may not always be acknowledged because there is the ever present tendency to minimize marital conflicts between elderly couples (Roy, in press). Then there is the myth that elderly persons may not be responsive to psychotherapeutic intervention. Mrs. A and Mr. A not only were anxious and eager participants in couple therapy, which lasted several months and was comprised of eight sessions, they emerged from treatment with a sense of equity in their relationship. Mrs. A reported significant improvement in her headaches.

Mrs. B., Age 72 Years: When All of Us Are Sick

Mrs. B, a rather gentle and soft spoken woman had a history of osteoarthritis. She was referred to the pain clinic for her unresponsiveness to treatment and deteriorating mood. Once her family situation was explored and understood, her mental state became eminently comprehensible and treatable. The first and foremost issue that had to be acknowledged was that this woman until recently was an active writer and contributed to many literary journals. Her pain deteriorated over the previous two years forcing her to abandon her writing career. In addition, her husband, a well known man in the business world, was showing early signs of organic brain syndrome. Their 42 year old son had failed to completely recover from a head injury and was becoming increasingly forgetful. These factors, in all probability, contributed to the worsening of her pain and mood.

Mrs. B had led a full life, travelling all over the world with her husband. They entertained a great deal and were surrounded by friends. That was in the past. Mrs. B's current situation was close to disastrous. She no longer had a sense of mastery over her environment. Her husband was not capable of even holding a simple conversation, and he would get angry with her for no apparent reason. The marriage had not been without problems. Mrs. B gradually withdrew inward and at times considered suicide.

This case is instructive for avoiding hasty diagnosis. The family circumstance, which revealed a rather hopeless and deteriorating situation, accounted for much of Mrs. B's distress. Compliance with treatment for her arthritis was not important. Physical pain, she explained, was of no consequence to her. She could tolerate her physical pain if her family situation were not so hopeless. Her life's efforts were unfolding before her eyes. Her pain itself had only a marginal effect on the family. The point is that it is not enough to examine the impact of pain alone on family relations. It is almost always pain in conjunction with other issues that tells the whole story. Did her pain contribute to further decline in family relations? Perhaps it did to the extent that pain compromised her ability to attend to the increasing demand placed on her by her husband and son. She was, of course, neglecting her pain problem by going off her medication. Despite the fact that she was referred to a pain clinic, in common with the previous case, pain was not the central issue for her.

Distance from the pain clinic, and the mental status of her husband, made any kind of family approach impractical. Mrs. B was seen in supportive psychotherapy for several months. She responded very well. Her mood improved as did her pain condition. She was showing some level of acceptance for the mental condition of her son and husband. She had been overly fearful of her husband's condition. His condition remained confined only to minor memory loss. A point of note is that pain and emotions coexist and improvement in one often leads to an improvement in the other.

Mr. C., Age 72 Years: This Is Too Much Kindness!

Mr. C., a very pleasant man, was referred to the pain clinic with a complaint of low back pain which radiated down his left side. The pain at times was so intense that he would be rendered immobile for days. Even on good days, his movements were restricted. Medical findings were essentially negative. His wife of some forty years was very alarmed by his condition. She became overprotective of this man and insisted that he should spend all his time in bed 'till he gets better'. She vented a great deal of anger on the health care professionals for their inability to help her husband. This couple had a married daughter whose attitude towards the patient was a mirror reflection of the mother's.

Mr. C felt rather thwarted by all this attention, but was reluctant to express his frustration lest he appear ungrateful. His wife and daughter, for all practical purposes, had taken over this man's life.

The total situation was further complicated by Mr. C's increasing level of depression. He found himself caught in a vicious cycle of pain, depression, enhanced feelings of inadequacy augmented by the reinforcement of his sick role and pain behaviors and more pain and depression. Pain reinforcing behavior by family members is a well understood phenomenon and has been subjected to rigorous research. One interesting observation is that the quality of marriage and the reinforcing pain behavior by the well spouse enjoy a direct relationship. The better the quality of marriage, the higher is the probability of reinforcement of pain behaviors by the spouse. Clinically this proposition makes eminent sense. It is natural for a concerned spouse to discourage the patient from performing tasks that might exacerbate the pain. Less means better. This is usually an undesirable state of affairs and not always amenable to change.

Mrs. C and the daughter were adamant in their belief that rest was the answer to Mr. C's aches and pain. He could not even drive himself to keep his hospital appointments. He was growing increasingly resentful about his unsolicited dependency, but could not communicate his anger and frustration to his family. They were only trying to be helpful, he said. This situation creates a classical dilemma. A systematic approach to help family members disengage from pain reinforcing behavior combined with encouraging the patients to find their physical limits usually works. The situation can get enormously complicated if the spouse is invested in maintaining and indeed encouraging dependency in the patient. In Mr. C's case there might have been such an element. All our efforts to engage Mrs. C and the daughter met with much resistance and in fact, they never came. The pain clinic staff did what they could to encourage and boost Mr. C's morale and increase his level of activity. These efforts, however, were basically undone by his loved ones.

TREATMENT ISSUES

The first two patients responded well to treatment. Mr. and Mrs. A surprised themselves by their capacity for compromise and change. In the course of treatment, they virtually renegotiated their marriage. Maintaining space, yet finding common interest was at the heart of their therapeutic pursuit. The Problem Centered Approach to couple therapy, a method widely employed by this author to treat chronic pain patients and their families, has its emphasis on the family or couple defining their own problems as well as seeking their resolution. It has a special appeal for many individuals, especially those who tend to be self-directed and savor the challenge of overcoming odds (Roy, 1989). Mr. and Mrs. A agreed that they had a marriage worth saving. They agreed that Mr. A would abide by the house rules. The rules he did not approve could be renegotiated. Mrs. A would respect Mr. A's somewhat slackened attitude to clothes.

Mrs. B's sudden and medically unexplainable deterioration of pain was on reflection not so inexplicable. Rather, negative life events had intruded in her life. She stopped taking her medication. In the pain literature an association has also been found between negative life events and onset of a new pain problem or deterioration of an existing pain condition (Roy, 1992). Another point of note was that her support system was on the verge of disappearance with both her husband and son becoming ill. Loss of support is a major cause for depression in older adults. A rather striking point about this case was the presence of a host of clinical and conceptually sound hypotheses that could so easily account for the changes in Mrs. B's pain condition. Mrs. B responded very well to supportive psychotherapy, the principal focus of which was to help her deal with her real and potential losses.

The treatment issues in Mr. C's case were self-evident. He was simply kept in the chronic sick role 'for his own good' by people who truly cared for him. Since the family members could not be engaged in treatment, the second and rather unsatisfactory choice was to help him to find his right level of functioning. The outcome was less than satisfactory.

These three cases were selected to emphasize that the problems in family relations faced by elderly pain patients were often unrelated to their age. The issues faced by these three patients are indeed commonly observed in the more traditional 40 plus year old somewhat prototypical chronic pain patient. Perhaps, there has been too much of a tendency in the recent past to view the elderly patient as a breed apart. This population was homogenized, their critical faculties under rated, their health viewed as universally deteriorating and their emotions and intelligence completely at the mercy of rapidly dying brain cells. Of course, nothing could be further from the truth. On the other hand, it will be naive to assume that old age and chronic pain do not give rise to some special problems. One specific situation which is faced on a regular basis by this author is when both partners have chronic pain problems, a common situation in old age. Here the burden of family responsibility generally tends to fall on the wife.

Space does not permit a comprehensive examination of the problems of conducting a family or couple assessment involving an elderly pain sufferer. Norms established by standard measures of family functioning often exclude the elderly population. Chronic illness is another dimension that requires reorganization of family roles and functions not readily recognized by the proponents of effective or healthy family functioning. The unfortunate combination of old age and chronic pain requires adjustments in family functioning that are often at considerable variance with the 'ideal' (Roy, 1990). Nevertheless, a close scrutiny of these couples and families often reveals the desirability of the family equilibrium achieved through trial and error and lack of choice. For example, the wife of Mr. D, a 73 year old man with multiple and debilitating pain problems, refused to involve him in the day to day management of the household and carried a lion's share of the roles and tasks, from cleaning the house to balancing the books. She relied more on her son to provide practical help. The arrangement was satisfactory to all parties. An argument can be made, however, that on the basis of this or that method of family assessment, the role distribution in this family was unfair or that decision making on the part of Mrs. D was autocratic. Both conclusions would be erroneous. In fact, a more plausible and realistic view of the situation would be that without her willingness to assume those responsibilities, this family would have either disintegrated or presented almost insurmountable problems for the caregivers. Equity or equality was not the issue between the couple. The most important consideration was the availability of support for the wife to enable her to bear the extra burden.

CONCLUSIONS

The central purpose of this paper has been to demonstrate that elderly chronic pain sufferers merit as much as anyone else of having their family situation explored and therapeutic measures implemented if problems are identified. Problems are often influenced by the age factor. It is the same factor, however, that deters adoption of psychological therapies for the elderly patient. On the other hand, it is acknowledged that many of the relationship issues of elderly pain sufferers are the same as those of younger patients, justification for denying psychological intervention may not be so self-evident. Exploration of interpersonal issues needs to be incorporated as part of routine investigation with elderly patients. Adoption of psychological interventions with them is equally imperative. Ageism is no justification for denying the elderly pain patient the benefits of psychotherapy.

REFERENCES

Ahern, D., Adams, A. & Follick, M. (1985). Emotional and marital disturbance in spouses of chronic low-back pain patients. *Clinical Journal of Pain, 1*, 69-74

Bishop, D., Epstein, N., Keitner, G., Miller, I., & Srinivasan, S. (1986). Stroke: Morale, family functioning, health status and function capacity. *Archives of Physical Medicine and Rehabilitation, 67*, 84-87.

Chenworth, B., & Spencer, B. (1986). Dementia: The experience of family caregivers. *The Gerontologist, 26*, 267-272.

Cook, A., & Roy, R. (in press). Attitudes, beliefs and illness behavior. In R. Roy (Ed.), *Chronic pain in old age: A biopsychosocial perspective*. Toronto: University of Toronto Press.

Edinberg, M. (1985). *Mental health practice with the elderly*. Englewood Cliffs, NJ: Prentice Hall.

Epstein, N., & Bishop, D. (1981). Problem-centered systems therapy for the family. In A. Gurman & D. Kniskern (Eds.), *Handbook of family therapy* (pp. 444-482). New York: Brunner/Mazel.

Feurstein, M., Sult, S., & Houle, M. (1985). Environmental stressors and chronic low back pain. *Pain, 22*, 295-307.

Flor, H., Turk, D., & Rudy, T. (1987). Pain and families: Assessment and treatment. *Pain, 30*, 29-46.

Flor, H., Turk, D., & Scholz, O. (1987). Impact of chronic pain on the spouse: Marital, emotional and physical consequences. *Journal of Psychosomatic Research, 31*, 63-72.

George, L., & Gwyther, L. (1986). Caregiver well-being: A multidimensional examination of family caregivers of demented adults. *The Gerontologist, 26,* 253-259.

Hughston, G., Christopherson, V., & Bonjean, M. (1989). Aging and family therapy: An introduction. *Journal of Psychotherapy and Family, 5,* 1-12.

Kerns, R., & Turk, D. (1984). Chronic pain and depression: Mediating role of the spouse. *Journal of Marriage and Family, 46,* 845-852.

Lasoski, M. (1986). Reasons for low utilization of mental health services by the elderly. *Clinical Gerontologist, 5,* 1-18.

Madanes, C. (1981). *Strategic family therapy.* San Francisco: Jossey-Bass.

Maruta, T., & Osborne, D. (1978). Sexual activity in chronic pain patients. *Psychosomatics, 20,* 241-248.

Maruta, T., Osborne, D., Swanson, D., & Halling, H. (1981). Chronic pain patients and spouses: Marital and sexual adjustment. *Mayo Clinic Proceedings, 51,* 307-310.

Mohamed, S., Weisz, G., & Waring, E. (1978). The relationship of chronic pain to depression, marital and family dynamics. *Pain, 5,* 282-292.

Olson, D., Portnoy, J., & Lavee, Y. (1985). *FACES III: Family Social Science.* St. Paul, MN: University of Minnesota Press.

Ouslander, J. (1982). Physical illness and depression in the elderly. *Journal of American Geriatric Society, 30,* 593-599.

Poulshock, S., & Deimling, G. (1984). Families caring for elders in residence: Issues in management of burden. *Journal of Gerontology, 39,* 230-239.

Ratna, L., & Davies, J. (1984). Family therapy with the elderly mentally ill: Some strategies and techniques. *British Journal of Psychiatry, 145,* 311-315.

Romano, J., & Turner, J. (1985). Chronic pain and depression: Does the evidence support a relationship? *Psychological Bulletin, 97,* 18-34.

Rowat, K., & Knafl, K. (1985). Living with chronic pain: The spouses' perspective. *Pain, 23,* 259-271.

Roy, R. (Unpublished Manuscript). Chronic pain, old age and couple functioning. University of Manitoba, Winnipeg.

Roy, R. (1986). Marital conflicts and exacerbation of headache: Some clinical observations. *Headache, 26,* 360-364.

Roy, R. (1988). Impact of chronic pain on the family: A systems perspective. In R. Dubner, G. Gebhart, & M. Bond (Eds.), *Proceedings of the 5th World Congress on pain.* Amsterdam: Elsevier.

Roy, R. (1989). *Chronic pain and the family: A problem-centered perspective.* New York: Human Sciences Press.

Roy, R. (1990). Chronic pain and 'effective' family functioning: A re-examination of the McMaster Model of Family Functioning. *Contemporary Family Therapy, 12,* 489-503.

Roy, R. (1992). *The social context of chronic pain sufferer.* Toronto: University of Toronto Press.

Roy, R. (in press). Family therapy with the elderly chronic pain patient. In R. Roy

(Ed.), *Chronic pain in old age: A biopsychosocial perspective.* Toronto: University of Toronto Press.

Roy, R., & Thomas, M. (1987a). Elderly persons with and without pain: A comparative study. *Clinical Journal of Pain, 3,* 102-106.

Roy, R., & Thomas, M. (1987b). Pain, depression and illness behavior in a group of community based elderly persons: Elderly persons with and without pain. *Clinical Journal of Pain, 3,* 207-211.

Roy, R., & Thomas, M. (1989). Chronic pain and marriage relations: An empirical investigation. *Contemporary Family Therapy, 11,* 277-285.

Roy, R., Thomas, M., & Berger, S. (1990). A comparison of British and Canadian pain subjects. *Clinical Journal of Pain, 6,* 276-283.

Shanas, E. (1984). Old parents and middle age children: The four and five generation family. *Journal of Geriatric Society, 17,* 7-19.

Sorkin, B., Rudy, T., Hanlon, R., Turk, D., & Steig, R. (1990). Chronic pain in old and young persons: Differences appear less important than similarities. *Journal of Gerontology: Psychological Sciences, 45,* P64-P68.

Steuer, J. (1982). Psychotherapy with the elderly. *Psychiatric Clinic of North America, 5,* 199-213.

Thomas, M., & Roy, R. (1989). Pain patients and marital relations. *Clinical Journal of Pain, 5,* 359-362.

Vendendries, G. (in press). A geriatrician's personal view on pain management in the elderly. In R. Roy (Ed.), *Chronic pain in old age: A biopsychosocial perspective.* Toronto: University of Toronto Press.

Nonpharmacologic Interventions for the Management of Chronic Pain in Older Women

Paula R. Mobily, PhD, RN

SUMMARY. Chronic pain can induce tremendous suffering, seriously affect the quality of life, and impair optimal daily functioning in older adults. Advances in the conceptualization and treatment of pain support the use of a multimodal approach to pain management incorporating both pharmacologic and nonpharmacologic interventions for the most effective management of chronic pain. Nonpharmacologic interventions, used concomitantly with pharmacologic approaches, typically result in more effective pain control, less reliance on medications, fewer side effects, less clinical impairment and an increased sense of personal control over pain.

In the past, chronic pain was thought to be an inevitable concomitant of aging and something that simply must be tolerated. More recently this view is being challenged and quality of life is becoming an increasingly important issue for those who work with older adults. Chronic pain can induce suffering and seriously affect the quality of life of elderly persons; however, there is growing recognition that older adults can benefit tremendously from more aggressive management of the chronic pain they experience. Advances in

---

Paula R. Mobily is Assistant Professor, The University of Iowa, College of Nursing, 388 NB, Iowa City, IA 52242.

[Haworth co-indexing entry note]: "Nonpharmacologic Interventions for the Management of Chronic Pain in Older Women." Mobily, Paula R. Co-published simultaneously in *Journal of Women & Aging* (The Haworth Press, Inc.) Vol. 6, No. 4, 1994, pp. 89-109; and: *Older Women with Chronic Pain* (ed: Karen A. Roberto) The Haworth Press, Inc., 1994, pp. 89-109. Multiple copies of this article/chapter may be purchased from The Haworth Document Delivery Center [1-800-3-HAWORTH; 9:00 a.m. - 5:00 p.m. (EST)].

the conceptualization and treatment of pain support the use of a multimodal approach, incorporating both pharmacologic and non-pharmacologic interventions, for the most effective management of chronic pain in this population.

Traditionally, the principle approach in treating chronic pain has been pharmacologic. However, nonpharmacologic interventions have particular value in the management of pain in the elderly population and interest in their use is increasing. Pharmacologic management of pain for older adults is often complicated by age-related physiologic changes affecting pharmacokinetics and pharmacodynamics, problems of polypharmacy, and idiosyncratic drug reactions (Butler & Gastel, 1980; Ferrell, 1991; Harkins, Kwentus & Price, 1984; Portenoy & Farkash, 1988). Older adults are more sensitive to the effects of narcotic analgesics and can more easily develop toxic side effects, including pseudodementia, because of pharmacokinetic changes leading to relatively long half-lives of these drugs (Cohen, 1986; Kaiko, Wallenstein, Rogers, Brabinski & Houde, 1982). Nonpharmacologic interventions, used in combination with pharmacologic approaches will result in more effective pain control, less reliance on medications, fewer side effects and less clinical impairment (Ferrell, 1991; Foley, 1990; Middaugh, Levin, Kee, Barchiesi & Roberts, 1988; Owens & Ehrenreich, 1991). It should be noted, however, that nonpharmacologic methods are adjunctive therapies and, for most chronic pain problems, are not substitutes for pharmacologic treatment.

Many pain specialists and geriatricians advocate the use of nonpharmacologic techniques for elderly clients (Butler & Gastel, 1980; Harkins et al., 1984; Hunt, 1980; Ferrell, 1991; Kwentus, Harkins, Lignon & Silverman, 1985), but health care providers often perceive older adults to be indifferent or unwilling to use cognitive-behavioral nonpharmacologic interventions, in particular (Portenoy & Farkash, 1988). Nonetheless, empirical evidence reveals that older patients often are very responsive to these interventions. In a study comparing characteristics of younger and older chronic pain patients, Sorkin and colleagues (1990) found that older individuals were equally as likely to report the use of physical nonpharmacologic techniques for pain relief (e.g., TENS, heat, massage), but less likely to report use of cognitive-behavioral nonpharmacologic techniques (e.g., relaxation, imagery, distraction) than their younger counterparts. However, they found that elderly clients were as likely as younger clients to accept and complete treatments involving both physical and cognitive-behavioral strategies. They contend that age should not be a significant consideration when offering clients multimodal treatment for chronic pain that focuses on cognitive-behavioral as well as physical nonpharmacologic modalities.

Similarly, in a study of the responses of geriatric and younger clients to a multidisciplinary chronic pain rehabilitation program including both physical and cognitive-behavioral interventions, Middaugh et al. (1988) found that geriatric clients can benefit from these programs at least as much, if not more, than younger patients, and that there were no differences in response to treatment between women and men. Further, they note that older clients are often more interested and more compliant than their younger counterparts, are often more realistic in their expectations, are willing to work hard for degrees of improvement, and are also relatively free of work-related issues that hinder progress for younger patients.

Mention of these studies is not meant to imply that there will not be individual differences in the acceptance and use of nonpharmacologic interventions. Cognitive-behavioral strategies, in particular, often necessitate continuous effort by the client in order to be effective and require clients to have a greater degree of confidence in their ability to manage their pain through their own personal skills and resources. Not all clients will have the personal desire for control or the self-efficacy for managing their own pain and will prefer using externally mediated nonpharmacologic strategies such as those classified here as cutaneous stimulation interventions. Many of the cognitive-behavioral techniques described, such as relaxation and imagery, require high levels of cognitive function. This must be a consideration in the selection and use of appropriate strategies. Finally, other factors important in selecting interventions for managing chronic pain for older adults include the pathophysiologic basis of the pain, functional status, social and financial support and developed coping strategies (Ferrell & Ferrell, 1991; Portenoy & Farkash, 1988).

It must be noted that, in general, very limited empirical data exists on the use of nonpharmacologic interventions for older adults, and virtually no data addresses gender-related differences in use or outcomes. Because of these limitations, the discussion that follows addresses nonpharmacologic management of pain for older adults, in general, and will address, specifically, interventions with available empirical and clinical data that reveal special considerations relevant to elderly women.

THEORETICAL FRAMEWORK:
THE GATE CONTROL THEORY OF PAIN

Although the state of scientific knowledge related to pain continues to evolve, the Gate Control Theory of Pain, formulated and later modified by Melzack and Wall (1965, 1982), provides a powerful theoretical basis for the use of multimodal interventions for pain management. In essence, pain is recognized as a complex, multidimensional experience interrelating three components: the sensory-discriminative (physical); the affective-motivational (psychological); and the cognitive-interpretive (cognitive) aspects of the individual's perception. This theory acknowledges the interplay of the dorsal horn, the brain stem and the cerebral cortex in modulating, enhancing and integrating the experience of pain.

According to the Gate Control Theory, there is a gating mechanism in the dorsal horn of the spinal cord that allows pain to be reduced or modulated at four points: (1) the peripheral site of pain; (2) in the spinal cord itself; (3) in the brain stem; and (4) in the cerebral cortex. Use of nonnarcotic analgesics, application of heat and cold, and local anesthetics can alter the release of nociceptive substances and decrease accompanying muscle spasm at the peripheral site of pain. In the spinal cord, direct electrical stimulation, massage, and application of heat and cold can stimulate large nerve fibers thereby interfering with transmission of pain impulses. Interventions that can effectively reduce or eliminate the transmission of pain impulses in the brain stem include electrical stimulation, acupuncture, and administration of narcotic analgesics. Finally, cognitive-behavioral techniques such as cognitive therapy, relaxation, imagery, music therapy, distraction, and hypnosis, as well as administration of narcotic and narcotic antagonist analgesics, are interventions that work primarily through action in the cerebral cortex (Donovan, 1989). This broader perspective of pain has provided powerful rationale for using both pharmacologic and nonpharmacologic interventions in the management of chronic pain.

COGNITIVE-BEHAVIORAL INTERVENTIONS

Cognitive-behavioral interventions are relatively new strategies for managing chronic pain, but they are becoming more integral components of pain management. Theoretical postulates, as well as clinical and empirical data (Slater & Good, 1991; Turner & Romano, 1990), indicate that these can be very beneficial in the management of chronic pain, including older adults with chronic pain (Applebaum, Blanchard, Hickling, & Alfonso, 1988; Carstensen, 1988). The cognitive-behavioral approach to managing chronic pain focuses on elements involved in helping the client to cope with the pain being experienced by altering the interpretation of the sensation of pain and enhancing self control (Miller & Jay, 1990). Cognitive-behavioral interventions, including cognitive therapy, relaxation, imagery, distraction, hypnosis and biofeedback, offer a variety of techniques to help those suffering from chronic pain better understand their individual psychological and social responses to pain and to develop effective coping responses (Saxon, 1991).

Despite increasing evidence of the efficacy of cognitive-behavioral interventions in the management of chronic pain, older adults are often considered poor candidates for their use and are seldom given ample opportunity to benefit from them (Portenoy & Farkash, 1988). Certainly, factors must be considered that would compromise cooperation with therapy including cognitive deficits and expressed mistrust of psychologic formulations, as well as financial limitations that would limit long-term involvement with health care professionals. Although it is likely that these factors would eliminate a proportion of elderly persons with chronic pain, empirical data (Keefe & Williams, 1990; Middaugh et al., 1988; Sorkin et al., 1990) and clinical experience suggest that many elderly clients are willing to try cognitive-behavioral interventions and can benefit from them. Advanced age alone should not preclude the use of these techniques.

Cognitive-behavioral interventions can be classified into five general categories (Sturgis, Dolce & Dickerson, 1987):

1. Techniques that alter physical function and improve the over-all level of functioning such as relaxation training, autogenic training, and biofeedback;
2. Contingency or behavior modification programs that involve application of learning principles to increase the use of ap-propriate pain management behaviors and decrease use of fre-quency of inappropriate pain-maintaining behaviors;
3. Psychological techniques and interventions to help reduce the impact of affective or emotional factors contributing to pain such as anxiety, depression, frustration, anger and irritation;
4. Behavioral techniques and interventions that teach the client how to pace activities to control pain since overexertion and fatigue contribute to pain perception; and
5. Coping and adaptive strategies and skills to manage pain and potentially painful situations.

Comprehensive discussion of all of the cognitive-behavioral modal-ities available is beyond the scope of this paper. The following discussion focuses on three general interventions known to be ef-fective in the management of chronic pain for elderly persons: cognitive therapy, relaxation therapy and imagery.

Cognitive Therapy

Chronic pain is more than just a sensory experience. Due to the interplay of cognitive, behavioral, affective and contextual vari-ables, chronic pain is often accompanied by debilitating emotional and behavioral symptoms including depression, anger, activity avoidance, substance abuse, and family discord. As noted previous-ly, cognitive factors contribute to an individual's appraisal of the chronic pain experience that, in turn, influences how the individual perceives and subsequently responds to pain. Many of the problems noted above can be traced to ineffective or otherwise self-defeating methods of coping with pain and/or pain-related disability (Ciccone & Grzesiak, 1988).

Cognitive therapy for pain control refers to interventions or strategies that influence pain through the use of the individual's thoughts or cognitions (Edgar & Smith-Hanrahan, 1992). The goal of these interventions is to modify or prevent maladaptive thoughts and appraisals associated with the pain experience, i.e., "to effect a profound and lasting change in the way (clients) think about pain" (Ciccone & Grzesiak, 1988, p. 159). Attention is focused on identifying and replacing dysfunctional beliefs and distorted information processing. Information from the higher centers of the brain affects the pain gate in the dorsal horn of the spinal column, therefore, emotional states and cognitions affect the actual perception of pain and consequently play an important part in the overall experience of pain.

A variety of techniques can be used in working with elderly individuals with maladaptive or dysfunctional responses to the chronic pain experience including cognitive restructuring, self-statement training, stress inoculation training, and problem-solving techniques. Cognitive strategies often incorporate a three-phased approach to implementation: (a) reconceptualization of pain and awareness of how pain has controlled thoughts, feelings and beliefs; (b) application of one or more new, more effective cognitive approaches and coping strategies; and (c) rehearsal of cognitive strategies until ease and proficiency is reached and pain is more effectively controlled (Weisenberg, 1987). The reader is referred to the works of Ciccone and Grzesiak (1988); Fordyce (1976); Hanson and Gerber (1992); Lazarus and Folkmann (1984); Keefe and colleagues (1990); and Turk, Meichenbaum, and Genest (1983) for a more comprehensive discussion of specific techniques.

Little empirical data on the effectiveness of cognitive therapy for older adults or age-related outcomes is available. In a study involving older adults, Puder (1988) evaluated the effects of a 10 week training program that incorporated cognitive therapy. Results indicated that the treatment decreased the interference of pain on activity, increased individual ability to cope with pain, and decreased use of some medications. Because age was found to be unrelated to outcomes, Puder advocates the use of cognitive therapy for management of chronic pain for adults of all ages. Similarly, studies by Parker and colleagues (1988) and O'Leary, Shoor, Lorig and Holman (1988), incorporating large numbers of elderly clients, evaluated the effects of cognitive treatments for rheumatoid arthritis and demonstrated improvements in multiple pain-related outcomes such as psychological functioning, functional status, and confidence in personal ability to manage pain. No gender-related differences were reported in these studies. As noted by Portenoy and Farkash (1988) and Helme and Katz (1993), compelling evidence exists that maladaptive behaviors can be identified and successfully targeted for change through a systematic program of cognitive interventions. These techniques can have a substantial impact on the experience of pain and the degree of psychological, social and physical impairment experienced.

Relaxation Therapy

One of the cognitive-behavioral approaches most frequently used for managing chronic pain is relaxation therapy. Chronic pain, by its very definition, implies a chronically stressful experience. Stress reactions often lead to autonomic and/or muscular responses associated with painful sensations. Noxious sensations, in turn, can cause muscle spasms, constriction of blood vessels resulting in decreased blood flow to tissues, and secretion of pain-producing substances that can cause or augment existing pain (McCafferey & Beebe, 1989; Ross, Keefe, & Gil, 1988). The emotional response to these occurrences can further exacerbate the physical response contributing to a spiral of pain, anxiety and muscle tension. Interventions that promote relaxation are effective in reducing or modulating pain by interrupting this spiral of events. In addition to managing pain, anxiety, and muscle tension, associated benefits of relaxation interventions include the improvement of sleep problems associated with chronic pain, decreased fatigue, enhanced sense of personal control over the pain, and enhanced mood (Haley & Dolce, 1986; McCafferey & Beebe, 1989). A variety of different relaxation interventions are available, including such techniques as progressive muscle relaxation, passive muscle relaxation, autogenic training, biofeedback, meditation and self hypnosis, among others. Three techniques, progressive muscle relaxation, passive muscle relaxation, and autogenic training seem to be most effective for elderly chronic pain clients.

Progressive Muscle Relaxation (PMR). Progressive muscle relaxation (PMR), a systematic technique of tensing and releasing of gross muscle groups while attending to the differences in sensation between tension and relaxation (Bernstein & Borkovek, 1973), is frequently used for managing chronic pain. Two skills are important for effective use of this intervention: the ability to discriminate between tensed and non-tensed muscles, and the ability to control the amount of tension by relaxing specific muscle groups. Through PMR, clients become more aware of, and therefore more in control of, their tension levels. PMR was originally developed by Jacobsen (1938); however, his approach is long and often impractical in clinical use. Jacobsen's technique was refined and shortened by Bernstein and Borkovek (1973). Since then, numerous alternative procedures have been developed incorporating alternative methods for relaxing muscle groups, alternative muscle groups to be relaxed, variable numbers of training sessions, practice sessions, and sessions required for effectiveness, and the role of the instructor (live versus taped instructions). Excellent discussion of techniques can be found in training manuals by Bernstein and Borkovek (1973) and McCafferey and Beebe (1989).

Progressive muscle relaxation is not appropriate for all clients. In particular, clients with conditions in which muscle tensing might produce physiologically injurious consequences are not candidates for PMR. These conditions include neck or back orthopedic injuries in which hyperextension of the upper spine creates pain and could further complicate the condition; and clients with increased intracranial pressure, capillary fragility, bleeding tendencies, or severe acute cardiac difficulties with hypertension (Scandrett & Uecker, 1992; Snyder, 1992).

Passive Muscle Relaxation. For those clients in which PMR is contraindicated, an alternative form of this technique, known as focused or passive muscle relaxation is appropriate. Passive muscle relaxation is similar to PMR, but without active contraction of muscle groups (Bernstein & Borkovek, 1973). This technique often proves valuable for those who have increased pain with tensing of muscles, or dislike the feelings of tension involved in PMR. Clinical experience suggests that elderly clients, in particular, may respond more positively to passive muscle relaxation because of increased pain elicited by inducing muscle tension.

Autogenic training. An alternative form of relaxation for chronic pain is autogenic training (Schultz & Luthe, 1969). This technique generally involves suggestion of the relaxed feelings of heaviness and warmth. The sensation of heaviness has been found to correlate with relaxation of muscles and warmth is associated with a psycho-physiologic perception of the vasodilation of the peripheral vessels (Schultz & Luthe, 1969). Thus, autogenic training results in increased blood flow to the extremities and an increased sense of warmness or heaviness, thereby inducing relaxation and reduction of pain (Catalano, 1987). This technique may be particularly suited to elderly chronic pain sufferers since it involves passive relaxation rather than the tensing and releasing of muscles that often exacerbates pain.

A critical aspect of the appropriate use of relaxation is an appreciation of its limits. Relaxation is most appropriate as an adjunctive intervention for chronic pain management. Relaxation interventions alone rarely will be effective enough for the successful management of chronic pain; they should not be used as a substitute for other therapies that might more directly attenuate pain. Moreover, these interventions are difficult to use when pain is severe and focusing attention on bodily tension or pain actually may heighten the individual's perception of pain rather than reducing it (Snyder, 1992).

Empirical support for the use of relaxation for elderly chronic pain patients is provided by a number of studies. In an investigation of patient preferences for pain treatment modalities following a 28-day pain treatment program that included elderly subjects, Kleinke (1987) found that relaxation therapy was the intervention most liked and was significantly correlated with pain reduction. Although the data were not analyzed based on preference and outcome by age and gender, Kleinke concluded that since relaxation therapy was uniformly favored and correlated with reduction of pain, it can be recommended as an integral modality for individualized treatment programs. The value of relaxation therapies in the management of chronic pain can be found in comprehensive analyses of empirical studies by Hyman and colleagues (1989), Linton (1986), and Malone and Strub (1988). Again, the reader is cautioned that age and gender-related outcomes are seldom addressed.

Clinical experience suggests, however, that in working with elderly clients, simple or brief relaxation techniques may be more acceptable and more beneficial.

Imagery

In the context of pain management, imagery is using one's imagination to develop an image or images to modify or relieve pain. Imagery can take two distinctly different approaches: directed toward the pain, with the emphasis on transforming the pain; or directed away from pain as the client uses imagination to concentrate on a situation in which pain is not present. Fernandez (1986) classified pain management strategies involving imagery by the nature of the images that can be evoked: (a) incompatible emotive imagery in which imagery is used to create emotions incompatible with pain (e.g., images that arouse humor or self-assertiveness); (b) incompatible sensory imagery in which individuals evoke "pure" sensory sensations not associated with emotions (e.g., imaging grassy, green meadows or the gentle warmth of the sun); and (c) transformative imagery where the features of pain are transformed or altered (e.g., imagining pain as a color and converting it to another less intense color, transforming pain into a fantasy object such as a bird and have it fly from the body and out of sight, or imaging a ball of healing energy that is circulated in the area of pain and takes away the sensation of pain). Although imagery can involve all five senses, often visual or auditory images are more easily used for the management of chronic pain (Sodergren, 1992). Relaxation usually precedes and/or accompanies imagery thereby facilitating image development and contributing to pain management by decreasing muscle tension and anxiety. Excellent presentation and discussion of specific training techniques can be found in the works of McCafferey and Beebe (1989) and Turk, Meichenbaum, and Genest (1983).

Imagery can be either self-guided or other-guided. Empirical support is variable with respect to which approach is more beneficial for chronic pain management. Clinical experience suggests that elderly clients may prefer other-guided imagery provided directly by the health professional or made available through taped recordings since they often prefer to be more passive participants in their health care. Although many clients will relate easily to visualization and imagery techniques, others do not. Some elderly clients may be unwilling to use imagery because they do not think they have the ability, fear lack of control, or are uncomfortable with psychologic formations. The ability to use imagination techniques, the willingness of the client to be guided in them, and the motivation to practice are critical factors for the successful use of this technique.

Although there is considerable support for the use of imagery in the management of chronic pain in general, data are quite limited with respect to using imagery for managing chronic pain in older adults. Hamm and King (1984) investigated the effects of guided imagery in a sample of elderly chronic pain sufferers. Following a 13 week trial, subjects using guided imagery reported a significant decrease in mean pain intensity. A study by Davis and colleagues (1990) of pain management techniques used by individuals with rheumatoid arthritis and osteoarthritis revealed that only 32 percent of those over 65 years of age reported using imagery, and younger adults were significantly more likely to identify this technique as helpful. However, the investigators maintain that this finding may be related more to level of exposure to this method rather than the ability or willingness of the older adult to use it. Based on support for this technique with younger chronic pain sufferers, as well as the reported effectiveness of imagery for other symptoms in older adults, they suggest greater use and testing of this technique for the older adult with chronic pain. Given that imagery has proven effective in managing chronic pain; and since it can be used independently, is minimally time consuming, low risk, and inexpensive, consideration of its use as an adjunctive therapy is certainly warranted in individual cases.

CUTANEOUS STIMULATION INTERVENTIONS

Cutaneous stimulation is an important noninvasive method for managing chronic pain that involves stimulating the skin and underlying tissues in order to moderate or relieve pain. A variety of different modalities, such as the application of thermal agents, transcutaneous electrical nerve stimulation (TENS), and massage are commonly used cutaneous stimulation interventions. In general, the Gate Control Theory suggests that cutaneous stimulation interventions reduce pain by interfering with the transmission of pain impulses through activation of the large diameter fibers that close the gate to pain messages carried by small fibers. It is also postulated that certain types of cutaneous stimulation may increase release of endogenous opiates (endorphins), thereby decreasing pain (McCafferey & Beebe, 1989). Used as adjunctive modalities, these interventions can be effective for the immediate reduction of pain during stimulation and also for varying periods following stimulation.

As noted by McCafferey and Beebe (1989), the importance of cutaneous stimulation interventions for the management of pain in older adults cannot be overstated. Not only can these methods be very beneficial in managing chronic pain, but they are easily performed, inexpensive, and noninjurious to the client when used properly; and they can readily be taught to the client and/or significant others enabling them to use many of these interventions independently. Selection of the site(s) most appropriate for cutaneous stimulation is an important consideration for their ultimate effectiveness. These techniques are effective not only when applied directly to the site of pain, but they can be extremely effective when applied to a site distal to, proximal to, or contralateral to the site of pain, as well as to trigger points, or on or around acupuncture or acupressure points.

Thermal Agents

A wide range of thermal agents, incorporating both heat and cold, is available for the management of chronic pain including hot and cold packs, hydrotherapy (i.e., tub baths or shower sprays), and paraffin baths (i.e., application of heat to a specific area by immersion in paraffin), as well as those agents requiring more sophisticated equipment such as infrared therapy, shortwave diathermy, microwave diathermy and ultrasound. In addition to stimulating large fibers to close the pain gate, thermal agents can produce analgesia via other mechanisms as well.

Heat can indirectly reduce pain through vasodilation resulting in improved tissue nutrition and elimination of cellular metabolites that stimulate pain impulses (Mehta, 1986). This can be especially helpful following an acute inflammatory response. When muscle spasm is the source of pain, heat is thought to effect gamma fiber activity in the muscle resulting in a decrease in the sensitivity of the muscle spindle to stretch. Further, heat can trigger pain-inhibiting reflexes through temperature receptors (Lehmann & DeLateur, 1982a). Finally, application of heat over a peripheral nerve can directly reduce pain by increasing pain threshold (Michlovitz, 1990).

Cold, or cryotherapy, is thought to produce analgesia through multiple mechanisms as well. Cryotherapy reduces pain by slowing the conduction velocity and synaptic activity of small unmyelinated fibers that conduct pain impulses from peripheral sites, by decreasing muscle tone and spasticity, and by decreasing release of pain-inducing chemicals when applied to a recently injured area (Lehmann & DeLateur, 1982b; Michlovitz, 1990).

Central to the use of therapeutic heat and cold for older adults is recognition of factors contributing to increased risk of thermal injury including: (a) decreased reactivity of the hypothalamic thermoregulatory system; (b) decreased autonomic and vasomotor responses; (c) atrophy of the skin with reduction in circulation; loss of sweat glands; and (d) decreased perception of thermal gradients (Kauffman, 1987). Other considerations are warranted as well. Heating of large body surfaces and the resulting vasodilation may place hazardous demands on cardiac output (Kauffman, 1987). Conversely, cold can produce a temporary increase in systolic and diastolic blood pressure which can pose a risk for hypertensive clients (Michlovitz, 1990). Additionally, cold applications are contraindicated for elderly clients with arterial insufficiency due to peripheral vascular disease (McCafferey & Beebe, 1989). Finally, mechanical stiffness of joints, aversion to cold, and cold intolerance may limit applications of cold with some older clients. Many of these concerns can be alleviated with careful selection and precautionary use of these thermal modalities. In general, operating temperatures for heating agents should be lowered for use with elderly clients while those for cooling agents should be raised. Both hot and cold packs may require additional insulation with greater thickness of dry toweling and treatment times may need to be shortened.

Research examining the effectiveness of thermal agents in controlling chronic pain has been relatively extensive; however, there are few studies that have included elderly individuals specifically. In general, treatment effectiveness for thermal agents used for managing joint pains from osteoarthritis and rheumatoid arthritis has been demonstrated with elderly clients (Barr, 1993). In addition to demonstrated effectiveness, the study of pain management for older adults with rheumatoid arthritis and osteoarthritis by Davis and colleagues (1990) cited earlier, found that heat application and use of a heated pool, tub or shower was one of the four methods identified by older adults as most helpful in relieving pain. Clinical practice indicates that cold is often more effective in managing chronic pain, particularly pain related to muscle or joint pathology. Moreover, alternating heat and cold, such as with contrast bathing, is often more effective than the use of either alone. Given the effectiveness of cold, in particular, its use for elderly clients is warranted and should be encouraged despite potential reluctance of the client to do so.

TENS

Transcutaneous electrical nerve stimulation (TENS) involves the stimulation of cutaneous and peripheral nerves via electrodes on the surface of the skin. TENS can be a very effective adjunctive intervention for the management of chronic pain in elderly clients. This intervention has been found to be effective for relief of low back pain, diabetic neuropathies, shoulder pain or bursitis, fractured ribs, postherapeutic neuralgia, myofascial pain, phantom limb pain and advanced painful malignancies among others (Ferrell & Ferrell, 1991; Hunt, 1980; Jay & Miller, 1990; Kwentus et al., 1985; Portenoy & Farkash, 1988; Thorsteinsson, 1987). However, well-controlled studies assessing control of chronic pain with long term use for older adults are sorely lacking.

TENS generally falls into two categories: conventional TENS and acupuncture-like TENS. Conventional stimulation preferentially activates low threshold primary afferent fibers thereby inhibiting transmission of nociceptive information in the dorsal horn of the spinal cord. The higher intensity acupuncture-like TENS activates not only low threshold primary afferents, but also small diameter nociceptive primary afferents thought to produce a type of counterirritation in which one noxious stimulus inhibits pain produced by another (Bushnell, Marchand, Trembley, & Duncan, 1991). It is also thought that TENS may activate deep fibers followed by endorphin release in some cases.

Although there are few side effects when using TENS, there are some special considerations for its use. TENS therapy is contraindicated for clients using demand-type synchronous cardiac pacemakers. Further, it has been suggested that electrical stimulation be avoided on the anterior chest of clients with cardiac histories, over the carotid sinuses, or over the larynx (Mannheimer & Lampe, 1984). In order for TENS therapy to be effective, it is critical that the client or their significant other(s) be thoroughly trained. Although this is true for all clients, it is especially true for use with elderly clients. Many older adults, and particularly older women, are uncomfortable using an electrical device and will not utilize it effectively without encouragement and careful instruction.

Important parameters in using TENS are selection of the best site(s) for placement of electrodes (i.e., directly over the pain, acupuncture points, spinal nerve roots, proximal or contralateral sites) and adjustment of the electrical current amplitude and pulse pattern. Meticulous searching and adjustment may be necessary for optimum pain control, often requiring an experienced therapist to initiate therapy and train clients or their caregivers. When considering TENS therapy for older adults, a thorough, carefully controlled trial period is recommended, typically a month or longer. Other important variables are that the TENS unit selected be "user friendly" and that all of the hardware, software and repair services necessary be readily available (Barr, 1993).

A number of additional cutaneous stimulation techniques can be effective in managing chronic pain including massage, acupressure and vibration. Readers interested in a comprehensive discussion of these techniques are referred to McCafferey and Beebe (1989).

CONCLUSIONS AND IMPLICATIONS

Management of chronic pain for older adults can often be challenging. Chronic pain can impact the quality of life and seriously impair optimal daily functioning of elderly individuals. Fortunately, the last two decades have witnessed substantial advancements in the conceptualization and treatment of chronic pain. These advances offer the opportunity for significant improvement in pain and pain-related disability, as well as overall quality of life. Optimal management of chronic pain in older adults often requires a multidisciplinary, multimodal approach. Nonpharmacologic interventions are important adjunctive therapies that can enhance pain control, decrease reliance on medications, and, because many of these techniques can be used independently, provide an increased sense of personal control over pain.

Older adults are often very responsive and accepting of nonpharmacologic strategies. There are a few basic principles for the effective implementation of these interventions that may prove helpful. Initially, a thorough assessment of the client's situation by a qualified health professional is important. This practitioner can then work with the client to select the strategy or strategies that would be most beneficial in managing the pain while capitalizing on the interest, motivation and other personal characteristics of the individual as well as important situational factors. Involvement of family members or significant others is often extremely beneficial in selecting interventions and ensuring correct use and long term compliance. Once an intervention(s) is selected, it is important that the use and benefits be explained thoroughly, followed by a period of time devoted to practice until the basic principles for use are mastered or individual adjustments are made. Provision of written information outlining use of these techniques is important for day to day reference, particularly during the initial period.

Available research, though limited, supports the use and effectiveness of nonpharmacologic interventions for elderly individuals. Many of the interventions discussed have been well researched in younger populations; however, additional research with elderly clients is needed to evaluate process and outcome measures and to determine approaches that are particularly effective for this population. Finally, long-term outcomes of these strategies also need to be evaluated and compared. Through future research, a more comprehensive, rational, scientifically-based process of pain management for the elderly population will be possible.

REFERENCES

Applebaum, K.A., Blanchard, E.B., Hickling, E.J., & Alfonso, M. (1988). Behavioral treatment of a veteran population with moderate to severe rheumatoid arthritis. *Behavior Therapy, 19*(2), 489-502.

Barr, J.O. (1993). Conservative pain management for the older patient. In A. A. Guccione (Ed.), *Geriatric physical therapy: Principles and practice* (pp. 283-306). Chicago: Mosby-Year Book.

Bernstein, D.A., & Borkovek, T.D. (1973). *Progressive relaxation training: A manual for the helping professions.* Champaign, IL: Research Press.

Bushnell, M.C., Marchand, S., Trembley, N., & Duncan, G.H. (1991). Electrical stimulation of peripheral and central pathways for the relief of musculoskeletal pain. *Canadian Journal of Physiology and Pharmacology, 69*(5), 697-703.

Butler, R.H., & Gastel, B. (1980). Care of the aged: Perspectives of pain and discomfort. In L.K. Ng & J.J. Bonica (Eds.), *Pain, discomfort and humanitarian care: Proceedings of the national conference* (pp. 297-311). New York: Elsevier.

Carstensen, L.L. (1988). The emerging field of behavioral gerontology. *Behavior Therapy, 19*(1), 259-281.

Catalano, E. (1987). *The chronic pain control workbook.* Oakland: New Harbinger.

Ciccone, D., & Grzesiak, R. (1988). Cognitive therapy: An overview of theory and practice. In N. T. Lynch & S.V. Vasudevan (Eds.), *Persistent pain: Psychosocial assessment and intervention* (pp. 133-161). Boston: Kluwer.

Cohen, J.L. (1986). Pharmacokinetic changes in aging. *American Journal of Medicine, 80* (Suppl 5A), 31-38.

Davis, G., Cortez, C., & Rubin, B. (1990). Pain management in the older adult with rheumatoid arthritis or osteoarthritis. *Arthritis Care and Research, 3*(3), 127-131.

Donovan, M. (1989). Relieving pain: The current bases for practice. In S. Funk, E. Tornquist, M. Champagne, L. Copp, & R. Wiese (Eds.), *Key aspects of comfort: Management of pain, fatigue, and nausea* (pp. 25-34). New York: Springer.

Edgar, L., & Smith-Hanrahan, C. (1992). Nonpharmacologic pain management. In J.H. Watt-Watson & M. I. Donovan (Eds.), *Pain management: Nursing perspective* (pp. 162-202). St. Louis: C.V. Mosby.

Fernandez, E. (1986). A classification system of cognitive coping strategies for pain. *Pain, 26,* 141-151.

Ferrell, B.A., & Ferrell, B. R. (1991). Principles of pain management in older people. *Comprehensive Therapy, 17*(8), 53-58.

Ferrell, B.A. (1991). Pain management in elderly people. *Journal of the American Geriatrics Society, 39,* 64-73.

Foley, K.M. (1990). Pain management in the elderly. In W.R. Hazzards, R. Andres & E.L. Bierman, (Eds.), *Principles of geriatric medicine and gerontology* (pp. 281-303). New York: McGraw-Hill.

Fordyce, W.E. (1976). *Behavioral methods for chronic pain and illness.* St. Louis: Mosby.

Haley, W.E., & Dolce, J.J. (1986). Assessment and management of chronic pain in the elderly. *Clinical Gerontologist, 5*, 435-455.

Hamm, B., & King, V. (1984). A holistic approach to pain control with geriatric clients. *Journal of Holistic Nursing*, 2(1), 32-37.

Hanson, R.W., & Gerber, K.E. (1992). *Coping with chronic pain: A guide to patient self-management.* New York: The Guilford Press.

Harkins, S.W., Kwentus, J., & Price, D.D. (1984). Pain and the elderly. In C. Benedetti, C.R. Chapman, & G. Moricca (Eds.), *Advances in pain research and therapy: Vol. 7* (pp. 103-122). New York: Raven Press.

Helme, R., & Katz, B. (1993). Prescribing for the elderly: Management of chronic pain. *The Medical Journal of Australia. 158*(5), 478-481.

Hunt, T.E. (1980). Pain and the aged patient. In W.L. Smith, H. Merskey, & S.C. Gross (Eds.), *Pain, meaning and management* (pp.143-158). Jamaica, NY: Spectrum.

Hyman, R., Feldman, R., Levin, R., & Malloy, G. (1989). The effects of relaxation training on clinical symptoms: A meta-analysis. *Nursing Research, 38*(4), 216-220.

Jacobsen, E. (1938). *Progressive relaxation.* Chicago: University of Chicago Press.

Jay, L., & Miller, T. (1990). Chronic pain and the geriatric patient. In T. Miller (Ed.), *Chronic pain: Vol. II* (pp. 821-838). Madison: International Universities Press.

Kaiko, R.F., Wallenstein, S.L., Rogers, A.G., Brabinski, P.Y., & Houde, R.W. (1982). Narcotics in the elderly. *Medical Clinics of North America, 66,* 1079-1089.

Kauffman, T. (1987). Thermoregulation and use of heat and cold. In J.O. Littrup (Ed.), *Therapeutic considerations for the elderly* (pp. 69-91). New York: Churchill Livingstone.

Keefe, F.J., Caldwell, D.S., Williams, D.A., Gil, K.M., Mitchell, D., Robertson, C., Martinez., S., Nunley, J., Beckham, J.C., Crisson, J.E., & Helms, M. (1990). Pain coping skills training in the management of osteoarthritic knee pain: A comparative study. *Behavior Therapy, 21*, 49-62.

Keefe, F.J., & Williams, D.A. (1990). A comparison of coping strategies in chronic pain patients in different age groups. *Journal of Gerontology: Psychological Sciences, 45*, P161-P165.

Kleinke, C. L. (1987). Patients' preferences for pain treatment modalities in a multidisciplinary pain clinic. *Rehabilitation Psychology, 32*(2), 113-120.

Kwentus, J. A., Harkins, S.W., Lignon, N., & Silverman, J.J. (1985). Current concepts of geriatric pain and its treatment. *Geriatrics, 40*, 48-57.

Lazarus, R.S., & Folkmann, S. (1984). *Stress, appraisal, and coping.* New York: Springer.

Lehmann, J.F., & DeLateur, B.J. (1982a). Diathermy and superficial heat and cold therapy. In F.H. Krusen, F.J. Kottke, & P.M. Elwood (Eds.), *Handbook of physical medicine and rehabilitation* (2nd ed.) (pp. 275-350). Philadelphia: Saunders.

Lehmann, J.F., & DeLateur, B.J. (1982b). Cryotherapy. In J.F. Lehman (Ed.), *Therapeutic heat and cold* (3rd ed.) (pp. 561-602). Baltimore: Williams and Wilkins.

Linton, S. (1986). Behavioral remediation of chronic pain: A status report. *Pain, 24*, 125-141.

Malone, M., & Strub, M. (1988). Meta-analysis of non-medical treatments for chronic pain. *Pain, 34*, 231-244.

Mannheimer, J.S., & Lampe, G.N. (1984). *Clinical transcutaneous electrical nerve stimulation.* Philadelphia: F.A. Davis.

McCafferey, M., & Beebe, A. (1989). Pain in the elderly: Special considerations. In M. McCaffery & A. Beebe (Eds.), *Pain: A clinical manual for nursing practice* (pp. 308-322). St. Louis: C.V. Mosby.

Mehta, M. (1986). Current views of non-invasive methods in pain relief. In M. Swerdlow (Ed.), *The therapy of pain* (2nd ed.) (pp. 115-131). Boston: MTP Press.

Melzack, R., & Wall, P.D. (1965). Pain mechanisms: A new theory. *Science, 150*, 971-979.

Melzack, R., & Wall, P.D. (1982). *The puzzle of pain.* New York: Basic Books.

Michlovitz, S.L. (1990). *Thermal agents in rehabilitation* (2nd ed.). Philadelphia: F.A. Davis.

Middaugh, S., Levin, R., Kee, W., Barchiesi, F., & Roberts, J. (1988). Chronic pain: Its treatment in geriatric and younger patients. *Archives of Physical Medicine and Rehabilitation, 69*, 1021-1026.

Miller, T., & Jay, L. (1990). Pharmacologic and nonpharmacologic approaches to pain management. In T. Miller (Ed.), *Chronic pain: Vol. II* (pp. 525-572). Madison: International Universities Press.

O'Leary, A., Shoor, S., Lorig, K., & Holman, H.R. (1988). A cognitive-behavioral treatment for rheumatoid arthritis. *Health Psychology, 7*(6), 527-544.

Owens, M.K., & Ehrenreich, D. (1991). Literature review of nonpharmacologic methods for the treatment of chronic pain. *Holistic Nursing Practice, 6*(1), 24-31.

Parker, J., Frank, R., Niels, C., Smarr, K., Buescher, K., Phillips, L., Smith, E., Anderson, S., & Walker, S. (1988). Pain management in rheumatoid arthritis patients: A cognitive-behavioral approach. *Arthritis and Rheumatism, 31*(5), 593-601.

Portenoy, R.K., & Farkash, A. (1988). Practical management of non-malignant pain in the elderly. *Geriatrics, 43*(5), 29-47.

Puder, R. (1988). Age analysis of cognitive-behavioral group therapy for chronic pain outpatients. *Psychology and Aging, 3*, 204-207.

Ross., S.L., Keefe, F.J., & Gil, K.M. (1988). Behavioral concepts in the analysis of chronic pain. In R.D. France, & K. Krishnan (Eds.), *Chronic pain.* (pp. 105-114). Washington, DC: American Psychiatric Press.

Saxon, S. (1991). *Pain management techniques for older adults.* Springfield, IL: Charles C Thomas.

Scandrett, S., & Uecker, S. (1992). Relaxation training. In G.M. Bulecheck & J.C.

McCloskey (Eds.), *Nursing interventions: Essential nursing treatments* (2nd ed.) (pp. 22-48). Philadelphia: W.B. Saunders.

Schultz, J.H., & Luthe, W. (1969). *Autogenic therapy Vol. I: Autogenic methods.* New York: Grune & Stratton.

Slater, M., & Good, A. (1991). Behavioral management of chronic pain. *Holistic Nursing Practice, 6*(1), 66-75.

Snyder, M. (1992). Progressive relaxation. In M. Snyder (Ed.), *Independent nursing interventions* (2nd ed.) (pp. 47-62). Albany, NY: Delmar.

Sodergren, K. (1992). Guided imagery. In M. Snyder (Ed.), *Independent nursing interventions* (2nd ed.) (pp. 95-109). Albany, NY: Delmar.

Sorkin, B., Rudy, R., Hanlon, R., Turk, D., & Stieg, R. (1990). Chronic pain in old and young patients; Differences appear less important than similarities. *Journal of Gerontology: Psychological Sciences, 45*, P64-P68.

Sturgis, E.T., Dolce, J.J., & Dickerson, P.C. (1987). Pain management in the elderly. In Carstensen, L., & Edelstein, B.A. (Eds.), *Handbook of clinical gerontology* (pp. 190-203). New York: Pergamon.

Thorsteinsson, G. (1987). Chronic pain: Use of TENS in the elderly. *Geriatrics, 42*(12), 75-82.

Turk, D.C., Meichenbaum, D., & Genest, M. (1983). *Pain and behavioral medicine: A cognitive-behavioral perspective.* New York: The Guilford Press.

Turner, J.A., & Romano, J.M. (1990). Cognitive-behavioral therapy. In J.J. Bonica (Ed.), *The management of pain* (2nd ed.) (pp. 1711-1721). Philadelphia: Lea and Febiger.

Weisenberg, M. (1987). Psychological intervention for the control of pain. *Behavior Research and Therapy, 25*(4) (Special issue), 301-312.

Chronic Pain and Older Women:
An Agenda for Research and Practice

Karen A. Roberto, PhD

SUMMARY. Drawing upon the available research literature, this article highlights the research and practice issues that must be addressed if we are to be responsive to the chronic health problems, and subsequent pain, that often confront individuals as they age. This list should by no means be seen as exhaustive, but rather as a starting point from which to further our understanding of chronic pain in the lives of older women.

In the United States, the health care delivery system has been successful in treating and curing acute diseases, decreasing the incidence of most infectious diseases, and developing new drug therapies and surgical procedures that have decreased the death rate from many chronic diseases. At the same time, however, we have seen increases in the morbidity rates for arthritis, heart disease, and other chronic conditions commonly found among older adults (Rothenberg & Koplan, 1990). As our population ages, we can expect that an increasing percentage of men and women will confront their later years with chronic health problems.

Chronic illness brings with it a host of associated symptoms and problems that must be understood in order to effectively treat and

Karen A. Roberto is Professor and Coordinator, Gerontology Program, University of Northern Colorado, Greeley, CO 80639.

[Haworth co-indexing entry note]: "Chronic Pain and Older Women: An Agenda for Research and Practice." Roberto, Karen A. Co-published simultaneously in *Journal of Women & Aging* (The Haworth Press, Inc.) Vol. 6, No. 4, 1994, pp. 111-116; and: *Older Women with Chronic Pain* (ed: Karen A. Roberto) The Haworth Press, Inc., 1994, pp. 111-116. Multiple copies of this article/chapter may be purchased from The Haworth Document Delivery Center [1-800-3-HAWORTH; 9:00 a.m. - 5:00 p.m. (EST)].

manage the condition itself. Persistent or prolonged pain is one such feature of chronic disease. In later life, it is estimated that 25 to 50% of community-dwelling older adults (Brattberg, Mats, & Anders, 1989; Crook, Rideout, & Browne, 1984) and between 45 and 80% of the nursing home residents (Ferrell, Ferrell, & Osterweil, 1990; Roy & Michael, 1986) suffer as a result of chronic pain problems. Yet, the issue of chronic pain among older adults has received little attention in the research literature.

This gap in our knowledge base is even more apparent when searching for information as to the influence of chronic pain on the lives of older women. An electronic search of the scientific litera-ture using a variety of databases (e.g., Medline, Psychlit), revealed a paucity of titles that would suggest that older women were the primary target population for recent studies. Even when older adults are the focus of the research, or are included as part of larger samples, similarities and differences between the pain experiences of older men and women are seldom explored.

We can no longer ignore the influence that living with chronic pain has on the lives of older adults. Drawing upon the information provided by the contributors to this volume, and others who have written about pain in later life, the following highlights the research and practice issues that must be addressed if we are to be responsive to the chronic health problems, and subsequent pain, that often con-front individuals as they age. This list should by no means be seen as exhaustive, but rather as a starting point from which to further our understanding of chronic pain in the lives of older men and women.

RESEARCH DIRECTIVES

Methodology Issues

Most of our knowledge about chronic pain in later life is based on the findings of cross-sectional studies. The continuation of these types of studies is important as they allow us to explore age, gender, and other differences in chronic pain among various groups of individuals. Further advancement of our understanding of the corre-lates and consequences of living with chronic pain in later life, however, requires the implementation of longitudinal designs. We must begin to examine if, and how, the chronic pain experience of older adults changes over time.

There is also a need for the use of more advanced sampling procedures. Chronic pain studies often employ small, convenience samples of individuals under the age of 75. The use of larger, random samples that include both men and women spanning a wider age-range will significantly enhance our knowledge of chronic pain among the "old-old" and strengthen the generalizability of future findings. In addition, we must broaden our samples by including not only those older adults living in the community but also those individuals residing in long-term care facilities.

Qualitative as well as quantitative methodologies must be employed to capture the experience of living with chronic pain. Qualitative investigations will provide us the opportunity to explore older individuals' interpretation of the influence chronic pain has on various aspects of their lives (e.g., functional abilities, self-perceptions, social relationships).

The assessment of chronic pain in later life also deserves greater attention. Many of the commonly used measures lack established norms for older samples. When assessing pain, be it in the laboratory, the clinic, or as part of our field research, we must recognize the special characteristics of the older population that may influence their perceptions and interpretations of pain (e.g., co-morbidity, pain-dependent functional limitations, mood-state). Turk and his colleagues (this volume) recommend a multi-method approach to the assessment of chronic pain in later life, but caution that the reliability and validity of the instruments used within each domain need to be established for use with an older population.

Areas of Study

The study of chronic pain in later life is in its early stages of development. Theories of chronic pain have been proposed based on observations of younger pain patients. Additional work needs to be done to substantiate these models with older populations.

Further research is needed in all content domains (i.e., physical, psychological, social) as we prepare for a potentially growing population of elders with chronic pain problems (see All, this volume; Gold, this volume). Questions to be addressed in relationship to the chronic pain experiences of older women (compared to older men) include:

- Is there a biological marker for pain?
- Does physical response and recognition of pain change with age?
- How do personal beliefs and health behaviors influence perceptions of chronic pain?
- What are the psychological implications of living with chronic pain (i.e., depression, anxiety, hopelessness)?
- What are the most successful coping strategies used to adapt to and manage chronic pain?
- How does living with chronic pain influence interpersonal relationships (and vice versa)?
- How successful are pain clinics in treating older adults?
- What are the long-term outcomes of both pharmacologic and nonpharmacologic treatments for chronic pain?

PRACTICE ISSUES

Education

Education must be provided for older individuals with chronic pain. Older adults would benefit from supportive health education programs that focus on the issues resulting from their chronic pain. Workshop or support group formats are currently popular ways of providing information and support to individuals with chronic conditions. Additional strategies, such as easy to read pamphlets and newsletters, and phone-support groups may need to be developed to reach older women whose chronic pain limits their abilities to attend community programs.

Self-management training models for older chronic pain sufferers also need to be further developed. Self-management is defined as "learning and practicing skills necessary to carry on an active and emotionally satisfying life in face of a chronic condition" (Lorig, 1993, p. 11). These types of programs are aimed at helping participants make informed choices by enhancing their knowledge of their conditions and their problem-solving skills. Professionals working with older persons with chronic pain need to encourage and educate them to do more for themselves and to take a more active part in their treatment decisions. Taking more responsibility for their personal health and well-being promotes a sense of independence and self-efficacy among older adults as they learn to effectively cope with their chronic conditions (Mettler & Kemper, 1993).

To be in a position to better treat and assist older men and women with chronic pain, more specific education about aging and chronic pain is needed for health care and human service professionals. The physical, psychological, and social aspects of chronic pain in later life must be included in undergraduate and graduate curricula and in continuing education programs.

Management

Pharmacologic strategies are commonly used to manage chronic pain in later life. As a result of physiologic and biomedical changes associated with aging (see Morris & Goli, this volume), older adults are particularly at risk for adverse effects from drug therapy. Health care providers need to be aware of these possible reactions when prescribing drug regimes for chronic pain. In addition, older adults need to be better informed about the possible side-effects of their treatments and encouraged to inform their physician if side-effects occur.

Several nonpharmacologic approaches have proven successful with older populations (see Mobily, this volume). Primary care physicians need to continue to be encouraged to refer older pain patients to health care providers with special skills in pain management for older adults. In addition to focusing on the physical aspects of chronic pain, practitioners need to recognize the psychological and social consequences of living with chronic pain. Individual, marital, and family counseling should be viewed as viable options for older individuals having problems coping as a result of their chronic pain (see Roy, this volume).

A multidisciplinary approach to the treatment and management of chronic pain may prove to be the most effective strategy for working with older adults. Whether treatment is sought through a pain clinic or family physician, the complexities of aging require health care and other practitioners to apply a "holistic" approach to the care of older men and women experiencing chronic pain.

REFERENCES

Brattberg, G., Mats, T., & Anders, W. (1989). The prevalence of pain in a general population: The results of a postal survey in a county of Sweden. *Pain, 37,* 215-222.

Crook, J., Rideout, E., & Browne, G. (1984). The prevalence of pain complaints among a general population. *Pain, 18,* 299-314.

Ferrell, B., Ferrell, B., & Osterweil, D. (1990). Pain in the nursing home. *Journal of the American Geriatric Society, 38,* 409-414.

Lorig, K. (1993). Self-management of chronic illness: A model for the future. *Generations, 17*(3), 11-14.

Mettler, M., & Kemper, D. (1993). Self-care and older adults: Making healthcare relevant. *Generations, 17*(3), 7-10.

Rothenberg, R., & Koplan, J. (1990). Chronic disease in the 1990s. *Annual Review of Public Health, 11,* 267-296.

Roy, R., & Michael, T. (1986). A survey of chronic pain in an elderly population. *Canadian Family Physician, 32,* 513-516.

Index

Activities of daily living, 2,35. *See also* Functional abilities; Functional disability
Acute pain, 3,9,26,36,45,48,62
Adverse drug reaction, 18. *See also* Side effects
Age groups. *See* Old-old; Young-old
Age-related changes, 3,17-18,27,33, 36,38,90
Aging:
    consequences of, 4,37,43,44,76
Analgesic medications, 28-29,31,48, 79,90. *See also* Nonsteroidal anti-inflammatory drugs (NSAIDS)
    alternatives to, 49
    narcotic, 65,66
    nonnarcotic, 92
    sensitivity to, 18,90
Ankylosing Spondylitis, 45,47
Anti-depressant medications, 49,67
Arthritis, 2,26,27,45,46-47,51,81,111
    osteoarthritis, 19,27,46,48,81,100, 103
    rheumatoid arthritis, 19,27,46-47, 96,100,103
Assessment, 31-36,64,65,113
    behavioral, 36
    functional, 35-36
    physical, 33
    psychosocial, 33-35,79
Assistive devices, 51
Autogenic training, 96,98-99

Back pain, 5,19,26,27,34,44-45, 47,75,79,82,103

Breast cancer, 21,60-61,70

Cancer pain, 20,69-70,103
    management of, 64-68
    psychosocial issues of, 62-64
    types of, 61-62
Chronic conditions, 5,27-28,48, 114-115
Chronic illness, 1-2,10,43,50,51,85, 111-112
Cognitive Behavioral Intervention, 68,90-91,92,93-100
Cognitive Therapy, 94-96
Cold, 5,50,92,101,102,103
Coping, 28,32,63,70,94,115
    active, 48,52,53
    as a process, 52
    as a trait, 52-53
    mechanisms, 65
    passive, 48,52,53
    strategies, 30,68,91,114
    with musculoskeletal pain, 48-53, 54
Couple therapy, 76,81,84
Cryotherapy. *See* Cold
Cutaneous Stimulation Interventions, 100-104

Depression, 5,21,28,29,33,37,38,49, 74,75,77,78,83,84,94,114
    estimates of, 4
    and cancer, 62,63,64
Diet, 54

Education, 51,114-115
Ergonomics, 5,51

Exercise, 47,48,50-51,54

Facial pain, 19-20,103
Family, 50,73,84,85,86,105. *See also*
        Spouse
    and cancer, 63-64,65
    counseling, 115
    elderly, 76-78
    impact of pain on, 29,75,82
    responses of, 32
    relations, 84
    therapy, 76
Family Adaptability and Cohesion
        Evaluation Scale, 75,77
Fibromyalgia, 5,26,47
Functional abilities, 28,35,36,113.
        See also Activities of daily
        living
Functional disability, 28,37. *See also*
        Activities of daily living

Gender differences, 4,17,19,26,28,
        29,44,54,92,96,98. *See also*
        Men
Geriatric Depression Scale, 33

Headaches, 5,26,27,34,47,79,80,81
Health care providers, 31,36,54,55,
        60,65,66,82,90,93,105
    education for, 114-115
    misconceptions of, 30,65
    responses of, 32
Health Care Professionals. *See*
        Health care provider
Health locus of control, 52-53
Heat, 5,16-17,50,90,92,101-102
Hip fractures, 19. *See also*
        Osteoporosis
Hope, 63,64,69
Hopelessness, 63,114
Hospice, 64,66,67

Human service providers, 69,115
Human service professionals. *See*
        Human service providers

Imagery, 68,91,93,99-100

Life expectancy, 1,37
Loneliness, 4
Lumbar degeneration, 19
Lumbar Spinal Stenosis, 47

Marital. *See also* Spouse
    conflicts, 78,81
    relationship, 74,80
    satisfaction, 4
Massage, 48,51,90,100,104
McMaster Model of Family
        Functioning, 75
Men. *See also* Gender differences
    and osteoporosis, 45,54-55
    and depression, 29
    and falls, 19
    and lower back pain, 44
    and osteoarthritis, 19
    number of, 1
    chronic health problems of, 2,27-28
    pain perceptions of, 3
    pain mechanisms of, 26
    pain threshold of, 16
Middle-age, 4,21
Multidisciplinary programs, 5,30,
        53-54,74,91,105,115
Musculoskeletal conditions, 2,47
Musculoskeletal pain
    causes of, 44-47
    coping with, 48-53
    treatments for, 53-54
Multiaxial assessment of pain, 32-33,35

National Oncology Nursing Society,
        69

Neck Pain, 5,46,97
Neuroanatomy, 12-13
Neurophysiology, 13-15
Nonsteroidal anti-inflammatory
    drugs (NSAIDS), 48-49,
    66,67
Nursing home residents, 2,9,112

Old-old, 1,38,78,113
Opioids, 13,15,16,18,26,38,66
Osteomalacia, 19
Osteoporosis, 18,27,44,45,46,48,54

Pain. *See also* Back pain; Cancer
        pain; Musculoskeletal pain;
        Neck pain; Pelvic pain;
        Theories of pain; Treatment
        for pain
    behaviors, 12,26,36,83
    clinics, 30,34,37,38,73,74,75,76,
        77,79,80,81,92,115
    definitions of, 2,10,16,61-62,96
    descriptions of, 10,12
    management of, 5,10,30,48-53,55,
        99,115
    perceptions of, 3,9,13,15,26,32
    sensitivity, 3,16,17,26
    severity, 29,31,34,35
    threshold, 16-17,26,64-65,68,102

Pelvic Pain, 20
Physiological Changes, 15,17,18
Post-menopausal women, 45
Psychological problems, 4,38. *See
        also* Depression
Psychological treatment, 5,74,76
Psychological therapy. *See*
        Psychotherapy
Psychotherapy, 31,74,82,84,86
Psychosocial issues, 33,62-64,69

Relaxation Therapy, 5,91,93,96-99
    and muscle relaxation, 68
    passive, 97,98
    progressive, 96-97

Self-efficacy, 91,115
Self-management, 114-115
Side effects, 5,48,49,66-67,90,104
Sleep:
    disturbances, 4,21,28,64
    problems, 47,49
Social activities, 2,77
Social relationships, 4,113
Social support, 29,34,37
Social network, 63
Spouse, 4,75,77,83. See also Marital,
        relationship

Transcutaneous electrical nerve
        stimulation (TENS), 5,
        51,90,100
    acupuncture-like, 103-104
    conventional, 103
Theories of Pain:
    Gate Control Theory, 12,92-93,101
    Learning Theory, 12
    Pattern Theory, 11
    Specificity Theory, 10
Thermal agents, 100,101-103
Treatments for pain. *See also* Pain,
        management of
    Nonpharmacologic, 5,67,68,
        90-92,105,114,115
    Pharmacologic, 5,31,48-49,53,
        65-67,90,114,115

Well-being, 1,52,63,65,115
West Haven-Yale Multidimensional
        Pain Inventory (MPI), 34
World Health Organization, 66

Young-Old, 1,38,78

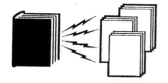

Haworth
DOCUMENT DELIVERY
SERVICE
and Local Photocopying Royalty Payment Form

This new service provides (a) a single-article order form for any article from a Haworth journal and (b) a convenient royalty payment form for local photocopying (not applicable to photocopies intended for resale).

- *Time Saving:* No running around from library to library to find a specific article.
- *Cost Effective:* All costs are kept down to a minimum.
- *Fast Delivery:* Choose from several options, including same-day FAX.
- *No Copyright Hassles:* You will be supplied by the original publisher.
- *Easy Payment:* Choose from several easy payment methods.

Open Accounts Welcome for . . .
- Library Interlibrary Loan Departments
- Library Network/Consortia Wishing to Provide Single-Article Services
- Indexing/Abstracting Services with Single Article Provision Services
- Document Provision Brokers and Freelance Information Service Providers

MAIL or *FAX* THIS ENTIRE ORDER FORM TO:

Attn: **Marianne Arnold**
Haworth Document Delivery Service
The Haworth Press, Inc.
10 Alice Street
Binghamton, NY 13904-1580

or FAX: (607) 722-1424
or CALL: 1-800-3-HAWORTH
(1-800-342-9678; 9am-5pm EST)

PLEASE SEND ME PHOTOCOPIES OF THE FOLLOWING SINGLE ARTICLES:

1) Journal Title: _____

    Vol/Issue/Year: _____ Starting & Ending Pages: _____

    Article Title: _____

2) Journal Title: _____

    Vol/Issue/Year: _____ Starting & Ending Pages: _____

    Article Title: _____

3) Journal Title: _____

    Vol/Issue/Year: _____ Starting & Ending Pages: _____

    Article Title: _____

4) Journal Title: _____

    Vol/Issue/Year: _____ Starting & Ending Pages: _____

    Article Title: _____

(See other side for Costs and Payment Information)

COSTS: Please figure your cost to order quality copies of an article.

1. Set-up charge per article: $8.00
   ($8.00 × number of separate articles) _____

2. Photocopying charge for each article:
   1-10 pages: $1.00 _____
   11-19 pages: $3.00 _____
   20-29 pages: $5.00 _____
   30+ pages: $2.00/10 pages _____

3. Flexicover (optional): $2.00/article _____

4. Postage & Handling: US: $1.00 for the first article/
   $.50 each additional article _____
   Federal Express: $25.00 _____
   Outside US: $2.00 for first article/
   $.50 each additional article _____

5. Same-day FAX service: $.35 per page _____

6. Local Photocopying Royalty Payment: should you wish to copy the article yourself. Not intended for photocopies made for resale. $1.50 per article per copy (i.e. 10 articles × $1.50 each = $15.00) _____

GRAND TOTAL: _____

METHOD OF PAYMENT: (please check one)

❏ Check enclosed   ❏ Please ship and bill. PO # _____
(sorry we can ship and bill to bookstores only! All others must pre-pay)

❏ Charge to my credit card: ❏ Visa; ❏ MasterCard; ❏ American Express;

Account Number: _____ Expiration date: _____

Signature: *X*_____ Name: _____

Institution: _____ Address: _____

City: _____ State: _____ Zip:_____

Phone Number: _____ FAX Number: _____

MAIL or *FAX* THIS ENTIRE ORDER FORM TO:

Attn: Marianne Arnold
Haworth Document Delivery Service
The Haworth Press, Inc.
10 Alice Street
Binghamton, NY 13904-1580

or FAX: (607) 722-1424
or CALL: 1-800-3-HAWORTH
(1-800-342-9678; 9am-5pm EST)